Advanced Sciences and Technologies for Security Applications

The series Advanced Sciences and Technologies for Security Applications comprises interdisciplinary research covering the theory, foundations and domain-specific topics pertaining to security. Publications within the series are peer-reviewed monographs and edited works in the areas of:

- biological and chemical threat recognition and detection (e.g., biosensors, aerosols, forensics)
- crisis and disaster management
- terrorism
- cyber security and secure information systems (e.g., encryption, optical and photonic systems)
- traditional and non-traditional security
- energy, food and resource security
- economic security and securitization (including associated infrastructures)
- transnational crime
- human security and health security
- social, political and psychological aspects of security
- recognition and identification (e.g., optical imaging, biometrics, authentication and verification)
- smart surveillance systems
- applications of theoretical frameworks and methodologies (e.g., grounded theory, complexity, network sciences, modelling and simulation)

Together, the high-quality contributions to this series provide a cross-disciplinary overview of forefront research endeavours aiming to make the world a safer place.

The editors encourage prospective authors to correspond with them in advance of submitting a manuscript. Submission of manuscripts should be made to the Editor-in-Chief or one of the Editors.

More information about this series at http://www.springer.com/series/5540

Henry Prunckun

Editor

Cyber Weaponry

Issues and Implications of Digital Arms

 Springer

Editor
Henry Prunckun
Research Criminologist
Australian Graduate School Policing and Security
Sydney, Australia

ISSN 1613-5113   ISSN 2363-9466 (electronic)
Advanced Sciences and Technologies for Security Applications
ISBN 978-3-319-74106-2   ISBN 978-3-319-74107-9   (eBook)
https://doi.org/10.1007/978-3-319-74107-9

Library of Congress Control Number: 2018933519

Printed on acid-free paper

This Springer imprint is published by the registered company Springer International Publishing AG part of Springer Nature.
The registered company address is: Gewerbestrasse 11, 6330 Cham, Switzerland

For Orren

Foreword

The adaptation of digital technology is shaping to be the single most important influence on how human beings conduct their lives. In the twenty-first century, the cybersphere has created endless opportunities for the improvement of the human condition: how we feed and clothe ourselves, how we treat disease, poverty, and natural disasters. It has given us new ways to entertain ourselves and to explore happiness and the quality of life. Algorithms help fuel modern technological and scientific progress, both addressing the grand conceptual challenges and making our household appliances work more efficiently. Algorithms facilitate the delivery of critical services and in hundreds of other ways improve the quality of life. They do our banking for us even as they are opening our garage doors and monitoring our heart rates on bushwalks, all guided by the cyber-enabled GPS gadgets on our wrists. Importantly, cyberspace has helped democratize information, revolutionizing the way people receive and impart information and how they communicate between themselves.

At the same time, the cybersphere has created new vulnerabilities with potentially devastating impacts on our daily lives, our safety, and our well-being. Society is rapidly learning that cyberspace is providing a new vector for criminality and fraud affecting both great and small. It is already challenging traditional Western liberal notions of privacy. The so-called democratization of information can also mean the democratization of misinformation—accelerating confusion between objective facts and the conman's spin, making achieving the consensuses that democratic decision-making requires more difficult.

Conducting business over the Internet is having an impact on the way nation states approach their first responsibility: protecting the lives and safety of their citizens. In terms of national security, cyberspace has become the *fifth domain of warfare* after land, sea, air, and outer space. Warfare in the twenty-first century will be fought in cyberspace long before a kinetic shot is fired; it will inform and condition both actual armed conflict and its aftermath.

Warfare in cyberspace has three important facets: the collection of intelligence; the sabotage, disruption, or degradation of the opposition's cyber-dependent war-fighting capabilities (which can include not simply weaponry but also critical infrastructure); and the ability to mislead and misinform through half-truths and concocted stories that are promulgated via social media. In short, the Internet, and our dependence upon it, offers a new vector through which to weaken an opponent's national resilience and war-fighting capability. Each of these facets has already been used by nation states, both in actual armed conflict and, alarmingly, in circumstances that fall short of armed warfare.

So, potentially damaging are the consequences of cyber-attack and so great the cost to nations having to fix the cyber vulnerabilities. We have allowed these shortcomings to open up because we have rushed pell-mell into cyber dependence. Societies and their governments now need to focus not simply upon repairing the damage, but on how innocent populations can be spared from the ravages of cyber-induced disasters, breakdowns, and damage, whether inflicted by nation states or non-state actors.

The response to cyber threats will be complicated, not least because prophylaxis inevitably lags the inventiveness of those who use the Internet to do harm. It will involve sophisticated technical solutions to protect our cyber-connected devices from infiltration and malicious activity; it will involve cultural or behavioral change in the way we respond to threats from cyberspace; it will involve legislation to force industry and cyber service providers to protect both privacy and the sustainability of the critical infrastructure which now depends on cyberspace. It will also require international cooperation to set norms and rules to govern both the offensive and defensive uses of cyber-technology, much as humankind has had to develop norms and rules to govern a range of transnational issues: the world's oceans, the natural environment, the use and proliferation of nuclear weapons, the management of contagious diseases, and how we address serious and organized crime.

The technological development of cyberspace and its rapidly expanding uses, together with mountains of data it generates, have become self-sustaining. This is not yet the case with the doctrines that ought to accompany the development of the Internet phenomenon. Our defense experts are still exploring the war-fighting capabilities developed for use in the cybersphere, as well as the technology and doctrines needed to defend ourselves against cyber-attack. We need to devote more intellectual effort to analyzing this technology's impact, the vulnerabilities it creates, and how best to mitigate the vulnerabilities. That intellectual effort must turn also to the ethical and moral dimensions and the obligations of the state to protect the privacy and the safety of its citizens against cyber-induced catastrophes.

With these critical issues in mind, I congratulate Dr. Henry Prunckun and his fellow contributors for their collaborative efforts in bringing together and analyzing so many strains of the cyber dilemma and, in doing so, making their arguments and research findings available to scholars, researchers, students, and policy-makers in such an easily read form.

Chair, Foreign Investment Review Board   David Irvine BA(Hons), AO
(since 2017)
Director-General, Australian Security Intelligence
Organisation (2009–2014)
Director-General, Australian Secret Intelligence
Service (2003–2009)

Preface

Without a doubt, cyberspace has become *the* battlespace for confrontations. However, to conduct cyber operations, a new armory of weapons needs to be employed. No matter how many or how sophisticated an aggressor's kinetic weapons are, they are useless in cyberspace. This fact places, at least in theory, those with an inferior set of kinetic arms, or those without arms at all, on a footing that allows them to go head-to-head with all contenders.

So, contrary to popular opinion, the use of cyber weapons is not limited to nation states, though this is where news reports seem to focus. The reality is that there isn't a sector of the political economy that is immune to cyber-attacks. In this sense, an *attack* could be part of a limited cyber warfare, cyber espionage, or cybercrime. Some attacks read like Hollywood screenplays: "A group of hackers use a stolen cyber-weapon to try to extort money from people worldwide. The attack cripple [d] hospitals, causes ambulances to be diverted, and [surgical] operations to be canceled. Then, a lone security researcher stumbles across a way to halt the bug in its tracks. Yet, this is exactly what happened..."[1]

This book addresses the use of cyber weapons by national security agencies, the military, law enforcement, and the business sector—with the latter including those agencies termed *nongovernment organizations*. It looks at the milieu of the cyber weapons industry and the belligerents who use them; it also looks at what distinguishes these hardware devices and software programs from those that are used in general computing.

The text is divided into two sections, each examining a specific aspect of the topic—contextual issues of cyberspace in the new battleground, defensive cyber weapons, offensive cyber weapons, and dual-use weapons—and finally, it looks at the implications these weapons systems have for practice.

The book's concise chapters will appeal to scholars as well as students in the field because it incorporates practical case examples along with policy discussion. Course

---

[1]"The Worm that Turned," *The Economist*, May 20, 2017, p. 10.

instructors will find several learning aids that should be useful for lectures or student assignments. These learning aids will also be of interest for readers who are perusing professional development outside the classroom. To enhance these learnings, each chapter is accompanied by references to the subject literature. Where appropriate, the chapters are accompanied by tables or figures that illustrate points being made. Finally, there is a comprehensive index to help readers quickly locate the material.

I am optimistic that this text will find wide application, appealing to those in fields such as computing/information technology, national security/intelligence, military science, police/law enforcement science, political science, and law/criminal justice/criminology.

Sydney, Australia   Henry Prunckun

About the Study Questions

Here is some advice about the study questions listed at the end of each chapter and how to approach and ultimately answer them:

Explain/list/describe: This type of question asks you to outline the factors associated with the issue under study.

Argue: This type of question asks you to present factors about the issue being investigated, but requires you to select one of the factors so that you can defend it.

Discuss: This type of question asks you to form a view (or judgment) after weighing up the for and against factors and then draw a conclusion(s).

Acknowledgment

The editor would like to thank the U.S. Department of Defense for the use of the visual information that appears in this book, but would like to point out that its appearance in this text does not imply, or constitute, the department's endorsement.

Contents

Chapter 1
Weaponization of Computers

Henry Prunckun

1.1 Weaponization

A prisoner sat on a locker-room bench drying herself after showering. She soon saw a group of prisoners approach and surround her. She looked around for the guard, but she was not in sight. Her heart raced; her breath became shallow. Despite no words having been spoken by those menacing her, she knew she was about to be given a beating.

If she was to survive, she needed help. But, with no one else to assist her, her only hope was for a weapon; something that would help equalize the odds. Nonetheless, being in a prison discounted this option—there were no guns, knives, or clubs. So, she reached for one of her socks, drop a bar of soap into it and swung it a circle over her head. She was now armed.

A device that is used to inflict harm on a person is considered a *weapon*, or *arm*. Arms are used to damage buildings, roads, and other forms of infrastructure. Weapons are used in a variety of positive ways, from helping to hunt for food, to humanly putting-down injured animals. But, arguably, the main purpose is to provide an effective means to harm an opponent. The effectiveness comes from the gain, or advantage, the weapon provides—in the case of our prisoner, it is in the potential delivery of the weight contained in the sock, and the mechanical advantage the leverage supplies, as well and the added speed of the delivery. A blow to the face or head will result in a greater degree of injury than the impact of a fist, and there is no pain or damage to the person delivering the blow.

Yet, a bar of soap and a sock are not weapons. However, they were weaponized—that is, they were combined to form a device that was a weapon. Depending on the circumstance and what is available, many everyday objects can be weaponized in

H. Prunckun (✉)
Australian Graduate School of Policing and Security, Charles Sturt University, Sydney,
Australia
e-mail: hprunckun@csu.edu.au

© Springer International Publishing AG, part of Springer Nature 2018
H. Prunckun (ed.), *Cyber Weaponry*, Advanced Sciences and Technologies for
Security Applications, https://doi.org/10.1007/978-3-319-74107-9_1

this way. Cars can be used to run-down people; pencils can be used as spikes to stab an opponent; drinking glasses can be used to lacerate attackers, and wine bottles filled with gasoline can be used to. . .

Chemicals, viruses, and radiological material can also be weaponized. History is littered with examples of chemical agents being used in war, and it is known that several countries hold stocks of biological weapons. At the time of writing eight countries[1] were conformed to have nuclear weapons—China, France, India, North Korea, Pakistan, the Russian Federation, the United Kingdom, and the United States. Radiological weapons are devices that are designed to spread radioactive material in densely populated areas. Acknowledged as less a hazard than a nuclear device, it is posited that this type of weapon has more psychological effect than physical harm—it is likely to be used to cause panic according to terrorist doctrine—"kill one, frighten ten-thousand." Nevertheless, there is plenty of sources of radiological material—it is held in places like dentists' offices, university laboratories, hospitals and clinics, and a person can make the equivalent of a Molotov cocktail with just a few components. Recall, it isn't the explosion that is the worry, it is the spread of the invisible radiological energy that will cause panic and economic injury. These weapons are referred to as *dirty bombs*.

This is all clear when dealing with the physical world—a person can visualize how they might go about arming themselves against attackers with an improvised weapon, but what about in the cybersphere? How does a person attack an opponent in the world of the Internet—a world constructed of optical fibre cables, routers, switches, ethernet cables, servers, and millions of computers? And, how does a person defend themselves in this world? A bar of soap and a sock just won't be enough.

1.2   Weaponizing Computers

Civilization occupies all the continents. All major islands are inhabited. The oceans and skies are populated with vessels and craft carrying people. Space is occupied by scientists aboard the International Space Station, and if today's visionary entrepreneurs are successful, space will have its tourists before too long. In all of these environments we can see examples of weaponization. We have taken motorized vehicles and mounted machine guns and cannon for offensive operations, and armoured plating for protection. We have done the same with aircraft and watercraft, and call them bombers, fighters, and warships. We have provided soldiers with rifles that once were used for hunting game, but the enhancements to these mean that they can now deliver a projectile hundreds of yards with precision; or in such rapid sequence that the number of rounds fired per minute sounds implausible.

---

[1]It is presumed that Israel has nuclear weapons, but this has not been established with any certainly.

A world exists in copper and optical fibre cables, magnetic disks and flash memory devices. Digital information that is created in this world by converting thoughts into representations through mechanical actions. These data are then stored on these devices. To communicate what has been created, it is transmitted via cables, and radio waves. But, is this really a *world?* Perhaps not, because the mechanical interface with the computer and the storage devices of a computer system exist in the physical world. So too do the apparatus that are used to transmit the electronic information—cables and the ether are in the physical world. Therefore, it is not really a world, but a metaphor that helps to conceptualize computer technology. Cyberspace is no more a world than books are a world. Yet, when we talk about "getting lost in the world of books," or "living in the cybersphere," we understand what is being implied.

If we accept the premise that information—ideas converted into digital representations—is the reason computer technology exist, then we can reason that the disruption of any process from mechanically entering the information (say, via a keyboard, mouse, e-pen, or voice command) to the reading, viewing, and/or listening to that information by the recipient, can form a target if the information is deemed to be a hazard. We can interdict and prosecute the two ends of this *kill chain*[2] without the weaponization of computers. We can, for example, arrest those involved with creating the information and receiving the information, and this will remove any risk this information presents. Take the case where a person concocts a plan to attack people at a busy city market. The planner transmits his plans over the Internet and are stored on a social media website. Others read it, and a conversation ensues; this dialogue culminates with four people carrying out the plan.

Arresting the planner would immediate remove the key to the illegal activity by denying the information on which the attack is founded. Arresting those reading the information would also achieve the same result. However, the laws of evidence, constitutional liberties, and the doctrine of due process could impinge on doing this, especially if the planner is domiciled in a country outside the target country, and those viewing the information are also in different countries.

Like transmitting information using radio waves, this information can be located (intercepted), and countermeasures that disrupt or destroy the data anywhere along the kill chain can be developed. After all, we are operating in the physical world—*cyberspace* is only a metaphor. This is done by taking what is normally used in electronic data processing and computer technology, and, like the fictional prisoner in our previous illustration, weaponizes these artefacts. The result is harm caused to the digitized information, and/or the means of creating, storing, using, or transmitting it.

---

[2]The term *kill chain* is used in the military. It refers to the attack process, or a *chain* of events and decisions. The process comprises: (1) identifying a target; (2) determining its location or position; (3) decision whether to attack; (4) and either standing-down, observing further, and/or using the data for intelligence, or to attack the target. Viewed in reverse, if an opposition's kill chain can be disrupted, the theory is that a successful attack is not possible.

1.3 How Is Weaponizing Done?

Clearly, there is no scope to use bars of soap and socks to improvise a weapon where computer technology is concerned. The digital world is characterized by electrical currents, wires, and tiny electronic components mounted on printed circuit boards. Sure, a person can hammer-away at a computer with an improvised soap-blackjack, but realistically, that isn't likely to result in a successful attack.

However, if an opponent's computer could be rendered inoperable without the need to be present, then the chances of success increase. This is done using the same infrastructure that processes and transmits information, only these "improvisations" are malicious.

Weaponization is done by two approaches—a software approach and a hardware approach. The first is by creating a program that when run, will perform an action that is not desired by the owner/operator. The terms *virus, worm, Trojan* are types of programs that are classified as *malware*—shorthand for malicious software. These can be standalone programs or parts of larger programs that allow the scribe to carry-out harmful tasks.

The hardware approach is where an electronic device is used to create harm. A keystroke logger is a type of device that is placed in-circuit with a computer and will record the mechanical input from the computer's keyboard. No elaboration is needed to understand the ramifications of doing this.

Consequently, like placing a bar of soap in a sock, when a person wires a simple recording device to a computer they have weaponised the device. When a software application is written to perform a destruction function, it has been weaponized. When a piece of software and hardware have been configured to operate in unison to act destructively, the system has been weaponized.

1.4 Who Does It?

Just as anyone can use a pencil as a spike, so too can anyone weaponized a computer. Who does this is best understood if these weapon developers are viewed on a spectrum. This spectrum could be described as the casual developer who creates a self-defence weapon because of genuine necessity—like the earlier prisoner example. At the other end of the spectrum are the world's global outlaws—societal malcontents who operate with psychopathic motives, or those who use simplistic philosophical arguments to justify their reasons.

There are also all those in between—those who are curious to see if they can do it (like a teenager who makes a zip-gun in his father's home workshop); those who are out for revenge (the employee who feels she was fired without cause); or to make a quick dollar (scammers and fraudsters); or those whose duty it is to protect society—law enforcement and intelligences agencies. Of course, there are more categories of weapon developers—

both defensive and offensive—but this list presents some idea of the range of people who engage in it.

1.5 Implications for Policy and Practice

1.5.1 Legislative Control

If anyone can "do it," it raises the question of who has these weapons. During the Cold War, the US and the Soviet Union kept close count of each other's nuclear weapons. Processes and procedures were put in place to verify what the each reported—some of these were covert intelligence gathering activities because the stakes were too high to not know what each side held in their arsenal.

On a smaller scale, domestic gun manufacturers are required to report the numbers and distribution of firearms; retail sales are recorded; and purchasers are registered. Although not perfect, authorities can estimate the numbers of guns in circulation. Though, on this point, the analogy ends. Although authorities know approximate numbers of guns in society, and their likely distribution—legal and illegal ownership—verification, in the sense of nuclear weapons, is not possible. And, this is an issue for policy and practice. As Prunckun questions in a later chapter; can society control these software programs through legislation, and should there be legal restrictions placed on the use of hardware devices? Enforcement might be an issue, but does that mean no controls at all? Governments face problems in policing firearms, but that doesn't mean a repeal of all gun laws, which is, arguable, the case now with cyber weapons—a somewhat lawless situation?

1.5.2 Malware Marketplaces

Herr argues in his chapter that it isn't so much the payload of a cyber weapon that should be the central concern for policy-makers, but the factors surrounding the computer source code—making them reliable, accurate, and their distribution through malware markets. If the environment for their proliferation could be understood, then it follows that strategies for effective control can be devised.

If we look, again, at firearms, every school student understands how a firearm works; but what makes the device reliable and accurate, and how can these enhancements make a standard armament worthy of deployment against a target? This understanding is the information necessary to succeed as a weapons maker; whether it is a firearm or a cyber weapon. It is also necessary for regulators to know to be able to control these processes.

1.5.3   Need for Self-Defence

Although the cybersphere is a world analogous to a place created in the pages of a book—a virtual world—the interface between these electronic devices and software programs affects the physical world. Just as publishing a book has real-world affects—the ideas expressed in the words can result in action, or inaction—so too can the information in computer systems. After all, that is why information is put into these systems; to do something with it; to use that information to manage some aspect of society.

It is in this vein that a people would seek protect for their ideas and intellectual property—in whatever form that exists. Thomas, Low and Burmeister's chapter discusses how a Red Team-type exercise can provide computer users with information to protect their systems from criminals and state-based espionage. Known as *penetration testing*, this is a purposeful attack on an IT installation with software applications and hardware devices to test the system's robustness.

This approach is somewhat controversy because it could be said that possession of these programs and electronic devices are offensive weapons, even though they are being used defensively. Therefore, shouldn't policy take this into account? But, what about the integrity of the "pen" testers themselves? Should they be licensed to assure their personal integrity, and that they are able to control the applications they use and the devices they deploy? This is analogous to situations where law enforcement officers can use fully-automatic firearms, but the average citizen cannot.

1.5.4   Personal Privacy

Debate about Internet privacy has been argued in many forums for a long time. One side of the debate is that people using the Internet have a right to privacy. There is legal precedent for this in the Fourth Amendment to the US Constitution and under other legal traditions found in other jurisdiction's that are based on the philosophical principles found in the theory of natural rights.

Regardless, a person's right to privacy is not absolute. The test as to whether a person has an expectation to privacy is based on what is observable by the five senses in, or from, a public place—the plain view doctrine. A right to privacy is also abolished when a court issues a law enforcement agency with a search warrant, or a law enforcement officer exercises a legal power to conduct search without a warrant.

This raises the question as to whether everything done on the Internet is private? Blog posts can be seen in the same way pinning a notice to a public bulletin inboard can. So, should online shopping be considered the same as shopping in a mall or department store? Can browsing various websites for a summer vacation destination, or anything else, be considered the same as window-shopping? When these activities are carried-out in the physical world, they are conducted in public view; so, can the same public observation be an expectation when viewing goods and services on the Internet?

No doubt the courts will wrestle with this issue for some time, but what about the issue of a person installing a key-logger into a USB port of someone else's computer? This may overstep the bounds and not only be a breach of privacy, but constitute criminal thief (or a civil wrong for breach of contract if done in a business settling), and depending on the target, espionage. In the meantime, how does a person, business, NGO, or government department ensure privacy until courts provide clearer definitions of what is and isn't private? Irwin's chapter looks at how common computer security techniques and methods can be used to help overcome cyber-criminal activity.

1.5.5   Dual-Purpose Weapons

Dealing with cyber-criminal activity with some of the time-honored computer security approaches is fine, but these software programs and electronic devices can also be used by the same criminals they are meant to protect against. Referred to as dual-purpose weapons, they can be both defensive and offensive. Several chapters in this book touch on this issue. Like other cyber weapons issues, there is no clear answer as to how it is addressed because much of the problem lays in the mind of the person who is using the program or hardware—in legal circles this is known as *intent*.

Take as an example a person who buys a second-hand mainframe computer. She sets it up in her garage with her other computer and networking equipment. But, rather than using it to help her solve mathematical problems related to astrophysics, she uses it to solve password encryption problems related to a classified government database. Having a mainframe computer is not a problem, but weaponizing it in this way is.

1.5.6   Business Sector and Non-government Organizations

Self-protection also extends to the business sector and to non-government organizations. McGonagle and Whitford in their respective chapters discuss how commercial-in-confidence information requires the highest levels of protecting to ensure the viability of free-market economies. Likewise, organizations operating to provide aid and social-relief, and issue motivated groups aimed at bringing about democratic reforms using Internet technologies also require defense against those opposed to their work.

McGonagle and Whitford suggest two approaches to dealing with these issues—(1) the human factor; and (2) crime prevention through environmental design (CPTED). Both address a system's issue by way of human intervention. Although, not often thought of as part of an IT strategy, these people-centric vectors are often the weakest elements in a cyber-defense practice. Granted, the problems caused when people have a critical part to play in IT systems are not directly part of the cyber weapon debate, they do cause an indirect and consequential impact. That is, it is people who design, maintain, change, and use computer systems. Therefore, unless policy takes the human factor into account, the best cyber security will fail. How this is done needs consideration. Is there an argument to license computer users so they understand the gravity of their weak system in spreading viruses, for instance? Should computer be certified as "safe" to operate on the Internet? This could be done the way motor vehicles are inspected for road worthiness. And, in terms of crime prevention design, this too raises questions about the safety of systems, like fire rating public buildings. Would IT self-defence benefit from some form of CPTED rating?

1.5.7   Cyber War

It has been said that wars between nation state are less likely to be fought on battlefields and more likely to be fought where digital information is kept. This is hard to argue against. But, it is more than just raw data that is at stake; it is the way this information guides and control decision-making, as well as the systems that run the world—financial sectors and national economies; manufacturing and industry; transport; telecommunications; health, education and welfare; and the list goes on. All sectors that support a nation's military.

If we look back at what was termed *strategy bombing* by the Allies during the Second World War, we note that the targets were not only military, but infrastructure that supported the military's ability to conduct war. If we look at the list of commercial and non-military sectors just discussed, it is not difficult to see the nexus. If a foreign power wanted to cripple a country, it could do so by ways other than putting troops into action.

1.5.8   State's Obligation to Citizen Protection

Cyber war, or at least cyber skirmishes, have been carried out already. The world has witnessed the use of the Stuxnet worm that setback Iran's nuclear program. Unlike a cruise missile, no one knows with absolute certaintly who was responsible—there was no "smoking gun," yet the result was equal to what a conventional explosive

Fig. 1.1 The 2017 *WannaCry* ransom screen (Reproduced here in accordance with the legal doctrine of *ex turpi causa non oritur actio*)

could have done—it held-back the facility's scientific advancements. Hardly a "war," but a conflict that ended in physical damage to equipment nonetheless.

So, doesn't a government have an obligation to it citizens to protect them from harm from this vector? Take as an example, the 2017 cyber-attack known as the *WannaCry* virus (Fig. 1.1). Although there was no evidence that this malware attack was launched against a particular state, it did affect hospital and health facilities in the United Kingdom (amongst a wide range of other sectors in some 150 countries). Because the UK facilities lost their computerized systems, surgery was cancelled, forcing the National Health Service to carry-out emergency only treatment. If this was a state-initiated attack, it raises the question; if a kinetic weapon was used, what would be the response—should that be the same for a cyber weapon. Should the doctrine that would guide a physical attack be applied to a cyber-attack? Smyth discusses these and other cyber war issues in her chapter of this book.

1.5.9 Use in Disrupting Drug Trafficking

If cyber skirmishes are on the horizon, and we have seen what could be classified as the phenomena's antecedents—*WannaCry* and others—could using cyber weapons be an effective policy option for combating organized crime? Could using cyber weapons be used to, say, deal with the world-wide problem of illicit drugs? Prunckun explores this issue in one of his chapters. He contends that not only is it viable, it should be a feature of government policy. If his argument has traction, then a further question could be; why not extend the policy to other areas of crime control—people smuggling, arms trafficking, and terrorism?

1.5.10   Cyber Counterintelligence

To be able to execute offensive campaigns against military foes and the world's worst outlaws, information about such plans needs to be kept secret. Without secrecy plans will be prematurely known and countermeasures implemented. If we think back to the planning stage for the raid on bin Laden's Abbottabad compound. It would take little imagination to foresee what would have happen if counterintelligence wasn't operating at its best.

Stech and Heckman's chapter describes how defenders can used the principles of denial and deception—counterintelligence—to create an active cyber defense system. In counterintelligence terms, this is known as the *cyber deception chain*. It helps mitigate cyber espionage along the kill chain. Cyber counterintelligence has grown in importance with repeated revelations of Chinese cyber espionage. China is not the only country alleged to be launching aggressive espionage campaigns over the Internet, but reports suggest it's People's Liberation Army Unit 61398 is one of most belligerent. North Korea is said to have a group that specializes in cyber espionage and cyber-crime—Unit 180. It has proven difficult to obtain conclusive proof of what North Korea has done—because it is such a close society (a form of denial)—but at the time of writing it was alledged to have links to the such raids as the 2014 Sony Pictures Entertainment hack that resulted in the thief of confidential business information, and the 2016 cyber-thief of $US81 million from the Bangladesh central bank.

1.6   Cyber-Security Myth

Given the range of policy implication and ramifications for practice just surveyed, as well as many others that space limits here, the question that presents itself is, "Can computers be made secure"? The short answer is "no." The reasons are because hardware, and particularly software, are complex.

Those with ill-intent can intercept data traversing the Internet at a number of physical points along its path. Software comprises many hundreds of thousands, if not millions, of lines of source code. Just the odds of ensuring the security of that many instructions in every piece of software is slim. So, cyber-space is inherently insecure. It would be glib to say that the answer resides with better technological devices and/or more vigilant users, though both will go some way toward shoring-up the metaphoric barricades.

Given that the historical development of the Internet featured security as an afterthought, using it as a means of confidential communication is peppered with hazards. Now, with the dawning of the Internet-of-Things, it is likely that we are compounding these issues and spawning new implications. Almost thirty years ago Prunckun (1989: 49) pointed out this problem: "...once a [hacker] knows or even believes that [someone holds confidential information], half of his work is already done; his next step is to devise a method to acquire it." Paraphrasing strategic analysts' thinking on conflict, it could be said that he who has land will face war; he who has a computer connected to the Internet will face hackers. So, perhaps we need to heed the Latin motto, *praemonitus praemunitus*; or, forewarned is forearmed.

1.7 Principal Concepts

The principal concepts associated with this chapter are listed below. Demonstrate your understanding of each by writing a short definition or explanation in one or two sentences:

- Counterintelligence;
- Cyber deception chain;
- Dual-purpose cyber weapon; and
- Kill chain.

1.8 Study Questions

1. Explain what is meant by the plain view doctrine.
2. Describe a typical malware market place.
3. Describe the two approaches to cyber weaponization.
4. Discuss whether, in your view, privacy on the Internet could ever be achieved. Provide supporting evidence for-and-against, and why this evidence makes to draw the conclusion you have.

1.9 Learning Activity

Individually, or in a small group, brainstorm a list of software programs and/or hardware devices that could be weaponized—like the bar of soap and sock example in the text. Describe: (1) how the items in the list could be used as-is or in combination; (2) what a person with malicious intent expect to gain from weaponizing these items; and (3) how a law-abiding citizen or business weaponize these items for legitimate defence against a cyber-malcontent.

Reference

Prunckun H (1989) Information security: a practical handbook on business counterintelligence. Charles C Thomas Publisher, Springfield

Chapter 2
Human Nature and Cyber Weaponry: Use of Denial and Deception in Cyber Counterintelligence

Frank J. Stech and Kristin E. Heckman

2.1 Background

Secrets range in importance, from what someone might have bought you for your birthday, to the nuclear launch codes. Personal secrets are kept to avoid embarrassment and to avoid judgment, but business secrets, law enforcement secrets, and secrets relating to national security are kept to protect people's lives, as well as to safeguard society. These data are characterized as *intelligence*. In its simplest form, *denial* is a means of protecting intelligence secrets. This can be done by limiting the intelligence to those who need-to-know, while blocking others from finding out. This method is often thought of as *security*.

Security can take many forms; from locks, vaults and guards, to more sophisticated methods involving personnel vetting, confidentiality agreements, and the use of technology to facilitate the creation, storage, and transmission of secret information.

In the past, such technology might have involved tattooing a message to a person shaved head, waiting for their hair to regrow, then sending the "messenger" to the recipient with the instruction to shave his head and read the message (Kahn 1967: 81). Though this might have worked for Histiaeus in 499BC, communication in the Twenty-First Century is, by-and-large, via the Internet; so, more advanced means of keeping secrets is needed. To protect secrets, a branch of intelligence work has developed and is known as *counterintelligence*.

As with secrets, those wanting to discover these pieces of confidential information range from noisy neighbors to espionage agents. The former is of little concern because rudimentary methods can usually take care of their attempts to eavesdrop. But, the latter group is more concerning because history shows that these operatives will go to extreme lengths to obtain intelligence—sometimes at the cost of their own lives.

F. J. Stech · K. E. Heckman (✉)
MITRE Corporation, McLean, VA, USA
e-mail: kheckman@mitre.org

© Springer International Publishing AG, part of Springer Nature 2018
H. Prunckun (ed.), *Cyber Weaponry*, Advanced Sciences and Technologies for
Security Applications, https://doi.org/10.1007/978-3-319-74107-9_2

With the increase use of cyber weapons in Internet-based espionage, the need for cyber counterintelligence has become apparent. Historically, counterintelligence has had important impacts on politics and military operations, at least at the tactical and operational levels of conflict. Arguably, counterintelligence remains more art than science because of its focus on tricking human nature—the way people think, feel, and behave. Nevertheless, counterintelligence theory and practice have been extended to domains such as industry (Defense Security Service 2015; O'Connell 1994; Office of the National Counterintelligence Executive 2013) and finance (Skerry 2013). Nonetheless, there are relatively few explicit counterintelligence applications to cyber security reported in the open literature.[1]

Espionage in the cyber world has led to calls for greater cyber counterintelligence (Intelligence and National Security Alliance 2017; French and Kim 2009; Office of the National Counterintelligence Executive 2013), but there is little evidence that cyber counterintelligence is reducing what appears to be a steady increase in the number and scope of cyber espionage operations (Coleman 2014; Geers et al. 2014). Nonetheless, research developing systematic frameworks for cyber counterintelligence show promise in applying new approaches and technologies to cyber counterintelligence, applying cyber denial and deception methods, and employing the growing field of what is being referred to as *deception technologies*.

Typically, denial involves the concealment of information; hiding it from cyber spies. Deception involves misleading cyber spies; convincing them to believe what is false, is real—like cinema viewers do when they watch a Hollywood film. The process of deception also involves hiding the false information—that is, the non-disclosable deception information—to protect the operation, which revealed, might show cyber spies the real information.

Research (Heckman et al. 2015) has not found comparisons between active cyber defense (ACD) measures, and of cyber denial and deception tactics, techniques, and procedures (TTPs), intended to address cyber espionage. Therefore, this chapter is a first attempt to provide such analytic methods. A technical report titled *Cyber*

---

[1]In 2009, the United States published the *Comprehensive National Cybersecurity Initiative* (CNCI). The initiative outlined US cybersecurity goals that spanned multiple agencies, including the Department of Homeland Security, the Office of Management and Budget, and the National Security Agency. The 2009 CNCI included the goal (among others) of "...enhancing US counterintelligence capabilities and increasing the security of the supply chain for key information technologies." Specifically, the CNCI announced "Initiative #6. Develop and implement a government-wide cyber counterintelligence plan." The Initiative stated: "Initiative #6. Develop and implement a government-wide cyber counterintelligence plan. A government-wide cyber counterintelligence plan is necessary to coordinate activities across all Federal Agencies to detect, deter, and mitigate the foreign-sponsored cyber intelligence threat to US and private sector information systems. To accomplish these goals, the plan established and expanded cyber counterintelligence education and awareness programs and workforce development to integrate counterintelligence into all cyber operations and analysis, increase employee awareness of the cyber counterintelligence threat, and increase counterintelligence collaboration across the government. The *Cyber CI Plan* is aligned with the National Counterintelligence Strategy of the United States of America (2007) and supports the other programmatic elements of the CNCI."

Counterintelligence (Stech 2016) reviewed counterintelligence definitions, status, and frameworks; it then described a cyber counterintelligence framework and outlined applications of cyber counterintelligence to the concept of active cyber defense. The report emphasized using cyber denial and deception techniques to enhance active cyber defenses. This framework forms the foundational argument for this chapter by showing how cyber denial and deception is essential to thwarting cyber espionage.

This chapter describes how defenders might build a tailored active cyber defense system for cyber counterintelligence, referred to as the cyber deception chain, to mitigate cyber spy actions within the cyber espionage "kill chain." While the chapter describes a concept and not an operational system, the logic and details are provided of how the cyber deception chain may enable defenders to apply cyber denial and deception in their cyber counterintelligence playbook operations to mitigate a cyber espionage threat and thwart cyber spies.

The hypothetical case study in this chapter describes specific applications for cyber denial and deception techniques to counter the actual cyber espionage techniques recently used by advanced persistent threat (APT) attackers, known as APT28 and APT29,[2] in conflicts between Russia and Ukraine, and other nations. While the cyber counterintelligence defenses described in the case study are hypothetical, the cyber espionage attack mechanisms are real.

History shows that so long as there is espionage, counterintelligence is a wise investment. This chapter illustrates how cyber denial and deception can enhance cyber counterintelligence operations, and provides the analysis and details for considering such operations in government- or enterprise-wide cyber counterintelligence plans. Researchers are providing increasingly detailed concepts for implementing cyber counterintelligence in enterprises.[3] We recommend such concepts, combined with cyber denial and deception, to cyber defenders.

2.2 The Cyber Espionage Threat

Espionage and cyber espionage remain major national security threats. While there have been calls for enhanced cyber counterintelligence for some time, each year seems to bring new and even more dramatic examples of cyber espionage. Open-

---

[2]These two threat agents have been code named by different cyber threat intelligence organizations. APT28 and APT29 are the code names used by FireEye and other organizations, and are used in this report for convenience.

[3]For example, Duvenage et al. (2016) describe the organizational requirements for strategic, operational, and tactical/technical cyber counterintelligence operations; Victor Jaquire and Sebastiaan von Solms (2017) outline a capability maturity model for cyber counterintelligence organizations; Duvenage, Sebastian von Solms, and Manuel Corregedor (2015) describe a cyber counterintelligence process model; and Johan Sigholm and Martin Bang (2013) propose a interorganizational information exchange model for cyber counterintelligence.

source research on cyber counterintelligence is scant, and commercial technology products for cyber counterintelligence are few. With the continued, and seemingly increasing threat of cyber espionage, the need for cyber counterintelligence is evident. Fortunately, counterintelligence and cyber security concepts are being expanded systematically to frame cyber counterintelligence operational concepts, allowing deeper analysis and refinement. Active cyber defense measures, and cyber denial and deception tactics, techniques, and procedures, can be adapted and applied to counter cyber espionage tradecraft phases and steps.

Geers et al. (2014) examined the motives behind cyber-attacks and found that they included cyber espionage, a phenomenon that they characterized as "a full-blown war zone" in which "governments across the globe clash for digital supremacy in a new, mostly invisible theater of operations." Cyber-attacks are a "key weapon for governments seeking to defend national sovereignty and project national power." Cyber espionage is instrumental; that is, the motives for cyber espionage cover political, military, economic, and primarily informational goals. Libicki (Geers et al. 2014: 3) argued nation-states carry out cyber espionage exploits "to achieve certain ends, which tend to reflect their broader strategic goals."

Russia makes no distinction about cyber warfare as an instrument used in isolation from other levers of state power and influence. Russia uses cyberspace to conduct espionage as just one element of Russia's mechanisms to project influence, along with diplomacy and propaganda, economics, military action, and other instruments of state power (Giles 2014, 2016; Weedon 2015).

Geers et al. (2014: 3–4) characterized Russian cyber threats, relative to other nations, as "more technically advanced and highly effective at evading detection. . . . [whose] cyber tactics are more surgical, reliant on advanced technologies and the cutting-edge work of contractors who are driven by competition and financial incentives." Geers et al. (2014: 12) characterized Russian exploit code as "significantly stealthier than its Chinese counterpart." Russian cyber-attack tactics, techniques, and procedures include weaponized email attachments, frequently changed attack patterns, exploits, and data exfiltration methods to evade detection. Russian hackers, according to Geers et al. (2014), "go to extraordinary lengths to hide their identities and objectives [and] run 'false-flag' cyber operations, designing their attack to appear as if it came from Asia."

Various cyber security companies (e.g., Kaspersky, FireEye, F-Secure) have identified large scale cyber-espionage networks associated with the Russian Federation. Technical analyses reflect a series of targeted attacks against diplomatic, governmental, and scientific research organizations in different countries, mostly related to the region of Eastern Europe, member states of the former-USSR (e.g., Ukraine), and countries in Central Asia.

Two large scale cyber-espionage networks that have been identified as being associated with the Russian Federation have multiple code names in Western cyber threat intelligence, but will be termed in this chapter and case study as advanced persistent threats—*APT28* and *APT29*.

2.3 Counterintelligence Definitions, Status, and Frameworks

In this chapter, we assume the objective of cyber counterintelligence is to put the adversary at an information disadvantage at a decisive moment; that is, the adversary has intelligence that is purposely degraded, and inferior at critical decisive moments, relative to the information available to one's own side.

Sims (2009) defined intelligence as "the collection, analysis, and dissemination of information for decision-makers engaged in a competitive enterprise." Sims's definition also covers counterintelligence. The purpose of intelligence, in Sims's theory (Sims 2009), is to gain a decision advantage for the intelligence actor over rivals, either by giving one's own side superior information, "or by purposefully degrading the adversary's information so that his decision-making suffers relative to one's own." In either case, success is gaining better information for one's own decision-makers than the information available to the opponent at those crucial moments when idea and intent become action. Similarly, failure is not "getting it wrong," but inferior decision-making based on degraded intelligence. In short, counterintelligence causes the failure of intelligence by causing the loss of better information for adversary decision-making, or degrading adversary intelligence at critical moments.

There are, at least, three types of counterintelligence per Lowenthal (2009: 231, and Chap. 7):

- *CI collection*—gaining information about an adversary's intelligence collection capabilities against one's own country;
- *Defensive CI*—thwarting efforts by other intelligence services to penetrate one's intelligence service; and
- *Offensive CI*—having identified an adversary's espionage efforts against one's own system, trying to manipulate these efforts by doubling the adversary's agents, or by feeding the agents false information that they report home.[4]

Ehrman (2009: 2–20) wrote there are four basic types of counterintelligence operations:

- *classic penetration*: (or a mole operation[5]) an officer of the opponent's intelligence service is recruited by one's own side and provides information from within the opposition service;
- *double-agent operations*: a double agent appears to be working for the opponent's intelligence service but is controlled by one's own side, and provides intelligence to the adversary that ultimately benefits one's own cause;

---

[4]It is interesting that Lowenthal's 1992 overview of U.S. intelligence mentions counterintelligence only briefly, as a defensive FBI function, c.f., Mark M. Lowenthal (1992) *U.S. Intelligence: Evolution and Anatomy, Second Edition*. London: Praeger.

[5]The term *mole* was applied to spies in the book *Historie of the Reign of King Henry VII* written in 1626 by Sir Francis Bacon; W. Thomas Smith (2003). *Encyclopedia of the Central Intelligence Agency*. New York: Infobase Publishing, p. 171.

- *local surveillance*: counterintelligence operations to identify a target service's officers and through access agents or physical and technical surveillance to uncover opposition intelligence activities and contacts; and
- *counterespionage*: hunting and uncovering, or isolating and controlling, an opponent's spies, double agents, moles, and penetration agents.

Prunckun (2014) defined a logical model for counterintelligence that captures these offensive and defensive definitional elements for passive and active counterintelligence (Table 2.1).

While the four categories of counterintelligence measures in Prunckun's (2014) logical model are distinct, in actual counterintelligence operations, an intelligence organization would use all four categories in a coherent, integrated program against an adversarial espionage threat. That is, the denial and deception operations in the passive offensive category (for example, creating fictional sub-nets of high value targets with access to manufactured information to deceive the adversary) would have to be closely coordinated with the neutralization measures taken in the active offensive measures (e.g., operation of double agents against the adversary's espionage operations). These four categories of counterintelligence measures for adversary espionage operations can be translated from the physical world of HUMINT operations to the virtual world of cyber espionage operations. While the instrumentalities of both adversary and defender must be adapted from the physical to the virtual world, the basic concepts of espionage (such as acquiring and handling sources) and the categories of counterintelligence (detect, deter, deny and deceive, neutralize) still apply to counterintelligence operations in cyberspace aimed at thwarting cyber espionage.

2.4   Cyber Counterintelligence Framework in Active Cyber Defense

Any active cyber defense, and especially cyber counterintelligence using cyber denial and deception, should depend on intelligence about the attacker, attacker's objectives, and tactics, techniques, and procedures. Intelligence on the adversary allows defenders to select defensive techniques that will work best. Knowing the objectives of an adversary, for example, can help the defender create more interesting lures for a counter-penetration operation.

The Adversarial Tactics, Techniques, and Common Knowledge (ATT&CK™) model developed by MITRE provided a taxonomy and framework describing advanced persistent threats and behavior in an enterprise network during the post-exploit phases of the cyber-attack lifecycle.[6] The model incorporates technical

---

[6]This section relies on material from Frank J. Stech, Kristin E. Heckman, and Blake E. Strom (2016), "Integrating Cyber-D&D into Adversary Modeling for Active Cyber Defense," in Sushil Jajodia, V.S. Subrahmanian, Vipin Swarup, & Cliff Wang eds. (2016), *Cyber Deception: Building the Scientific Foundation*. Switzerland: Springer.

Table 2.1 A logical model of the four counterintelligence principles

	Defensive counterintelligence	Offensive counterintelligence
Passive CI	*Detection*: the act of noticing that an event has taken place and that the event is somehow associated with a breach or potential breach of confidential information.	*Denial & Deception*: misleading an opponent about some aspect of the agency's operations, capabilities or intentions (or those of its client) to make them act (or not act). Deception may cause confusion delaying an opposition's ability to react effectively, or to project a false understanding that wastes the opponent's time and resources. Double agent operations are classic examples of the latter.
Active CI	*Deterrence*: the ability to prevent an opposition from gaining access to information. Deterrence discourages the opposition from attempting to conduct a penetration operation or by preventing an opposition's data collection operation. Deterrence must impose *unacceptable damage*, be *perceived*, and be *credible* to the opposition.	*Neutralization*: Blocking an opposition's intelligence collection operation through "defeat" operations—that is, collapse, failure, rout, or ruin. Collection operations can be thwarted by destruction, paralysis, loss of interest, or loss of confidence that collection will be able to achieve its objectives. The opponent distrusts its own collected intelligence.

descriptions of tactics, techniques, and procedures of APT28 and APT29, details specific sensor data observables and indicators for each tactics, techniques, and procedures, describes detection analytics for the tactics, techniques, and procedures, and specifies potential mitigations. ATT&CK describes techniques that can be used against enterprise network environments.

While there is a great deal of research on initial exploitations and the use of perimeter-focused cyber defenses, there is a gap in knowledge about adversary's approaches after their initial compromise of an enterprise network. ATT&CK incorporates information on adversary tactics, techniques, and procedures gathered from various sources, including MITRE research, public threat intelligence, penetration testing, vulnerability research, and from RED (adversary) versus BLUE (defender) team exercises and experiments. ATT&CK collects knowledge characterizing the post-exploit activities of cyber adversaries. ATT&CK includes the tactics, techniques, and procedures adversaries use to make decisions, expand access, and execute their objectives. ATT&CK describes an adversary's steps at a high enough level to be applied widely across different hardware platforms, while maintaining enough details to be technically applicable to cyber defenses and research.

Additionally, effective defender cyber counterintelligence operations require effective operations security (OPSEC) for the defended enterprise, including active cyber operations security. For example, if the cyber security defenders of the enterprise network continue to use their compromised systems to discuss and plan their response to the intrusion, the espionage adversary will simply counter any new defenses. The attacking hackers will read the e-mail traffic of the cyber defenders, corporate officers, incident response companies, that is, "listening in" on how the defenders were going to expel the espionage intruders. Effective cyber operations security and cyber counterintelligence require secure means to compartmentalize knowledge of the cyber counterintelligence and cyber denial and deception operations, and out-of-band secure communications to control and coordinate such plans without the espionage adversaries listening in and adapting to the defenses.

The research literature provides a few guides to cyber counterintelligence operations. Duvenage and von Solms (2014) advocated cyber counterintelligence as an effective means to turn the tables on cyber adversaries, exploiting malicious cyber actions to the defender's advantage and adversaries' detriment. They argued that cyber counterintelligence must be properly conceptualized and implemented. Table 2.2 shows the Duvenage and von Solms conceptualization based on their use of the counterintelligence concepts in Prunckun (2014), Sims (2009), and Sims and Gerber (2009). Duvenage et al. (2016) elaborated this framework, adding a range of actions between active and passive that includes deny, detect, and collect for defensive mode cyber counterintelligence, and collect, disrupt, exploit, and destroy for offensive mode cyber counterintelligence. They further differentiate tactical/technical, operational, and strategic cyber counterintelligence.

The Duvenage and von Solms (2014) cyber counterintelligence concept envisions a three-tier strategic concept:

1. *Cyber CI as Cyber*: CI theory and practice applied to the cyber domain as a conceptual template for modelling cyber counterintelligence actions for safeguarding cyber interests. Cyber counterintelligence has offensive and defensive modes that are distinguishable but not separable.
2. *Cyber CI as part of multi-spectrum CI*: To be effective, cyber CI must interlock with all-field counterintelligence—defensively and offensively. Cyber counterintelligence cements an integrated approach to securing the cyber space. Cyber counterintelligence includes the modelling of cyber actions on counterintelligence, and the integration of these offensive and defensive actions with conventional counterintelligence.
3. *Cyber CI as part of business intelligence and strategy*: Effective cyber counterintelligence protects and promotes cyber threat intelligence operations and the enterprise business strategy. Cyber counterintelligence is integrated into the enterprise business strategy and cyber threat intelligence landscape.

Heckman et al. (2015) detailed the role that cyber denial and deception can play as part of a larger or more comprehensive active cyber defensive scheme and provide tactical and strategic concepts for using cyber denial and deception operations within an organizational or business context. While their framework does not explicitly describe cyber denial and deception applied to cyber counterintelligence operations, they do provide models for implementing cyber denial and deception in cyber defensive operations generally, which might include passive-active, offensive-defensive cyber counterintelligence operations.

Table 2.2 Modes of cyber counterintelligence (Cyber CI)

Modes	Passive cyber CI	Active cyber CI
Defensive mode	*Denies adversaries access to own information and generates information about adversaries*	
	Passive Defense: Denies the adversary access to information through security measures, systems and procedures.	**Active Defense**: The collection of information on the adversary to determine its sponsor, modus operandi, network and targets. Methods include physical and electronic surveillance, dangles, double agents, moles, and electronic tapping.
Offensive mode	*Aims to manipulate, mislead, degrade, control and neutralize adversaries*	
	Passive Offensive: Some forms of collection, deception, disinformation and disruption. Include 'dummies' and 'decoys'.	**Active Offensive**: The adversary is deceived and its interpretation manipulated. Disinformation can be channeled through (for example) double agents and 'moles'. Active-offensive CI could include some forms of collection and Covert Action. (Covert action aims to influence role-players, conditions and events without revealing the sponsor's identity.)

Based on: Petrus Duvenage and Sebastian von Solms (2014)

2.5 Cyber Denial and Deception Techniques and Technologies to Enhance Cyber Counterintelligence in Active Cyber Defense

Heckman et al. (2015) described the substantial opportunity that exists for advancing cyber defenses by adapting and applying classical denial and deception theory and techniques to cyber defensive operations.[7] Such adaptation and application entail connecting the method's classical theory and techniques to cyber defense in a framework that facilitates greater use of the techniques in routine cyber defense operations.

As adversaries' attack techniques evolve, defenders' cyber systems need to evolve to provide the best continuous defense. This ushers in a new paradigm, consisting of a highly-customized network defense based on understanding the specifics of adversary attacks. By knowing how to engineer cyber systems to better detect and counter the deception aspects of advanced cyber threats, and how to apply denial and deception against cyber-attackers, defenders will force adversaries to move more slowly, expend more resources, and take greater risks, while themselves possibly avoiding or at least better fighting through cyber degradation.

---

[7]See also, Neil C. Rowe & Julian Rrushi (2016) *Introduction to Cyberdeception*. Switzerland: Springer; and Sushil Jajodia, V.S. Subrahmanian, Vipin Swarup, Cliff Wang, eds. (2016) *Cyber Deception: Building the Scientific Foundation*. Switzerland: Springer.

Heckman et al. (2015) used a traditional framework called the denial and deception methods matrix (for describing the basics of denial and deception in the physical world) and extended the matrix to cyber security with a set of techniques for applying denial and deception in active cyber defense. Heckman et al. (2015) also proposed using the *deception chain* to plan, prepare, and execute cyber denial and deception operations. The deception chain is like an adversary's *kill chain*. That is, adversaries follow a common pattern of behavior to compromise valuable information in a target network. Adversaries generally employ a cyberattack strategy, divided into the six phases of the cyber kill chain or attack lifecycle. Like the cyber kill chain, the deception chain is not always linear. Progression through the phases can be recursive or disjoint as necessary for denial and deception planners and cyber defense operators to achieve their goals.

Defensive deception can be applied at each phase of the cyber kill chain, and deception operational goals may be associated with each of the six kill chain phases (Heckman et al. 2015).

Defensive teams need to plan counterintelligence deception campaigns rather than incidents. Key to this strategy is allowing the espionage adversary apparent successes that are covertly under the control of the defenders. These successes reduce the spy' incentive to innovate, and provides defenders with a channel to manipulate adversary espionage action in pursuit of a deception goal beyond the integrity of their own cyber operations. To enable this strategy, defenders can use the deception chain that encompasses the phases of planning, preparation, and execution of denial and deception operations.[8] Defenders can use this deception chain to develop adaptive and resilient courses of action as defensive responses.

2.6 Hypothetical Case Study

To gain an appreciation of what this theoretical discussion might look like in practice, this section presents a hypothetical case study. It is based on two cyber espionage attacks by advanced persistent threat (APT) actors that were associated with Russia (FireEye 2014), known as APT28 and APT29 (Stone 2016; Schmoker 2015a, b), against countries in Europe, in particular, Ukraine. Both APT28 and APT29 used cyber denial and deception tactics, techniques, and procedures in their attacks. What this case study demonstrates is the possible application of denial and deception methods against actual attacks. This is a hypothetical case study because not every attacker technique is addressed, nor are all the possible cyber denial and

---

[8]Further description of the cyber deception chain and its applications in active cyber defenses are in Kristin E. Heckman, Frank J. Stech, Roshan K. Thomas, Ben Schmoker, Alexander W. Tsow (2015) *Cyber Denial, Deception and Counter Deception: A Framework for Supporting Active Cyber Defense*. Switzerland: Springer.

deception tactics, techniques, and procedures described that might be used against attackers.

For this case study, consider this NATO cyber counterintelligence strategic goal and these operational objectives:

- Support NATO strategic deception goal: convince Russian authorities their cyber intelligence supports propaganda but is not ready for kinetic war against NATO;
- Active & Passive CCI Defense: Reduce and eliminate effectiveness of APT28 tactics, techniques, and procedures for espionage; Eliminate or counter APT28 and APT29 malware and tradecraft;
- Passive CCI Offense: Poison APT28 and APT29 intelligence stream with deception materials; eliminate, corrupt, or covertly take over control of attackers' command and control; and
- Active CCI Offense: Feed Russian espionage units with false information (e.g., feed APT29 false information about actions and effects of APT28, and vice versa). Support apparent intrusion successes with cyber and non-cyber strategic NATO deception operations.

Various active cyber defense cyber-denial and deception tactics, techniques, and procedures would support the NATO counterintelligence operations. Technologies to help NATO identify espionage attack indications and provide warning, and to detail aspects of APT28 and APT29 information operations, include:

- Methods: malware family analysis for overlaps of use (same campaign);
- Infrastructure: correlation of launch sites (different campaigns, same source); and
- Tactics, Techniques, and Procedures: development of threat classifiers {target type, approach and exploitation} and association to {goals, intent and objectives}.

Countermeasures to recognize and counter threat actions include:

- defensive personnel measures, such as counter social engineering alerts (e.g., known targeted URLs) and counter-spear-phishing measures; and
- defensive denial and deception methods, such as trolling "bait victims" for attacker recruitment, exploitation, penetration; and
- cloning APT28/APT29 compromised boxes to operate as honey-traps, baited with beacons, double-backed backdoors, etc.

Table 2.3 summarizes the hypothetical NATO cyber counterintelligence tactics, techniques, and procedures in the cyber counterintelligence matrix.

Possible countermeasure sets for APT28 and APT29 include:

- Technologies to identify indicators and warning and aspects of information operations;

Table 2.3 Hypothetical NATO Cyber CI Operations against cyber espionage threat

Modes	Passive cyber CI	Active cyber CI
Defensive mode	**Deny access and collect on espionage threat**	
	Passive defense:	**Active defense**:
	Harden endpoint and server configurations	Gather intelligence on ongoing intrusions
		Use honeypots to gather late-stage implants and unpatched exploits
	Share actionable indicators across NATO intelligence partners	Share indicators to force infrastructure and "toolkit" rotation
Offensive mode	**Manipulate, degrade, control and neutralize espionage threat**	
	Passive offensive:	**Active offensive**:
	Use honeypots to deliver deception materials	Counter-hack hop points and control servers
	Sinkhole APT28 hop points	Trolling "bait victims" to lure attackers to controlled boxes
	Identify APT28 operatives	Operating controlled boxes as double agents to inject beacons, double-backed backdoors, etc. into APT28 control environment

- – Malware families overlaps of use (same campaign);
- – Separation of launch sites (different campaigns, same source);
- – Target type, approach and exploitation (various goals, intent, objectives);
- • Countermeasures to recognize and counter threat actions;
  - – Counter social engineering alerts (e.g., known targeted URLs);
  - – Counter-spear-phishing measures;
  - – Defensive cyber denial and deception, for example;
    - • Troll bait victims for recruitment, exploitation, penetration, etc.; and
    - • Clone compromised boxes, operate as honey traps, baited with beacons, double-backed backdoors, etc.

One possible additional APT29 countermeasure set for technologies to identify indicators and warnings and aspects of information operations, is the intelligence exfiltrated (comparisons of topics, goals, intent).

While it is suggested that there are specific goals and objectives for the cyber defenders in this case study, others are also possible. For example, rather than a NATO operational counterintelligence goal of convincing Russian authorities their cyber intelligence supports propaganda, but is not ready for kinetic war with NATO; the operational counterintelligence goal might be to convince the Russian authorities that their cyber intelligence is highly effective and ready for kinetic war against NATO, and then use the NATO controlled cyber intelligence channel to conduct strategic deceptions against Russian forces in conflicts.

2.7   Conclusion

This case study describes an actual attempt to penetrate a cyber network by espionage agents. It shows how cyber denial and deception can enhance cyber counterintelligence operations through an example that outlines the analytical thinking that is needed to incorporate these measures in a cyber counterintelligence plan. For espionage agents seeking to discover confidential information rudimentary methods will unlikely be enough to safeguard these data. Skilled operatives go to extreme lengths to obtain intelligence, so cyber security needs to respond in kind. And, counterintelligence's denial and deception theory and practices could be the prefect reply.

2.8   Principal Concepts

The principal concepts associated with this chapter are listed below. Demonstrate your understanding of each by writing a short definition or explanation in one or two sentences:

- ATT&CK;
- APT28; and
- APT29.

2.9   Study Questions

1. Explain why you might think that any active cyber defense, especially cyber counterintelligence using cyber denial and deception, should rely on intelligence about the attacker, the attacker's objectives, and tactics, techniques, and procedures? Are there times when engaging in active cyber defense without attacker intelligence is better than no response? If so, provide an example. If not, explain why.
2. By comparing-and-contrasting traditional, kinetic counterintelligence and cyber counterintelligence, discuss the key differences as well as the similarities.
3. Explain how the denial and deception methods matrix could be used as a cyber counterdeception method. Explain how it could then be used as cyber intelligence to inform a cyber counterintelligence operation.

2.10   Learning Activities

1. Take the case study from this chapter and build on it. Use the open source intelligence on APT28/APT29 for this learning activity. What additional hypothetical NATO cyber counterintelligence tactics, techniques, and procedures would you include in the cyber counterintelligence matrix (see Table 2.3)? Identify additional countermeasure sets for cyber counterintelligence against APT28/APT29 (the MITRE ATT&CK website has many mitigations to consider).
2. Choose one NATO cyber counterintelligence operation for execution and illustrate how you, acting as a counterintelligence organization, would use all four cyber counterintelligence categories in a coherent, integrated program against the APT28/APT29 espionage threat.
3. Choose one NATO cyber counterintelligence operation that involves deception for execution. Use the denial and deception methods matrix and the deception chain to illustrate how you would plan, prepare, and execute that cyber denial and deception counterintelligence operation against APT28/APT29/Russia.

References

ATT&CK™ (2017) Adversarial tactics, techniques & common knowledge. Viewed 23 Sept 2017. https://attack.mitre.org/

Coleman R (2014) Combating economic espionage and trade secret theft: May 13 statement before the Senate Judiciary Committee, Subcommittee on Crime and Terrorism. Viewed 22 May 2017. https://www.fbi.gov/news/testimony/combating-economic-espionage-and-trade-secret-theft

Defense Security Service (2015) Counterintelligence best practices for cleared industry. Viewed 22 May 2017. http://www.dss.mil/documents/ci/CIBooklet.pdf

Duvenage P, von Solms S (2014) Putting counterintelligence in cyber counterintelligence: back to the future. In: Liaropoulos A, George T (eds) Proceedings of the 13th European conference on cyber warfare and security ECCWS-2014. Piraeus, Greece, 3–4 July 2014

Duvenage P, Jaquire V, von Solms S (2016) Conceptualising cyber counterintelligence—two tentative building blocks. In: Proceedings of the 15th European conference on cyber warfare and security, Munich, Germany, 7–8 July 2016, pp 93–102

Ehrman J (2009) Toward a theory of CI: what are we talking about when we talk about counterintelligence? Stud Intell 53(2):5–20

FireEye (2014) APT28: a window into Russia's cyber espionage operations? 27 Oct 2014. Viewed 22 May 2017

French G, Kim J (2009) Acknowledging the revolution: the urgent need for cyber counterintelligence. Nat Intell J 1(1):71–90

Geers K, Kindlund D, Moran D, Rachwald R (2014) FireEye Report. WORLD WAR C: understanding nation-state motives behind today's advanced cyber-attacks, FireEye, Inc. Viewed 22 May 2017. https://www.fireeye.com/content/dam/fireeye-www/global/en/current-threats/pdfs/fireeye-wwc-report.pdf

Giles K (2014) The next phase in Russian information warfare: report by the NATO Strategic Communications Centre of Excellence. Viewed 22 May 2017. http://www.stratcomcoe.org/download/file/fid/5134

Giles K (2016) Russia's 'New' tools for confronting the west continuity and innovation in Moscow's exercise of power: report by Chatham house. Royal Institute of International Affairs. Viewed 22 May 2017. https://www.chathamhouse.org/publication/russias-new-tools-confronting-west

Heckman K, Stech F, Thomas R, Schmoker B, Tsow A (2015) Cyber denial, deception and counter deception: a framework for supporting active cyber defense. Springer, Cham

Intelligence and National Security Alliance (2017) Counterintelligence for the 21st century. Viewed 22 May 2017. https://obamawhitehouse.archives.gov/the-press-office/2015/02/25/fact-sheet-cyber-threat-intelligence-integration-center

Kahn D (1967) The code breakers. Macmillan, New York

Lowenthal M (1992) U.S. intelligence: evolution and anatomy, 2nd edn. Praeger, London

Lowenthal M (2009) Intelligence: from secrets to policy. CQ Press, Washington, DC

O'Connell E (1994) Countering the threat of espionage. Security Management 38(5). Viewed 22 May 2017. https://www.questia.com/magazine/1G1-15501611/countering-the-threat-of-espionage

Office of the National Counterintelligence Executive (2013) Protecting key assets: a corporate counterintelligence guide. Viewed 22 May 2017. https://www.dni.gov/files/NCSC/documents/Regulations/ProtectingKeyAssets_CorporateCIGuide.pdf

Prunckun H (2014) Extending the theoretical structure of intelligence to counterintelligence. Salus J 2(2). Viewed 22 May 2017. http://www.salusjournal.com/wp-content/uploads/sites/29/2013/03/Prunckun_Salus_Journal_Issue_2_Number_2_2014_pp_31-49.pdf

Schmoker B (2015a) MITRE corporation briefing. Deception in the wild: a case study of APT28. MITRE. Viewed 22 May 2017

Schmoker B (2015b) MITRE corporation white paper. Denial and deception in a targeted espionage operation. MITRE. Viewed 22 May 2017

Sims J (2009) Defending adaptive realism: Intelligence theory comes of age. In: Gill P, Marrin S, Phythian M (eds) Intelligence theory: key questions and debates, United States. Routledge, New York, p 154

Sims J, Gerber B (eds) (2009) Vaults, mirrors, and masks: rediscovering US counterintelligence. Georgetown University Press, Washington, DC

Skerry M (2013) Financial counterintelligence: how changes to the U.S. anti-money laundering regime can assist U.S. counterintelligence efforts. Santa Clara Law Rev 53(205):217

Stech F (2016) MITRE corporation technical report MTR 160057. Cyber Counterintelligence, MITRE. Viewed 22 May 2017

Stech F, Heckman K, Strom B (2016) Integrating cyber-D&D into adversary modeling for active cyber defense. In: Jajodia S, Subrahmanian VS, Swarup V, Wang C (eds) Cyber deception: building the scientific foundation. Springer, Cham

Stone J (2016) Meet fancy bear and cozy bear, Russian groups blamed for DNC hack. Christian Science Monitor, 15 June. Viewed 22 May 2017. http://www.csmonitor.com/World/Passcode/2016/0615/Meet-Fancy-Bear-and-Cozy-Bear-Russian-groups-blamed-for-DNC-hack

Weedon J (2015) Beyond "Cyber War": Russia's use of strategic cyber espionage and information operations in Ukraine. In: Geers K (ed) Cyber war in perspective: Russian aggression against Ukraine. NATO CCD COE Publications, Tallinn

Chapter 3
The Human Element: The "Trigger" on Cyber Weapons

John J. McGonagle

3.1 Introduction

"Social engineering uses influence and persuasion to deceive people by convincing them that the social engineer is someone he is not, or by manipulation. As a result, the social engineer is able to take advantage of people to obtain information with or without the use of technology," so wrote Mitnick and Simon (2002: iv). But, the term these authors used—*social engineering*—is a corruption of its real meaning; the reference to planning for societal change by exerting influence over the behaviors of an entire population (Tolman 1909). What Mitnick and Simon were referring to is nothing more than a confidence trick. The authors should have also pointed out that the phenomenon is nothing new, and certainly not unique to the field of information technology.

Arguably, the first *reported* use of a "con" was by the *New York Herald* in July 1849 where that newspaper reported ". . .in its *Police Intelligence* column a series of four unsigned short reports about the arrest of a swindler, purportedly known as the 'Confidence Man,' (Braucher and Orbach 2015: 251)." The news article said that Samuel Thompson[1] convinced gullible people to hand over money and valuables by winning their confidence: "Have you confidence in me to trust your watch until to-morrow?" (Braucher and Orbach 2015: 256).

This chapter deals with the protection of information from penetration by confidence tricksters. It relies on the principles used in competitive intelligence to make this type of attack more difficult. Despite the high-tech environment in which businesses operate, paradoxically, cyber penetrations often rely on low-tech

---

[1]He is reported to have used other names, including William Thompson (Braucher and Orbach 2015: 252, fn. 16).

J. J. McGonagle (✉)
The Helicon Group, Blandon, PA, USA
e-mail: jjm@helicongroup.com

© Springer International Publishing AG, part of Springer Nature 2018
H. Prunckun (ed.), *Cyber Weaponry*, Advanced Sciences and Technologies for
Security Applications, https://doi.org/10.1007/978-3-319-74107-9_3

approaches, which can be surprisingly effective. Nonetheless, these attempts can be foiled by alert personnel. Several real-world cases demonstrate how experience-proven principles can be applied to remedy similar situations (McGonagle and Vella 1998; Vella and McGonagle 2017).

3.2 Rationale

Why use competitive intelligence as a model? Why not use some combination of offense, active defense, and passive defense? Active defense refers to a:

> ...spectrum of proactive cyber-security measures that fall between traditional passive defense and offense. These activities fall into two general categories, the first covering technical interactions between a defender and an attacker. The second category of active defense includes those operations that enable defenders to collect intelligence on threat actors and indicators on the Internet, as well as other policy [approaches] (e.g. sanctions, indictments, trade remedies) that can modify the behavior of malicious actors. Activities that produce effects solely within an actor's own networks are often referred to as passive defenses. They primarily involve the use of perimeter-focused tools like firewalls, patch management procedures, and antivirus software. These can be installed and left to function independently. Passive defenses can also include procedures like white or blacklisting and limiting administrative authorities. While passive defenses are necessary for a sound cyber-security regimen, they are insufficient by themselves to defend against the most advanced cyber-aggressors. (George Washington University 2016: v, xi, 9)

These concepts are certainly valid, but they do not focus enough on the human element; the reason behind most data breaches. In the cyber-sphere, this is the use of a pretext or subterfuge. These ploys come from a basket of "techniques employed by cybercriminals designed to lure unsuspecting users into sending them their confidential data, infecting their computers with malware or opening links to infected sites" (Kaspersky Labs).

> When individuals are targeted (for social engineering) the criminals are usually trying to trick you into giving them your passwords or bank information, or access your computer to secretly install malicious software–that will give them access to your passwords and bank information as well as giving them control over your computer. (Webroot)

But, as Prunckun (2015, 153) pointed out, *social engineering* is simply a "con": "The technique is nothing more than a ruse, subterfuge, or pretext. In fact, *pretext* is the term most used by private investigators—private investigators rely heavily on this technique as a means of gaining information about their targets." A pretext is a polite expression for a confidence trick.

Second, competitive intelligence has developed defensive principles that are simple, but proven in practice (McGonagle and Vella 1998; Vella and McGonagle 2017). They apply to protecting sensitive business data; nonetheless they can be applied to protecting information from hostile cyber penetrations. These are presented here as they apply to cyber-security:

Step 1: Identify the data that needs protection—these are usually the company's vital information assets. Try to determine what a cyber attacker might seek out. Using a dollar amount for each piece of information or collection of like data is one way to assess what the information is likely to be worth to a foe.

Step 2: Assess the company's data exposure. Know where the company's vital information assets are produced and stored, who has access to it (including third party contractors), and review why they require access. But in doing so, avoid finger-pointing—just be thorough in identifying the critical information.

Step 3: Work with third parties who have access to your company's information assets, or to the system(s)that hold them, so you can sensitize them to the need to protect it. And, regularly remind them of their obligations—nicely.

Step 4: Have IT personnel work with your corporate security staff. Reinforce protections against the accidental release of vital information assets and of any passwords. Use simple methods to warn employees against opening documents or links that they were not expecting to see; avoiding computer access from public spaces; never using USB drives (also called *jump* or *thumb* drives), which can easily be lost (or can used to carry virus infections); checking your web sites for dated access points; and making regular backups that are stored separately from your operating system.

Step 5: Make sure employees and third parties know who to notify if they suspect a possible leak or loss of any information assets. This is not an enforcement issue, but an awareness issue. Employees should not be disciplined because they bring an issue to management's attention—by doing so, they are helping the company protect other information assets.

Step 6: Do not over react. When in doubt, shut-down a system that might be compromised. But, do not try to protect everything from everyone, forever. If your company tries to do this, it is not likely to be able to conduct business. Be reasonable. (Vella and McGonagle 2017: 82–88).

3.3 Who

Before proceeding with a more in-depth discussion of cyber-security, our understanding would benefit from a quick overview of: (1) who gets attacked; (2) how this happens; and (3) why they are a target.

The statistics about data breaches because of hostile penetrations are overwhelming. One source reports that in 2016 there were 4149 breaches reported that exposed over 4.2 billion records: the business sector accounted for 51% of reported breaches, government 11.7%, medical 9.2%, education 4.7%, and unknown 23.4% (Risk Based Security 2017). Google Research analyzed over a billion emails passing through its email servers, and reported that corporate email addresses were 6.2 times more likely to receive phishing attacks than private email addresses. In addition, they were 4.3 times more likely to receive malware as compared to personal accounts. Nonprofit email addresses are 2.3 times more likely to be targeted than are corporate addresses. In the malware category, ransomware was the largest threat (Google 2017). And, news reports reflect these indicators: Symantec, a software security provider, estimated that ransomware increased 35 percent in 2015 as compared to the previous year (Symantec 2016: 6).

3.4 How

While the type of damage to corporate information varies, successful cyber-attacks appear to have one thing in common: "[n]inety-five percent of all security breaches at the workplace are because of human error" (Schiff 2017). However, taking a more positive perspective on what could be a dismal outlook, "private sector companies that implement basic practices of cyber hygiene can prevent the vast majority of malicious cyber activity" (George Washington University).

3.4.1 Attack Vectors

Hacking: This is "the unauthorized intrusion into a computer or a computer network. The person engaged in hacking activities is generally called a *hacker*, and what the hacker does is called a *hack*. A hacker may access data, change data, change system settings or security structures—all without the authority of the legal owner." (Technopedia)

Malware: "Malware includes viruses, spyware, and other unwanted software that gets installed on your computer or mobile device without your consent. These programs can cause your device to crash, and can be used to monitor and control your online activity. They also can make your computer vulnerable to viruses and deliver unwanted or inappropriate ads. Criminals use malware to steal personal information, send spam, and commit fraud." (US Federal Trade Commission 2015)

Phishing: "Another category of unwanted email is called phishing, a phonetic play on the word fishing. It refers to baiting, or luring, Internet users to click on links that take them to malicious websites." (Bayuk et al. 2012: 111). This enables the criminal to steal personal identity details or other vital information, such as credit card numbers. One columnist has detailed a phishing attack that works 90% of the time: it targets firms that frequently ship goods or have employees that travel often. Employees receive email messages that appear to deal with an airline reservation, a receipt for shipping, and the like. (Sjouwerman, April 2017a, b, c, d). Another involves "spoofed" emails, supposedly coming from the US Securities and Exchange Commission, (SEC) aimed them at company officials who file documents with the SEC. In some cases, corporate executives clicked on a fake Microsoft Word file attached to the email, which is made to appear as coming from the SEC's filing service. (Roberts 2017)

Ransomware: This software allows the cybercriminal to take control of a targeted system, encrypt it, and then threatens to destroy it if not paid a specific ransom by a specific time. A variation is when it threatens or includes the release of data or other files if the ransom is not delivered. "Phishing with spoofed email addresses is the No. 1 ransomware attack vector". (Sjouwerman, Feb. 14, Sjouwerman 2017a, b, c, d)

Spam: The "unsolicited and unwelcome advertisements sent to people via e-mail or posted in newsgroups." (Downing et al.: 448) The term has it origin in the British comedy, *Monty Python's Flying Circus* [1970].

Spear phishing: This is a variety of phishing because it is "a type of fraud carried out by sending out e-mails that pretend to come from a bank or corporation with which the victim has an account." (Downing et al.: 362)

Virus: A computer virus is "a computer program that automatically copies itself, thereby 'infecting' other disks or programs without the user knowing it, and then plays some kind of trick or disrupts the operation of the computer." When that program runs, the virus runs. (Downing et al.: 514)

Experience shows how common and dangerous human engineered-attacks can be:

- One Internet security firm reports that "Spear-Phishing Campaigns Targeting Employees Increased 55 Percent in 2015" (Symantec 2016: 6).
- Another one estimates that over 55% of identity thefts are due to hacking, skimming or phishing, that is involved confidence tricks. (ITRC 2015)
- While hacking is the most common breach type reported to Internet security firms (as of 2013), low-tech approaches continue to be used effectively and extensively. One source estimated that combining phishing, virus or Trojan web-based intrusions (including where data is potentially exposed through search engines, or on public pages), lost/missing/stolen hardware, fraud/swindles (the fraud usually being external and the con external), and lost/stolen/missing documents accounts for perhaps 40% of all intrusions. (Risk Based Security 2017: 4).

3.5 Why

3.5.1 Identify Vital Information Assets

This comprises two elements: what you must protect and what cybercriminals usually try to obtain, delete, or hold for ransom. The first includes what you are legally obligated to protect as well as what you need to protect to assure the continued operation of your business. The former group varies with industry, but will include things such as medical records, tax payer information, credit card numbers, etc. One way to do this is to visualize what data you would have to have saved or can rebuild (whether from hard copy records or from records in the possession of others) to continue your enterprise's operation (this should be recorded in the company's continuity plan). You may be surprised what you must protect (or retain) and what you do not. For example, from the perspective of the employee, there is a real question whether an employer has a legal duty to safeguard the personal information of its own employees. (Enslin v. Coca-Cola)

"[H]acking has become a lucrative industry." (Bremmer 2017: 14)

The second involves understanding what is sought and why. Cybercriminals seek one or more of three options: (1) to steal and then use, misuse, or sell the data; (2) to damage a target by deleting its data; or (3) a ransomware attack. However, one estimate is that less than 5% of the cases involve "wiping" corporate data (Makuch 2017).

To conceptualize this, the method of gaining access must be differentiated from what the intruder wants. Most often, an intruder wants records (data); secondarily, they may hold your data for ransom; and finally, they may just be seeking to destroy (wipe) your records. 42.6% of data breaches reported exposed email addresses and 38.1% exposed passwords. All the following fell below 20%: social security numbers, credit card numbers, phone numbers, financial account numbers, and medical data (Risk Based Security 2017: 4).

These attacks can take many forms on a wide variety of targets. "Some of the most common threats include website tampering, theft of data, denial-of-service attacks, and malicious code and viruses." (US Small Business Administration n.d.: 3) Consider, for example, the on-line warnings of the US Internal Revenue Service (IRS) about the variety of cyberattacks it is familiar with:

E-mail phishing schemes posing as potential clients, trying to trick [private tax] preparers into downloading malware onto their computers. Phishing e-mails that pose as IRS e-Services [a program that allows tax returns to be filed electronically and these records to be accessed] and attempt to steal e-Services users' usernames and passwords. Remote takeover schemes in which cybercriminals actually take control of preparers' computers and file fraudulent tax returns [where refunds are sent to others]. (US IRS)

In this example, cybercriminals were targeting personal data for identity theft, including opening new credit accounts as well as seeking direct access to the IRS to file false returns and collect refunds.

In another case, a cyber-security contractor was infected by the W-2 spear phishing scam. W-2 is a tax form showing an employee's name, Social Security number, and income earned. That scam involved sending emails to an employee that looked like they come from a C-level executive, asking for a file, with the W-2 tax information on all employees. As the targeted firm's CEO reminded its employees after the breach, a W-2 has "all the information to file fraudulent tax returns and [also] steal anyone's identity" (Sjouwerman 2017a, b, c, d).

3.5.2 Assess Your Vital Information Assets' Vulnerability

Consider the following eight issues (at a minimum):

1. Who has administrative rights to the corporate system? This type of access allows a user to make changes on a computer or a system that will affect other users of the computer or the system. That includes changing security settings, installing new software and hardware, accessing files, and even making changes to other users' accounts. These users, and their computers, are prime targets for hackers. Make sure you know who all of them are.
2. Who has the authority to ask others to send them large amounts of data? Are there any protocols in place as to how and when such requests can be made and how they must be confirmed? If not, they should be developed.
3. Do all systems get automatic updates of software? Can any person delay or even block this update process? Why? There needs to be a good reason because experience shows that software vulnerabilities are a key vector for penetration. Updates correct these vulnerabilities.
4. Are all employees required to change their passwords regularly? Are they required to use strong passwords, ones not based on personal information and include upper- and lower-case letters, numerals, and symbols? How is this policy prescribed for easy compliance?
5. Can anyone access other's data from a computers other than at the firm's offices? How? Why? If so, and there is a need, then policies to guide users in the use of proven security devices and software need to be developed.
6. Regular cyber-security training has helped many corporations with online line, self-paced subjects often the easiest methods. These have short quizzes at the end of the modules that provide management with feedback.
7. Is particularly sensitive data—such as trade secrets, electronic products, confidential files—stored in encrypted files? A policy for using encryption should be considered, with guidance on what data should be subjected to encryption, when, and for how long.
8. When any employee leaves the business, is his/her computer access automatically terminated? On departure, are all his/her electronic devices, including personal devices, checked to ensure that corporate passwords and information systems accesses are not taken away. If this is not the case, a policy that requires this as part of the employee's exit interview should be developed. A clause in their employment contact should also be considered that allows management to view their personal devices upon termination (this may require qualified legal advice as to how this is written).

3.5.3   Vital Information

It is important to know where the company produces and stores its vital information, who has access to it, and to review why they have that degree of access.

3.5.3.1   Basics

Determine where sensitive corporate data are stored. Every person or organization that has access to that location or to computers linked to that represent potential access points. For example, in April 2017, it was reported that Netflix was hacked by someone demanding a ransom in order to prevent the release of new episodes of its series. Netflix stated that this was due to a third-party hack of a "production vendor used by several major TV studios [which] had its security compromised" (Washington Post 2017: A6).

Next, establish who has administrative rights—this type of access is critical to protect. Then, determine who else has limited access to add, change, or delete data, without having administrative rights. This group of users typically includes those accessing or entering customer orders, supply chain and logistical operations and instructions, employees dealing with personnel and benefits, and customers entering or tracking their own orders.

Finally, review the company's website, and those firms linked to yours, for access points. "Websites are a critical element in major attacks: they are a way into the network, they are a way into sensitive data, and they are a way [for hackers] to reach customers and partners" (Symantec 2016: 23).

How many access points are there? Probably a bewildering number. But, the purpose of this effort is to identify the way that a cyber-criminal can access your data. And, that starts with knowing the variety of paths leading to it.

What does this survey show you? Take, for example, the healthcare industry. There, a review of IT staff identified the following as among their top areas of concern:

- 80% reported that employee security awareness is one of their greatest concerns;
- Exposure of their data due to partners or other third-parties was a important concern for almost 69%; and
- Securing wireless communications or BYOD (or Bring Your Own Device to work) was a high concern for 54% (Snell 2017).

3.5.3.2   IT Infrastructure

Information technology infrastructure has its own issues, but here too, the low-tech approach adds value. Consider this advice from a cyber-security firm:

For any infrastructure services, including file servers, web servers, and other Internet-connected devices:

- Stay informed about emerging threats.
- Keep systems up to date. . .
- Use integrated security software. . .
- Use a strong firewall. . .
- Employ multi-layer protection. . .
- [T]rain staff well.
- Control access. . .
- Always keep backups offsite. (Symantec 2016: 66).

3.5.3.3 Internet of Things

Access points continue to multiply. The Internet of Things (IoT) is rapidly spreading and, in doing so, is spreading concern. In 2015, Symantec reported seeing "growing numbers of IoT attacks in the wild. In numerous cases, the vulnerabilities were obvious and all too easy to exploit. IoT devices often lack stringent security measures. . ." (Symantec 2016: 16) Regardless, there are simple things that can be done. The U.S. Federal Trade Commission suggested:

> Don't just click 'next' when you set up your IoT device. Review the default settings carefully . . . and use the security features for your device. If it allows you to set up a code lockout ('three strikes and you're out') and enable encryption, you can add a layer of protection to your device.
>   Download the latest security updates for your IoT device. To be secure and effective, the software that comes with your device needs updates. . .
>   Change your pre-set passwords. The manufacturer may have assigned your device a standard default password. Hackers know the default passwords, so change it to something more complex and secure. (Lazarus 2016)

3.5.3.4 Public Networks and Social Media

Assume all public networks are vulnerable (Palmer 2016). It is not always possible, but if it can be avoided, do not transmit critical data over a public system, such as free hotel or restaurant Wi-Fi. An alternative is to use "your smartphone as a hotspot for your laptop . . . which offers [you] a secure connection" (Rubin 2016). Nevertheless, there is some good news in all this caution: "In recent years, [social media] sites have . . . made it much harder for the attackers to exploit them (Symantec 2016: 30)" (Fig. 3.1).

3.5.4 Reinforce Basic Protections

The most vital step is to have all employees focus on their passwords. This is because "seventy-six percent of attacks on corporate networks are due to weak passwords. . . ." Examples of weak passwords are a user's partner's or child's birth

Fig. 3.1 Cyber-security is essential for all devices connected to the Internet (Photograph by Traci Boutwell and courtesy of the U.S. Department of Defense)

date, his/her home town, a pet's name, or a favorite car—all facts that can easily be located by a search of social media. (Schiff 2017)

There are four keys features in creating a strong password and keeping it secure:

1. Use a long password because the longer the password, the more difficult it is to break. Consider using at least ten characters comprising upper- and lower-case letters, numerals, and symbols.
2. Avoid using the same password for multiple accounts. If a hacker obtains your password, they can then use it to take control of your other accounts.
3. Never share passwords on over the telephone, in texts, or by email. Beware of messages from businesses asking you for your password. "Legitimate companies will not send you messages asking for your password. If you get such a message, it's probably a scam" (US Federal Trade Commission 2011).
4. Passwords need to be stored in a secure place that is out of sight. Look around and see how many co-workers have their passwords on a Post-It note next to their workstations; or stuck to the underside of their keyboard, or at the back of their monitor. These are not secure locations even though they may be out of sight.

3.5.5 Improve Awareness

Creating and maintaining awareness is not a one-time effort. It requires participation by all employees and management as well. In the workplace, there are some unrealistic attitudes about IT that must be recognized and overcome. As one cyber expert put it, "(m)y concern is; because employees believe their IT departments filter emails, many are conditioned to receive spam 'at home,' but not at the office [w]hich makes end-users that much more likely to randomly 'click' while at work" (Cooper 2017).

> "Lack of training is one of the most significant information security weaknesses in most organizations." (US Small Business Administration: 5)

By way of example, take the problems that arose from the 2016 US election and hacking efforts that took place during this time. They illustrate the need to raise awareness about the human element in cyber-security:

- John Podesta, chair of Mrs. Clinton's presidential election campaign had his computer hacked and hundreds of his emails were made public through *WikiLeaks.* "*Wikileaks* founder, Julian Assange, revealed...that Clinton Campaign Chair John Podesta's email password was 'password'" (O'Brien 2017). The lesson here? Create and use obscure passwords. Even better, create robust passwords by combining letters, numbers, and symbols, such as in P@s$w0rdS, and then change them often.
- "One [Podesta] email in particular reveals that DNC [Democratic National Committee] officials had discovered their email system had been compromised. Yet, instead of taking cautionary steps to prevent future hacks, they sent out new passwords to the team—via email" (O'Brien 2016). The lesson in this? Never assume a single security breach is, or will, stay limited.
- Concerned that it might have been attacked like its opposite number, the Republican National Committee reportedly got information about what kinds of malicious emails to look for it. It then determined that that its electronic filters had blocked emails matching the ones it had been warned about (O'Brien 2017). What can we understand from this? Keep your company's spam filters and other protective protocols up-to-date, and do not be afraid to call for help.

3.5.6 *Act, But Do Not Over React*

When help is needed, make certain that you know what company data requires protection. There are four steps in doing this:

- Protect company data that is most difficult to replicate;
- Protect data that is crucial to business operations;
- Protect data that is already partially protected—remember, partial is rarely enough; and
- Protect sensitive data only as long as it is necessary. Lift protective security measures when they are no longer needed.

Then, back-up that critical data and isolate it—off-line and off-site.

> Your goal should be the ability to restore systems and data to what existed before any threat is realized. Make back-up copies of important information and restore weekly. Store a backup copy offsite for safe keeping. You should also test your backups to make sure that they actually work. (US Small Business Administration: 7)

Do not forget to exercise care when using old equipment—bear in mind the importance of disposing of old computers, smart phones, and media (i.e. CDs, hard drives, USB drives) securely. Just because you no longer use the device does not mean a third party cannot access the information that was once on it.

3.6   Best Practice

Best practice has become a universal method for producing superior results when compared to other ways of operating. Having a set of best practice policies and procedures helps companies maintain quality, and can be used as the basis for self-assessment. Reflecting on the eight steps for defending sensitive data, we can see that there are many aspects on the human element that should be addressed. This is because the human dimension is key to the execution of many cyber weapons.

To fortify cyber-security to make the human element attack vector less vulnerable, a best practice checklist can be postulated. At the core are three considerations: (1) employee training; (2) management of IT systems; and (3) engaging management. The following checklist represents a compilation of what experience has shown to be best practice. (Ambrose 2016; Berman 2017; Federal Communications Commission; Federal Communications Commission Cyber-security for Small Business; Federal Trade Commission 2011, 2015; Hackett et al. 2017: 75–76; KnowledgeBe4; Palmer 2016; Ruffini 2017; Schiff 2017; Sjouwerman 2017a, b, c, d; Stowell 2017; Toren 2014; US SBA, 1–8; and Winkler 2017)

1. **Routinely train employees and managers in basic, proven practices**:

   - Remind users to conceal personal information that may be available elsewhere to protect company assets. The most obvious example of providing personal information is via social media. That information is critical because they may tend to default to personal passwords.
   - Compel users to have strong, unique passwords, and to change them often. This could be done by coding a requirement to have a certain minimum length to every password (e.g., ten characters) and make it include a capital letter, a number, and a symbol. Also, consider requiring that, after a predetermined number of days, all users are required to change their password, a practice of some banks.
   - Require the IT department to back-up all sensitive data. Since cannot be known when data will be compromised, or how, that data needs to be backed-up.
   - Consider installing anti-phishing software, including software that can train employees to avoid these types of attacks. That way, users who are most vulnerable will be reminded to be careful.
   - Do not post critical documents online. A vetting policy that outlines how a document should be vetted before being made public should be considered.
   - Do not "surf the web" from an administrative account. This can open another attack vector.

- Never download software or files from an unknown website or from unknown email sources. Do not allow a website to install any software on your computer.
- Have employees using individual computers use screen locking, and always log-on and off, and power down the system at the end of the day. Unattended, idle computers on a system can be captured by outsiders. Close this attack vector too.
- Instead of clicking on a link in an email, type the site URL directly into the browser. Links may look legitimate, but when clicked, could download malware or direct the user to a scam site.
- Provide personal or confidential information only through secure sites, which are always identified with URL prefix of "https."
- Have all mobile telephone users' password protect their devices, encrypt their data (usually on a removable micro-SD card), and install security applications to prevent thieves from stealing information while the phone is on a public network. Also, create reporting procedures for lost or stolen equipment.
- Never plug a free USB drive, or one that has been "found," into the company's system. It is hypothesized that it was via a USB drive that the Stuxnet worm/virus was introduced to Iran's nuclear laboratory in 2010. Always assume that these devices are infected; have them checked by IT staff before putting them in to service.
- Alert employees to specific threats, like a new spear phishing campaign, or malware investigation. These alerts are carried in the news media as well as provided via security software developers. Advise users not to validate a suspicious email by sending a reply. Instead, call or send out a fresh message to an email address that is already known.
- Be wary of people asking to access who do not have a genuine need to know; and be alert for users with a need to know, but who are accessing data perhaps too frequently, or downloading more data than what would be expected in their position's role.
- Exercise extra caution when travelling. For example, avoid using free Wi-Fi at public hotspots because these offers may be spoofs. Also, many public Wi-Fi networks lack strong security protections. That makes it easier for hackers to capture users' passwords, and other sensitive data.

2. **Follow best practices in managing your IT systems at all levels**:

- Run reputable antivirus software and keep it up to date.
- Provide firewall security for all Internet connections.
- Use encryption/secure sockets layer (SSL) technology because it provides security, privacy, and data integrity for your websites as well as your users' personal information.
- Update your corporate operating systems and software as software developers release new products. Many times, the new patches are specifically designed to foil cybercrime.
- Where appropriate, enable two-factor authentication. This is an additional layer of security requiring a password and a username, plus something that

only that the user has access to. It could be a biometric, like a finger print, or the contents of a text message immediately sent to that person's previously registered smart phone when access is sought.
- Consider using a virtual private network (VPN). This allows a user to connect to the Internet by way of a server run by a VPN provider. That process assures that all data traveling between the user's computer, smart phone, or tablet, and server is securely encrypted.
- Backup sensitive data automatically, and on a regular schedule. Then store the e-copies either offsite or in the cloud; encrypt the backups if that is possible.
- Isolate your payment systems from other, less secure programs. Also, do not use the same computer to process payments and to access the Internet.

3. **Engage all levels of management**:
- Create and keep up to date a data disaster recovery plan, sometimes referred to as a business continuity plan. Such a plan should be flexible as well as scalable, since it must address a wide variety of disruption scenarios. These can range from situations where data center's overall integrity is untouched, to one where it is destroyed.
- Review the availability and costs of cyber liability insurance. This type of insurance is commonly available from major property/casualty insurers. It covers a business' liability for a data breach when the firm's customers' personal information, such as credit card or Social Security numbers, is exposed/stolen by a hacker. They usually cover expenses associated with these data breaches, including notification costs, credit monitoring, costs to defend claims by regulators, fines and penalties, and losses resulting from identity theft.
- Alert IT staff to the numerous free government resources that enable them to develop a training program or to vet your existing program against industry standards. In the US, these sources include the US Small Business Administration (US SBA), National Institute of Standards and Technology (Wilson and Hash 2003), the Federal Communications Commission (FCC, Cyberplanner), and the Federal Trade Commission (FTC 2011, 2015)

3.7 Conclusion

Although popular culture could lead one to conclude that cyber penetrations are all about devices and software exploits, the reality is that the human element plays a pivotal part. Without gullibility, it would be difficulty-to-impossible to penetrate a well-crafted cyber-security system. Like the first reported swindler who conned people in to giving them their watches, today's con artists are focused on bigger prizes—information. This chapter looked at data and the methods businesses can use to identify what is critical to their operations, and some simple, yet highly effective ways to protect it. These methods use the principles employed in competitive intelligence that states that, regardless of the high-tech environment in which corporations operate, cyber penetrations are usually facilitated by low-tech approaches via the human element.

3.8   Principal Concepts

The principal concepts associated with this chapter are listed below. Demonstrate your understanding of each by writing a short definition or explanation in one or two short sentences.

- Attack vectors;
- Best practice;
- Data breaches;
- Hostile penetrations; and
- Social engineering vs confidence trick/pretext.

3.9   Study Questions

1. Explain why a two-factor authentication system is an improvement over a simple password security system.
2. Explain why it is importance to include data back-up as part of a business's continuity plan.
3. Describe the steps involved in protecting information from hostile cyber penetrations.
4. Discuss how a business might go about developing a cyber-security training program.

3.10   Learning Activity

Referring to the section on best practice, use the three-point checklist presented in this section and apply it to a real-world situation. That is, apply the best practice principles to your workplace or a hypothetical workplace. In the case of the latter, this could be a place you formerly worked, or an amalgam of several past employers. The purpose is to develop a set of best practice policies and/or procedures that will help the business maintain data security.

References

Ambrose E (2016) The hidden dangers of free public Wi-Fi. August 3, 2016. http://www.aarp.org/money/scams-fraud/info-2016/dangers-of-free-public-wifi-ea.html?intcmp=AE-MON-CONP-SPOTLIGHT-SPOT1-FWN-TM816-TKOVR. Accessed 19 Apr 2017

Bayuk J, Healey J, Rohmeyer P, Sachs M, Schmidt J, Weiss J, Joseph (2012) Cyber-security policy handbook. Wiley, Hoboken

Berman J (2017) Don't wait for the Bait. Smart Meetings, April 2017. http://www.smartmeetings.com/technology-news/98427/dont-wait-bait-prevent-phishing. Accessed 13 July 2017

Braucher J, Orbach B (2015) Scamming: the misunderstood confidence man. Yale J Law Umanit 27 (2):249

Bremmer I (2017) The real cost of 'forced transparency'. Time, March 16, 2017, p 14

Chameleon Associates (2017) The method to the madness of criminal intent. February 9, 2017. https://chameleonassociates.com/cyber-security-methods/. Accessed 30 Mar 2017

Cooper BL (2017) Google: office inbox receives 6.2X more phishing and 4.3X more malware than your 779999Inbox at home. February 24, 2017. https://www.linkedin.com/pulse/google-office-inbox-receives-62x-more-phishing-43x-malware-cooper. Accessed 14 Apr 2017

Downing D, Covington M, Covington M, Covington C (2009) Dictionary of computer and internet terms, 10th edn. Barron's Educational Series, Inc, Hauppauge

Enslin v. The Coca-Cola Company et al. US district court for the eastern district of Pennsylvania., No. 2:14-cv-06476. Opinion 31 Mar 2017

George Washington University, Center for Cyber and Homeland Security (2016) Into the gray zone—the private sector and active defense against cyber threats. October 2016. https://cchs.gwu.edu/sites/cchs.gwu.edu/files/downloads/CCHS-ActiveDefenseReportFINAL.pdf. Accessed 19 Apr 2017

Google (2017) Targeted attacks against corporate inboxes—a gmail perspective RSA 2017. https://www.slideshare.net/elie-bursztein/targeted-attacks-against-corporate-inboxes-a-gmail-perspective-rsa-2017. Accessed 14 Apr 2017

Hackett, Robert, Jeff John Roberts (2017) The future of online security. Fortune, May 1, 2017, pp 75–76

Identity Theft Resource Center (ITRC) (2015) Data breaches increase 40 percent in 2016, finds new report from identity theft resource center and cyberscout. http://www.idtheftcenter.org/2016databreaches.html. Accessed 12 Apr 2017

Kaspersky Lab. Social engineering. https://usa.kaspersky.com/resource-center/definitions/social-engineering. Accessed 13 Apr 2017

KnowledgeBe4.https://info.knowbe4.com/kmsat-request-a-demo-1?ads_cmpid=216440141&ads_adid=10468528541&ads_matchtype=p&ads_network=g&ads_creative=171774788525&utm_term=security%20awareness%20training&ads_targetid=aud-290844403135:kwd-13521353&utm_campaign=&utm_source=adwords&utm_medium=ppc&ttv=2&gclid=Cj0-KEQjwzpfHBRC1iIaL78Ol-eIBEiQAdZPVKhfQfEfpHCS0xtdjHPSXI8_NdSf9gEp4q8f3SAnm7TgaAumg8P8HAQ. Accessed 6 Apr 2017

Lazarus A (2016) What you need to know to secure your IoT devices. December 7, 2016. https://www.consumer.ftc.gov/blog/what-you-need-know-secure-your-iot-devices. Accessed 19 Apr 2017

Makuch B (2017) Cyberwar—season 1. Viceland Network, Mar 2017. https://www.viceland.com/en_us/show/cyberwar

McGonagle JJ, Vella CM (1998) Protecting your company against competitive intelligence. Praeger, New York

Mitnick KD, Simon WL (2002) The art of deception. Wiley Publishing, Indianapolis

O'Brien C (2016) Oops: DNC continued to email passwords after they knew they'd been hacked. Townhall, Posted: 14 Sept 2016 10:00 AM. https://townhall.com/tipsheet/cortneyobrien/2016/

09/14/oops-dnc-continued-to-email-passwords-after-they-knew-theyd-been-hacked-n2217948. Accessed 24 Mar 2017

O'Brien C (2017) Assange: Podesta's Password Was 'Password'. Townhall. January 4, 2017 12:00 PM. https://townhall.com/tipsheet/cortneyobrien/2017/01/04/assange-podestas-password-was-password-n2267069. Accessed 24 Mar 2017

Palmer A (2016) How to ensure your mobile data is secure at meetings. (interview with Terver Roald), March 23, 2016. http://www.successfulmeetings.com/Strategy/Meeting-Strategies/How-to-Secure-Your-Mobile-Data-at-Meetings/?t=head&cid=eltrMtgNews. Accessed 30 Mar 2017

Prunckun H (2015) Scientific methods of inquiry for intelligence analysis, 2nd edn. Scarecrow Press, Lanham

Risk Based Security (2017) Data breach quick view report: 2016 data breach trends—year in review. January 2017. https://pages.riskbasedsecurity.com/hubfs/Reports/2016%20Year%20End%20Data%20Breach%20QuickView%20Report.pdf. Accessed 24 Mar 2017

Roberts JJ (2017) Fake SEC emails target execs for inside information. Fortune. March 7, 2017. http://fortune.com/2017/03/07/sec-phishing/. Accessed 13 Apr 2017

Rubin C (2016) Before You Use the Public Wi-Fi, Read This. Entrepreneur. November 2016. https://www.entrepreneur.com/article/283943. Accessed 6 Apr 2017

Ruffini A (2017) Stay safe and enjoy the event. Incentive. 10 January/February 2017

Schiff JL (2017) How to fend off cyberattacks and data breaches. March 29, 2017. http://www.csoonline.com/article/3186389/cyber-attacks-espionage/how-to-fend-off-cyberattacks-and-data-breaches.html. Accessed 30 Mar 2017

Sjouwerman S (2017a) Dominos still falling 3 years after Yahoo data breach. Reading Eagle, Business Weekly, 7. March 28, 2017

Sjouwerman S (2017b) New phishing attack works 90% of time. Reading Eagle, Business Weekly, 7, April 11, 2017

Sjouwerman S (2017c) Pew survey finds Americans weak on online security issues. Reading Eagle, April 18, 2017

Sjouwerman S (2017d) Scam of the week blends CWO Fraud, W-2 phishing. Reading Eagle, February 14, 2017

Snell E (2017) Employee healthcare data security awareness top industry threat. Health IT Security, April 18, 2017. http://healthitsecurity.com/news/employee-healthcare-data-security-awareness-top-industry-threat. Accessed 4 May 2017

Stowell HG (2017) Teller trouble. March 1, 2017. https://sm.asisonline.org/Pages/Teller-Trouble.aspx. Accessed 30 Mar 2017

Symantec (2016) Internet security threat report. Volume 21, April 2016. https://www.symantec.com/content/dam/symantec/docs/reports/istr-21-2016-en.pdf. Accessed 12 Apr 2017

Tolman WH (1909) Social engineering. McGraw Publishing Co., New York

Toren M (2014) 5 No-brainer tips to avoid getting hacked. Entrepreneur.com. February 17, 2014. http://www.nbcnews.com/id/54235589/ns/business-small_business/t/no-brainer-tips-avoid-getting-hacked/#.WPEn2IjyuUk. Accessed 14 Apr 2017

US Federal Communications Commission. Cyberplanner. https://www.fcc.gov/cyberplanner. Accessed 13 Apr 2017

US Federal Trade Commission (2011) Computer security. September 2011. https://www.consumer.ftc.gov/articles/0009-computer-security. Accessed 19 Apr 2017

US Federal Trade Commission (2015) Malware. November 2015. https://www.consumer.ftc.gov/articles/0011-malware. Accessed 19 Apr 2017

US Internal Revenue Service (2016) Protect your clients: security summit partners warn tax pros of cybercriminals, launch new awareness tips. IR-2016-163. December 7, 2016. https://www.irs.gov/uac/protect-your-clients-security-summit-partners-warn-tax-pros-of-cybercriminals-and-launch-new-awareness-tips. Accessed 19 Apr 2017

US Small Business Administration (n.d..) SBA Cybersecurity for Small Businesses. https://www.sba.gov/tools/sba-learning-center/training/cybersecurity-small-businesses. Accessed 30 Mar 2017

Vella CM, McGonagle JJ (2017) Competitive intelligence rescue: getting it right. Praeger, New York

Walsh B (2017) A safer, smarter grid. Time, April 10, 2017, pp 30–32

Washington Post (2017) Hack claims he's released new episodes of netflix series. Reading Eagle, April 30, 2017, p A6

Webroot (n.d.) What is social engineering? https://www.webroot.com/us/en/home/resources/tips/online-shopping-banking/secure-what-is-social-engineering. Accessed 24 Mar 2017

Wilson M, Hash J (2003) Building an information technology security awareness and training program. US Department of Commerce, National Institute of Standards and Technology. October 2003. http://nvlpubs.nist.gov/nistpubs/Legacy/SP/nistspecialpublication800-50.pdf. Accessed 6 Apr 2017

Winkler I (2017) Why awareness needs to teach scam detection and reaction. March 2, 2017. http://www.csoonline.com/article/3176531/security-awareness/why-awareness-needs-to-teach-scam-detection-and-reaction.html. Accessed 19 Apr 2017

Chapter 4
Cyber Defense for IMGs and NGOs Using Crime Prevention Through Environmental Design

Troy Whitford

4.1 Background

Since 2012, Russia has increased censorship of political opposition websites. China exercises strong controls over that country's online environment—any content that the state considers subversive, is censored. So, the UNHRC human rights resolution that advocates a citizen's right to unencumbered access to the Internet has not been supported by either Russia or and China. But there are other countries that have far more restriction to the sharing of ideas—take for instance, North Korea or Iran which has developed its own Internet separate from the broader World Wide Web (Tormsen 2015). However, countries like America promote increased access to the Internet in its foreign policy. This was an approach that was supported by both Secretaries of State, John Kerry and Hillary Clinton. But, how do groups seeking democratic reform in authoritarian states express their grievances without jeopardizing their safety?

This chapter discusses an approach Issue Motivated Groups (IMGs) and Non-Government Organizations (NGOs) can consider for organizing online support using Crime Prevention Through Environmental Design theory (CPTED).

4.2 Introduction

Cyber defense is essentially about maintaining secrecy or confidentiality of information. For governments, the risk comes from political, economic, and military threats. Domestically, authoritarian governments have responded to these threats by

T. Whitford (✉)
Charles Sturt University, Canberra, ACT, Australia
e-mail: twhitford@csu.edu.au

© Springer International Publishing AG, part of Springer Nature 2018
H. Prunckun (ed.), *Cyber Weaponry*, Advanced Sciences and Technologies for
Security Applications, https://doi.org/10.1007/978-3-319-74107-9_4

attempting to control the online environment. Events commonly referred to as the *Arab Spring*, and Internet filtering measures taken by military regimes like Thailand illustrate some of the measures—or rather countermeasures—authoritarian governments use against IMGs or NGOs that are trying to bring about social reform using (in part) Internet technologies.

Often, the aim of an IMG or NGO is to have their message widely known. Most of the counter activities of authoritarian governments have been to dismantle social networks and online community support for these democracy advocates. What is apparent is that while oppressive governments are concerned about cyber defense in terms of secrecy, IMGs and NGOs seek the opposite—there is greater advantage to be transparent (Whitford and Prunckun 2017). The nature of their goals is to gain and galvanise public support. Subsequently, cyber defense for democracy advocates is more often (and should ideally be) focused on avoiding government agency interference in peaceful protest or other non-violent activity. This chapter takes the perspective that the best cyber defense for these types of organizations is to create greater transparency. It makes this point in the context of adopting Crime Prevention Through Environmental Design (CPTED) principles, and advocates that this theory, with some modifications, can be adopted by IMGs and NGOs to provide security against government sponsored violence or provocative counter-protest operations. To understand the role of social media networks in IMG and NGO operations, this chapter will highlight some social media examples and strategies that emerged from the Arab Spring of 2011.

4.3 Role of Social Media in Protest

It has been said that social media allows for the creation of transnational communities (Crider 2015, p. 1). This is because social media allows for wide networks to be established that offer a greater opportunity to galvanize support for democratic movements. Randi Zuckerberg, the former director of marketing development for *Facebook*, considered the platform as a way to enabled social interactions that were not previously possible. She commented that social media is "democratic... it provides a platform for discussion and coordination for democratization." She described *Facebook* as providing a "forum where information can be quickly and efficiently published and this function takes on particular importance where these forums are absent from day to day political life or where individual liberties are curtailed" (Jose 2010: 178).

Papic and Noonan in their article on social media and protest, written for the private intelligence group, Strat for, highlight the schism between those that are online activists, and those who actually take to the street. Papic and Noonan is also argue that it is almost impossible to organize protests via social media and remain undetected from government monitoring. They reflect on the number of arrests which occurred early in the Egyptian April 6 movement, that were likely identified through the participants' *Facebook* sites (Papic and Noonan 2011). Papic and

Noonan provided an analysis of the strengths and limitations of using social media in organizing protests. But, their concern for secrecy is likely to be unnecessary if the aim is to build critical mass and ensure both domestic and international supporters are aware of actions taking place.

Amongst other critics, there is a view that social media did not play a key role in protest movements like the Arab Spring. But, even these critics do admit that without social media networks, the *Arab Spring* would have looked very different (Demidov 2011: 24). Overall, there is sufficient evidence to suggest that social media has an important role. Social media provides a platform for groups to express their views and gain support. Howard and Hussain (2013) used the example of a Tunisian vegetable merchant named Mohsammed Bouyaziz who set himself on fire in protest of against the Tunisian Government's policies. Howard and Hussain argue that the story of Bouazizi told through social media platforms such as *Facebook*, *YouTube*, and *Twitter*, had a role in generating the *Arab Spring*. Further, they write that *Facebook* was the *information infrastructure* required to support the independent IMGs from government and mainstream political parties (Howard and Hussain 2013: 2). It is acknowledged that the information infrastructure was not only used within the states where the protests were taking place, but also spread globally; which increased democracy advocates' visibility and gave it international attention. It is the opportunity to gain global support that gives power and security to IMGs and NGOs.

A notorious example of an IMG forming networks online to conduct its activist agendas is the *Anonymous* group. It deliberately works without a structured leadership and favors individuals directly carrying out specific actions (Stalder 2012: 1). Anonymous operates as what is termed a *temporary collective* that focuses on a particular action, which is driven by a social, political, or economic issue. It is suggested that there are three elements to these groups: "the promise," "the tools," and the "bargain." The promise is the proposed activity that must be achievable and interesting. The tools must be available to individuals online so they can participate in the action. The bargain is the conditions participants agree on before they start the action (Stalder 2012: 1). The loose affiliation of *ad hoc* groups that emerge to conduct a protest action disperses at its conclusion; and blended with no identifiable leadership or institution, provides it security from regimes and government agencies. Further, it is suggested that the cyber-attacks launched against the Tunisian government in 2011 by Anonymous made "Tunisian bloggers feel they could rely upon international solidarity" (Stalder 2012: 2) (Fig. 4.1).

During the Arab Spring, and other protests undertaken by IMGs, various governments have attempted to block social media networks from its users. But, slowing down the Internet or even turning it off also has repercussions for state agencies. Howard and Hussain (2013) argued that while states can own networks, they are rarely able to cut-off connections completely. Social networking sites such as *Twitter*, *Facebook*, *YouTube*, and other electronic forms of communication, such as emails, SMS or fax can still find their way through.

As Papic and Noonan (2011) wrote social media can instantly organise, train, and mobilize activists through online information. Social media networks perform an

Fig. 4.1 Social media and
mobile telephony are a
powerful combination
(Photograph by William
B. King and courtesy of the
U.S. Department of
Defense)

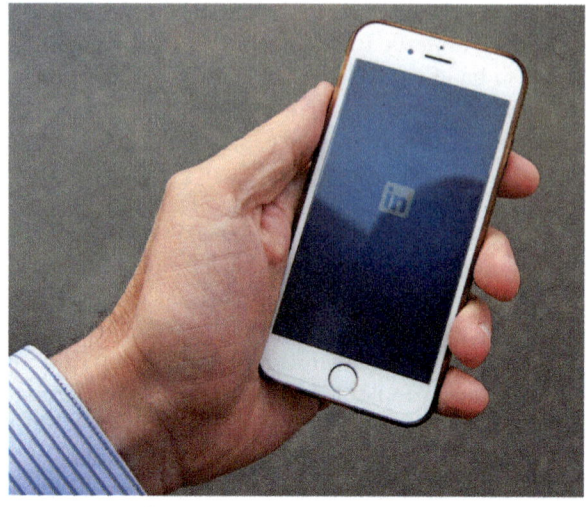

important function for IMGs and NGOs in organizing support and coordinating
efforts. Given the strength and application of social media, it would then be
worthwhile considering applying some principle of CPTED as a form of cyber
defence against authoritarian oppositions.

4.4 Background to CPTED

CPTED is a theory that suggests modifications to the physical environment can
reduce crime. It is a theory that has gained currency amongst security and policing
agencies, architects, and local/county governments. For the most part, it has been
reserved for the physical environment. But, with the advent of cyber communities
and online commerce, attempts to apply CPTED principles to the online environment are increasing. There are six principles that, with some modification, can
provide direction for IMGs and NGOs to operate in cyberspace. The principles of
CPTED are:

1. Surveillance;
2. Legibility;
3. Territoriality;
4. Ownership of the space;
5. Management of the space; and
6. Vulnerability (State of Queensland, Australia 2007)

Surveillance is about creating physical spaces that allows inhabits an opportunity to
see what is taking place around them; the creation of open spaces. Legibility is about
ease of negotiability of the space. Territoriality is about providing some physical

deterrent to the space, such as high fencing. Ownership of space is about developing a sense of proprietorship of the physical space. Management of the space is about keeping the physical environment well maintained, to encourage people to respect the space they are inhabiting. Vulnerability refers to making spaces well populated, under the idea that there is greater safety in numbers. These principles and its application to cyber defense for NGOs and IMGs will become more apparent later in the chapter.

The idea of using CPTED principles in the online environment go back as far as 1998. Sutton et al. (1998: 8), presented a conference paper on Internet crime prevention, to the Australian Institute of Criminology. The paper contended that CPTED literature outlines the role local communities can play in reducing the opportunity for crime. Further, it argued that the same principles of local communities can be applied to communities online. Through segregating by function, and creating separate spaces for separate internet activities, there would be a possibility to provide people with a sense of safety. A further analogy between CPTED in an online environment and the physical environment is done by advocating closed communities—that is, cyber spaces select their "residents" as well as establish rules and protocols within that community.

In an article published in *The Conversation* by Nigel Phair (2012), the Director of the Centre for Internet Safety at the University of Canberra, a connection was made between CPTED and the online environments. He made the comparason that shopping centres have space for the high traffic flow of pedestrians, along with physical and electronic surveillance to make people feel safe and those principles can be achieved in online shopping; through web design, product placement, and navigation.

Both the work of Sutton and Phair begin making the connections between the principles of CPTED and the online environment; however, both have used the concept with reference to crimes such as theft and fraud. This chapter takes the cyber CPTED model further, and recommends it to create safe environments for IMGs and NGOs protesting hostile regimes. Therefore, taking the theory in a slightly different direction and advocating for open rather, than closed online communities.

4.5 Developing a Cyber Defence Plan

Adapting transparency and CPTED requires a degree of planning. To illustrate the application of this approach, the following is an example of how it could work. It does not purport to be an infallible plan, but rather an opportunity to show how the elements could come together.

4.5.1 Creating the Network

Groups are often formed on one or two social media platforms. To ensure a transparent security, a range of social media platforms need to be incorporated. More traditional forms of communication should also be maintained such as email, fax, and SMS. Under certain circumstances, traditional mail services may be used and later relayed out through online international networks.

Multiple social media accounts could be developed by members both within the state and internationally. Using many social media platforms, these accounts should aim at achieving a high number of *followers* or *friends*. The accounts should detail the issue, and the purpose, and call for support. Information should be coordinated to ensure the message is targeted. It should also be able to gather information. This information should be collected and analysed, when necessary, for organisational purposes.

4.5.2 Gathering Information

Where the Internet can be used effectively, several repositories of information should be established. Sites such as *Google Maps* and *Ushahidi* can provide a place for collecting information. *Google Maps* can provide geographic information, while *Ushahidi* is a good platform for gathering information via a range of communications.

Google Maps can be used to label areas of conflict, protest action, or places of safety. These maps can be distributed not only to participating activists, but also to media and international supporters. Naturally, there are issues of security in highlighting safe areas or areas where medical assistance can be found during a protest; for instance, forceful government reaction. Nevertheless, if these are well known, there is a greater role that the media, and people with cell phones can play in documenting any subsequent political violence by the government.

Ushahidi was instrumental in reporting violence in Kenya after the election in 2008. Since, activists have used the platform to establishe a crisis map focusing on Syria, and documenting human rights violations that are taking place there. Essentially, *Ushahidi* works to facilitate crowd sourcing. This means it can assist in gathering supporters for issues. Yet, it needs to first be supplemented by another social media platform that can build a following. This could be a *Facebook* or *Twitter* account, etc. The *Ushahidi* platform can then obtain data from a range of communication technologies, including email, social media, and SMS. These data can be in the form of reports, observations, or surveys. The data can then be analysed and distributed to a wide network of supporters as well as the news media.

4.5.3 Sending Information

The greatest challenge for IMGs and NGOs is transmitting information from hostile environments. Government controls over the Internet and telecommunications makes this a challenge. Therefore, in environments where Internet activity is monitored or restricted, basic telephony using phone cards or fax can be used. SMS can still provide the opportunity to coordinate and plan. Essentially, the key is to be diverse in the choice of platform, and gather a variety of contact options. There are obvious benefits in mixing the technologies and various times of communication. Networks both inside and outside of the nation where activists are operating could be given relevant information, with an instruction to distribute it broadly across social media platforms and internationally.

4.6 Using CPTED

The principles of CPTED can be incorporated in several ways into the online environment. The following discussion outlines the principles and the approaches this theory presents for NGOs and IMGs. The connection between the physical environment and the virtual space is not seamless, but this illustrates the underlining application that it can create in developing a degree of cyber defense.

4.6.1 Surveillance

CPTED advocates that passive or natural surveillance is a key principle to design. Characteristically, it suggests that the environment should be designed in a manner that allows people to easily see the street or place in question. In terms of cyber defense, it is suggested that NGOs and IMGs create social media platforms that are visible to a wide number of online communities. This would likely involve using a range of social media—not just the well-known platforms such as *Twitter* and *Facebook*, though these should be included. *What's App*, *Viber*, *Line*, and *Instagram* are examples of others, and each should be used. The platforms should establish international networks built on a variety of social media platforms; and should include not only those associated with the cause, but the public, and variety of media agencies. The more people that are aware of their actions, the greater opportunity for them to be under "passive surveillance," and safe. The more people that are aware of their activities, the safer NGOs and IMGs will become when advocating democracy.

In *The Guide to Protecting the Tunisian Revolution* produced by the online activist movement Anonymous, the use of *Google Maps* was emphasised as a means to coordinate movements between groups. It suggested that using *Google*

Maps be kept undisclosed from opposing government agencies (Anonymous 2011). Nonetheless, a transparent approach using *Google Maps* can have several advantages for groups aiming to coordinate their movements, and can also mark where the military or government agencies may also be operating. It can provide a transparent view of the movement's locations of protestors, places where medical assistance can be sought, and where areas of danger may exist. This would allow the transnational community of supporters built through social media to assist in observing and reporting events taking place.

4.6.2   Legibility

Within the physical environment, legibility refers to the ability for individuals to find their way around the setting. The aim is for individuals to be more confident and assured in the environment, and therefore be less stressed or less concerned with being lost. In the cyber realm, and cyber defence in particular, the challenge is for members of IMGs and NGOs to be confident in using social media and other relevant platforms. Access to forums, sites, and various messaging platforms needs to be open to members with a variety of information technology literacy skills. Subsequently, each cyber community should use a range of platforms from conventional telephony and SMS; through to easily negotiated websites; then on to more complex platforms and event databases like *Ushahidi*. The more avenues available to contribute and receive information, the more equipped NGOs and IMGs are to analyse and respond to that information.

4.6.3   Territoriality

In the physical environment, territoriality is essential for control of a person's space. Fences, walls, gates, and other forms of barriers ensure there is a sense of control and safety. Similarly, closed Internet communities provide the same assurance. This can be done via a request to join the group and these new members vetted and given passwords to access the site. This, and other methods add to creating a sense of territoriality. However, because CPTED advocates identification, in the natural environment territoriality too often comes at the risk of losing the opportunity for passive surveillance. If the cyber community is too closed, its activities will not be seen, nor its work recognised. Territoriality within the cyber community may mean a closed Internet community and a closed expression of ideas reserved only for that online community. This has implications for achieving safety in transparency. Further, any ideas that are expressed need to be seen by the broader online community if the group is to gain credibility.

4.6.4 Ownership of the Space

Galvanising a transnational group requires giving each member of the group a sense of ownership in the movement's aims. In the physical environment, it is about providing the opportunity for individuals to feel a sense of community, and therefore taking ownership of that community. IMGS and NGOs are required to be more inclusive of the general online public, and less inward-looking. The power for protest movements are its people and wide support. Subsequently, the more inclusive the group, the more people will feel a sense of ownership in its aims.

4.6.5 Management of the Space

CPTED theory states that the management of space is about its maintenance. It advocates for clean and tidy spaces as a mechanism to encourage use. In the cyber security sense, the virtual space should be well organised and easily navigated, with regular sweeping of the site to ensure security from malicious software, denial of service attacks, and website defacement. There is little connection between the physical and virtual environment for this aspect; however, the point to be made is that social network interactions need to be well organised and allow for well-structured activities and accessibility.

4.6.6 Vulnerability

The principle of vulnerability relies on having populated physical spaces—streets, malls, parks, shopping districts, etc. The more people occupying a space, the greater the safety. Fundamentally, it is about isolated spaces making people more vulnerable. With respect to cyber defense, it is about not leaving individuals isolated. This can take several forms—from checking on the saftey of members who are in-country, to confirming that no harm has come to them before, during or after a protest. One way that this might be done is to post short video clips showing the non-violent action of the group as events take place. This should signal to the opposition that should harm come to the members in the future, the video of this incident will be viewed worldwide. In effect, a group can "populate" cyber space the way people populate physical space.

4.7   Agent Provocateur

The concept of vulnerability and supporting individuals leads to the problem of agent provocateurs. An agent provocateur is an individual who actively encourages another person or group to perform an illegal act, or act hastily without thought. Often, they are employed by government, law enforcement or security agencies. This may appear conspiratorial, but there are many examples of governments using such a tactics. In the 1960s, the Federal Bureau of Investigation launched a series of covert operations against political organizations. Known as COINTELPRO (Counter Intelligence Program) they were given the directive to expose, disrupt, and misdirect activities of various political movements. Other examples include an agent provocateur employed by SeaWorld in the United States. A person identifying himself as Thomas Jones took part in protests conducted by People for the Ethical Treatment of Animals (PETA), only to be identified as an employee of SeaWorld who was canvasing PETA activists about their intentions during their protests (Blake 2015). Earlier in 2014, undercover police infiltrated a protest in Oakland California, regarding a decision of a Grand Jury over a shooting death only, to be discovered, and resorted to drawing a gun on protesters (Watson 2014).

The intent of these examples is to illustrate that NGOs and IMGs are vulnerable to such tactics. Particularly, these tactics can be used through social media networks. There are signs worth acknowledging that can be identified as possible agent provocateurs (Heid 2011). These traits are also identifiable in social networking behavior.

An agent provocateur will often join a group with little background and will likely not be known by anyone in the group. The online discussions they take part in will be focused on debate with not much focus on undertaking action. The agent provocateur will aim to create disharmony, and seek to build relationships with people who are not satisfied with the group. Their goal is to divide the group, and propose support for radical activities that will negatively impact on the group. They may also serve as informers to government agencies. In terms of cyber defense using CPTED, being supportive of the membership in the vulnerability and ownership of space principles, can mitigate against a disaffected membership. Unusual behaviour should, however, be identified and countered where possible.

4.8   Conclusion

By using social media and developing networks, a degree of safety can be provided for NGOs and IMGs. Developed networks within social media can offer the opportunity to crowd source and galvanize supporters for an issue. The modes of organization can be as *ad hoc* as those of the Anonymous—forming primarily for specific action and then disbanding; or, more established modes through *Facebook* accounts and event recording platforms such as Ushahidi. Using social media platforms has its limitations, though. Social media platforms can train, plan, and organize activists. But, those online commitments must be met with an equal commitment to go out onto the streets or places of protest.

Using CPTED principles as a theoretical base provides IMGS and NGOs with the ability to use social media to develop cyber defense for their online environments. Because hostile governments will inherently have control over the Internet, IMGS and NGOs are at a disadvantage. But, by using CPTED principles, along with an awareness of possible agent provocateurs and reliance on information transparency, they are more likely to overcome some of these obstacles.

Along with a wide dispersal of information available, there should also be a range of technologies used: from the contemporary *Facebook*- or *Twitter*-style social media; to older forms, such as emails, and SMS; and even fax, telephony and traditional mail services. Unless, these groups are operating in a place like North Korea, it would highly improbable for even the most authoritarian regime to track and trace such a vast number of mechanisms by NGOs and IMGs to organise and report its activities, especially when a transnational network including media organisations are at work.

4.9 Principal Concepts

The principal concepts associated with this chapter are listed below. Demonstrate your understanding of each by writing a short definition or explanation in one or two short sentences.

- issue motivated group;
- crime prevention through environmental design;
- non-government organization;
- agent provocateur; and
- temporary collective.

4.10 Study Questions

1. Explain why social media could prove an effective way to conduct protest activities in countries that have authoritarian governments?
2. Discuss what some of the pros-and-cons might be in creating transparent on social media platforms regarding protest activities?
3. Explain how compatible is CPTED with the online environment and some of its limitations.
4. Explain what impact social media had on the Arab Spring.
5. Discuss why some see the group Anonymous as a leader in online activism. Describe what, if anything, makes it unique.

4.11   Learning Activity

Take the perspective of an IMG organizer and operationalize a social media strategy that provides training for your members, mobilization, and implementation of a street protest. Choose the types of social media you will use. Incorporate at least some aspects of the CPTED theory and explain how you will guard against agent provocateurs by the authoritarian regime. Finally, reflect on what maybe some of the risks of your plan and how they might be (if at all) addressed. Write your strategy as an action plan and your explanation as well as reflection in a few paragraphs.

References

Anonymous (2011) Guide to protecting the Tunisian revolution, part one: initial security. https://www.youtube.com/watch?v=imvfXtTkZv8

Blake M (2015) Agent provocateur? PETA claims SeaWorld employee infiltrated protests. https://www.rt.com/usa/273676-seaworld-spy-peta-protests/

Crider J (2015) Social media and protest movements. Number 13, Fall p 1. https://pdfs.semanticscholar.org/cc7f/689a495aeaba7cb99cfabc255b5b8696eced.pdf

Demidov O (2011) Social networks in international and national security. Security Index No 1 18 (98):24

Heid B (2011) How to identify an agent provocateur. http://takethesquare.net/2011/08/14/how-to-identify-an-agent-provocateur/

Howard P, Hussain M (2013) Information infrastructure and the organisation of protest in democracy's forth wave?: digital media and the Arab spring, Oxford Scholarship Online May

Jose V (2010) Accidental activists: using facebook to drive change. J Int Aff Fall 64:177–180

Papic M, Noonan S (2011) Social media as a tool for protest, Stratfor. https://www.stratfor.com/weekly/20110202-social-media-tool-protest

Phair N (2012) Cutting cybercrime is a question of smart design. The Conversation. https://theconversation.com/cutting-cybercrime-is-a-question-of-smart-design-9013

Stalder F (2012) Anonymous power. https://snuproject.wordpress.com/2012/02/22/anonymous-power-by-felix-stalder-via-viewpoint/

State of Queensland, Australia (2007) Crime prevention through environmental design guidelines for Queensland. https://www.police.qld.gov.au/programs/cscp/safetyPublic/Documents/CPTEDPartA.pdf

Sutton A, David T, Shane M, Fiona B (1998) Internet crime prevention paper presented at the conference: internet crime held in Melbourne, 16–17 February 1998, by the Australian Institute of Criminology. http://www.aic.gov.au/media_library/conferences/internet/sutton.pdf

Tormsen D (2015) 10 authoritarian government attempts to control the internet. http://listverse.com/2015/07/16/10-authoritarian-government-attempts-to-control-the-internet/

Watson S (2014) US protests infiltrated by agents provocateurs: undercover cops attempt to incite crime, pull gun on #ICan'tBreathe Protesters. http://www.globalresearch.ca/us-protests-infiltrated-by-agents-provocateurs-undercover-cops-attempt-to-incite-crime-pull-gun-on-icantbreathe-protesters/5419449

Whitford T, Pruncun H (2017) Discreet not covert: reflections on teaching intelligence analysis in a non-government setting. Salus J 5(1):4861

Chapter 5
Drinking from a Fire Hydrant: Information Overload As a Cyber Weapon

Craig Greathouse

5.1   Introduction

The issue that seems to resonate with scholars in the field of international relations and security studies would arguably be terrorism. But cyber war would at least be a contender for that crown. While the late-President Reagan raised the issue of cyber war after watching the film *War Games* (Kaplan 2017), today's occurrences are even more profound given the development of cyber weaponization. Events in the infosphere have become more apparent, given the purported external influences on the American presidential election in 2016. While the public understand the impact of identity theft and cyber-crime in general, for the first time the world gained an understanding of the potential disruptive effects of cyber war. Experts have long warned about the potential power of this form of warfare, but until recently that disruptive power has remained largely obscured.

To understand the impact of cyber capabilities, researchers have worked to develop typologies that provide guidance when examining the impact of cyber. In 2014, such a typology was proposed (Greathouse 2014), however the continuation of cyber weaponization dictates that a reassessment of this typology needs to occur to better understand the range of activities within cyber war. In developing this framework the underlying assumption is the role of *fog of war* matters, as postulated by Clausewitz (1984). In the past, the idea of fog of war focused on the impact of decisions when there was *limited information* during a conflict (Clausewitz 1984). However, in the current environment the idea of fog of war needs to be expanded to address not only the lack of information, but also an *overload of information*, as well as the potential *corruption of information* (Waldman 2010). The ability to overload an opposition force with information, or corrupted information, may provide advantages greater than just destroying data.

C. Greathouse (✉)
University of North Georgia, Dahlonega, GA, USA
e-mail: Craig.Greathouse@ung.edu

© Springer International Publishing AG, part of Springer Nature 2018
H. Prunckun (ed.), *Cyber Weaponry*, Advanced Sciences and Technologies for
Security Applications, https://doi.org/10.1007/978-3-319-74107-9_5

This chapter addresses the issue of the fog of war by examining Clausewitz' original argument in *On War* (1984) and by looking at the different interpretations about the traditional role of confusion. With fog of the war as the foundation, a reformulated typology of cyber war is proposed. This typology, while influenced by fog of war arguments, is influenced by events that have become known recently. This chapter also looks at occurrences of cyber war and assesses where they fall on the scale, and the potential policy impacts that may result. In examining this topic, this chapter focuses on conceptualizing a typology to help understand nuances related to cyber war. This chapter builds on work published in 2014 that laid-out a simple typology and looked at the potential of applying existing strategic thought to this issue of cyber war (Greathouse 2014). Given the revelations about potential capabilities since 2014, a reassessment is necessary.

5.2   Cyber War

The definition of *cyber war* used by Greathouse (2014: 24) was based on one created by Schaap (2009), but with expansion to include non-state actors. "Cyber war is the use of network based capabilities of a state or non-state actor to disrupt, deny, degrade, manipulate, or destroy information resident in computers or computer networks or the computers or networks themselves of another actor." The problem is this definition did not consider recent uses of cyber war to engage in actions beyond that of information and hardware, instead attacking the foundations of society. An evolved definition of cyber war is the use of network based capabilities of a state or non-state actor to disrupt, deny, degrade, manipulate or destroy information resident in computers or networks or the computers or networks themselves; in addition, cyber war can undermine the credibility of information within society through the distribution of alternative information through cyberspace that can destabilize governance and or society. In this chapter there is no distinction between cyber war and cyber warfare.

The inclusion of the distribution of misinformation through infosphere within the definition was necessary based on occurrences within the system. In 2011, the transmission of information into states within the Middle East was at odds with the information being presented in those societies (Miladi 2016). Information does not have to be false information, it can be information that conflicts with the accepted views of governing authority that is controlling the information which its citizens receive. An early variant of this approach would be Radio Free Europe, a shortwave radio station that was an alternative source of information to those living in Eastern Europe during the Cold War. Nevertheless, for this aspect to fall within cyber war, the transmission of information must occur in the infosphere.

The continued development of the infosphere puts a greater emphasis on the role of information within society, and has become by extension an important element of military capability, as well as vulnerability. The importance of information is not a new concept in military circles; it was addressed by Clausewitz (1984) in *On War*. He not only addressed issues about the lack of information, but about how too much information could also be a detriment.

5.3 Fog of War

Clausewitz stated that, "War is the realm of uncertainty; three quarters of the factors on which action is based are wrapped in a fog of greater or lesser uncertainty" (Clausewitz 1984: 101). Some have argued fog of war may be better understood as the *uncertainty of war* (Kiesling 2001). Waldman (2010) made the case that uncertainty was a significant issue for Clausewitz who considered the human side of war. Waldman also showed that "the Prussian general is well known for his emphasis on the interminable poverty of reliable information in war and his dismissive attitude regarding the substance and value of intelligence" (Waldman 2010: 348).

> ...the general unreliability of all information presents a special problem in war: all action takes place, so to speak, in a kind of twilight, which, like fog or moonlight, often seems to make things seem grotesque and larger than they really are. Whatever is hidden from full view in this feeble light has to be guessed at by talent, or simply left to chance. (Clausewitz 1984: 161)

Clausewitz provides a consistent argument that information is flawed and will have a significant impact on battles. An argument made by those supporting the technological Revolution in Military Affairs (RMA) is that the new developments in technology will remove the fog of war (Owens 2001). The ability to divine the enemy's intentions through more technology and intelligence will limit the impact of the fog of war and issues of uncertainty. Still, scholars like Betts (1978), Jervis (1968), and Handel (1989) have argued that there will be failures of intelligence which will not lift the fog of war because of human factors (Waldman 2010). "Also, one only has to factor in the enemy's almost certain efforts in the realm of counterintelligence, misinformation, deception, and so on—none of which can be definitively negated" (Waldman 2010: 349–350).

Waldman (2010) also pointed-out that Clausewitz understood that too much information can create as many problems as not having enough, "we know more, but this makes us more, not less, uncertain" (Clausewitz 1984: 117). While information is easily gathered it still needs to be analyzed, processed, and converted into knowledge (Waldman 2010: 351). So, while cyber war can be seen as a way to steal information, it may also be used to provide an information overload, which makes understanding what is real, and what is misleading or deceptive, difficult. The 2016 American presidential election provides an example of where it became difficult to determine what was factual and what was not because of the proliferation of information, combined with what might have been a Russian attempt to push promote particular pieces of information (New York Times Archive 2016/17). The 2017 French presidential run-off had a significant release of hacked information from Emmanuel Macron's campaign (Danadio 2017) prior to the media blackout. The question about whether the previous instances of attempted interference during the 2016 American presidential election and potentially the 2016 Brexit vote (House of Commons Report 2017, Syal 2017) represented a possible cyber-attack? The need for better understanding of the goals, actors, and level of disruption from cyber war has become even more apparent.

5.4   Typology

The original typology proposed by Greathouse (2014) attempted to capture the different levels of intensity within cyber war. The development of cyber capabilities by actors within the system and the emergence of new types of activities necessitates a redevelopment of the previous typology. Originally, there was only one scale on which cyber war was defined with cyber vandalism being the lowest level of activity; this was followed by cyber espionage, cyber-crime, denial of service, focused cyber-attack, with a massive cyber assault at the upper end of the scale (Greathouse 2014). The two lowest levels of the scale where not originally classified as cyber war. The evolution of activities in the infosphere since 2014 has forced a reassessment; actions by Russia in the Ukraine, and potentially the US, the 2017 French elections, the US with ISIS, and *Wikileaks* with its continued releases of purported American capabilities meant that espionage and vandalism have expanded, passing the threshold that hitherto precluded them from being considered as forms of cyber war. This is because they now have demonstrated their ability for destabilization.

As more research is conducted, a better understanding of the elements of cyber war are being brought to light. Valeriono and Maness (2014) revealed important ideas that should be incorporated in a revised cyber typology. They included a severity of cyber operations component with five types, including: (1) minimal damage; (2) targeted attack on critical infrastructure or military; (3) dramatic effect on a country's specific strategy; (4) dramatic effect on a country; and (5) an escalated dramatic effect on a country (Valeriono and Maness 2014: 353). The severity idea provides clarity for any typology especially when combined with their methods, which include vandalism, denial of service, intrusions, infiltrations, and advanced persistent threats it provides more understanding (Valeriono and Maness 2014: 353). This approach is based on the concept of cyber disputes that focuses on how to code disputes within the typology. The question becomes, can one disconnect severity and methods into separate spheres? Within the American presidential campaign of 2016 the methods for penetrating the Democratic email system were fairly simple (New York Times Archive 2016/17), though the impact may have been more significant. So, any typology needs to mesh methods and severity within one scale so there is no disconnect between what might be a simple method, but a profound outcome. *Severity* is not the best term to measure cyber impact, instead the focus should be on *disruption*, specifically the level of disruption that results from a cyber-attack.

Another element missing from Greathouse's (2014) previous typology is the impact of the types of actors in the system that can engage in cyber war. The original argument was that the barriers to entry into cyber activity are very low (Greathouse 2014). There are many non-state actors who have engaged in this form of conflict; they do not need the resources of a nation-state to be effective. *Wikileaks* has impacted many states with its release of information. This is in addition to the activities of terror groups like ISIS, which has a strong online presence and has used elements of social media to disseminate its divisive messages. But, in examining past activity, it is clear that the capacity of the actor in the infosphere still matters. Frank Cilluffo, the Director of Center for Cyber and Homeland Security, stated in 2016 during testimony before the US House of Representatives that nation-states were the greatest threat, followed by terrorist organizations, criminal organizations, and finally, hacktivists (Cilluffo 2016). While the barrier for entry is low, the capacity of the actor does matter, and this needs to be incorporated into the typology.

A revised typology will have three axes: one to represent the actors; the second to represent the type of activity taken; and the third to represent disruption to the target. This creates a three-dimensional framework with an X, Y, and Z dimension. The X axis is the type of activity ranging from simple cyber vandalism to a full-scale cyber weapons deployment aimed at complete disruption of the target. This axis is focused on the ends rather than the technical means, the origin point would represent no cyber-attacks. The Y axis would contain the actors of cyber war starting with individual hackers and expanding from the origin point to nation-states, which are the end point. The last axis—Z—again starts from the origin point, which represents zero disruption, to a complete collapse of the target. This axis is measured by the level of disruption that is created within the target, limited disruption falls lower on the scale with complete disruption being the ideal type at the upper-end. Cetron and Davies (2009) argued that cyber is a weapon of mass disruption. The end point would the maximum that could occur with cyber capabilities but the likelihood of that occurring would be low. This framework should provide a much more nuanced understanding of the capacity of actors and the potential for disruption within the system, it should also accommodate further evolution of cyber capabilities.

5.5 X Axis

The X axis is based on Greathouse' s (2014) previous typology, but revised with a clear focus on the ends rather than the technical means within cyber war. Focusing on the means gives the typology a limited shelf life given the pace of technological development and the existence of hidden capacities. Some of these technical means would include, trapdoors, trojans, backdoors, logic bombs, worms, and viruses among others forms of malware (Valeriono and Maness 2014). By looking at the goals of the actors—from cyber vandalism to full-scale attacks—this axis provides a better understanding about the level of engagement that the actor is focusing on.

The lowest level is that of cyber vandalism, an action which defaces websites and postings made by the target, but which causes no other impact. An example of this would be hijacking and changing the content on a webpage. This capability represents the lowest threshold to cyber activity and would be within the capability of most cyber actors. The next step on this scale is that of cyber-crime, previously cyber espionage was positioned at this point, but due to changes in capabilities cyber-crime is moved down. Cyber-crime is the use of cyber capabilities to engage in criminal activities that are driven by a profit motive for the actors involved. Actors can be singular, a small group, an organized crime syndicate, or it could at times be a nation-state. The argument for including cyber-crime revolves around the fact that it can have disruptive effects on a target. The level of disruption will tend to be lower than other forms of cyber-attacks; an example being the 2013 hack to the retail chain, Target. In this case, it was estimated that 110 million cardholders had their information stolen (McMullen et al. 2016).

Greathouse (2014:25) originally defined cyber espionage as "the use of electronic capabilities to gather information from a target. This step in the continuum is an extension of the activities that actors within the system engage in every day. It simply uses a new means to access different types of data which had previously not been available. The reason cyber espionage is placed so low on the [scale] is that it is an accepted and understood activity within the [infosphere]." The expansion of capabilities for cyber espionage was underestimated by Greathouse (2014) and the amount of information gained, which can be potentially distributed throughout the infosphere by an attacker, has increased. The impact of cyber espionage can vary widely depending on the actions of the attacker. If the attacker remains covert, the outcome may be just the loss of data (or the use of that data to benefit the attacker's employer or a third-party—for instance, a nation-state). If the attacker releases the information, the level of disruption can escalate. By way of example, take the case of the attack 2014 on Sony Pictures where information was compromised, but the impact escalated as worker information and project data were released onto the Internet. (Haggard and Lindsay 2015). *Wikileaks* would also be an example of cyber espionage as it purportedly published information that had been taken from American services about sources and methods as reported in 2017 by the *New York Times* (Shane et al. 2017).

The fourth waypoint on the X axis is the attacker focusing on achieving a temporary disruption of a particular system/s within the target. Temporary disruptions would include website denial of service attacks and networks. This point on the scale shows a level of escalation beyond that of nuisance/activism, which exists in cyber vandalism, or a profit motives that are at the center of cyber-crime. This type of activity could be characterized by the Anonymous attacks on websites like *PayPal* and *Amazon* that followed the *Wikileaks* disclosures of 2017 (Uitermark 2016). Another example would be the 2007 attack on Estonia where there were two periods where the attack disrupted activities in parts of Estonia (Tikk et al. 2010). This type of attack is of limited duration and scope, which differentiates it from other cyber activities.

The next point is a sustained cyber assault; this type of cyber-attack focuses on rolling-back the capacity of the target to make use of their networks for an extended period of time. This type of attack is similar to temporary disruption, but with a longer time frame. The length of time increases the intensity of the attack. The sixth waypoint in cyber war is the destruction of network capacity and/or information. This type of assault moves beyond the denial of usage to the destruction of the systems themselves. This act raises the bar in terms of the damage being done to the target. However, this type of attack would be limited in terms of the duration, with a narrow set of networks or data sources as targets. An example of this type of attack would be Stuxnet and its focused assault on the Iranian nuclear program. The Stuxnet worm was specifically targeted at the Iranian centrifuges with specific instructions about how to destroy the devices (Lindsay 2013).

At the top-of the scale is the massive cyber assault that is designed to destroy network capacity and information across a wide segment. This type of attack would be sustained over a longer time with the specific intent of destroying the targets ability to operate effectively. As of this writing, an attack of this magnitude has not been seen and there are questions about whether it is viable. A so-called cyber Pearl Harbor scenario has been raised by many (e.g. Clarke and Knake 2010; and Kaplan 2017), but little evidence exists as to its potential to be carried out.

The X axis in the proposed typology represents the range of possible options that are open to an attacker in terms of their ability to undermine the target. This expanded scale provides a better range of options than previously and it also provides waypoints to which more can be added in the future if necessary. With the focus on the goal of the attack, rather than the means by which the attacks occur, it allows this axis to maintain its credibility.

5.6 Y Axis

The Y axis provides a look at the different actors which may be an attacker within cyber war. At the lowest end of the scale there is the individual. While individuals may have the capacity to hack into numerous systems their ability to create botnets and other types of sophisticated attack methods is going to be lower, in general, than a group. While solo hackers have been able to create noteworthy viruses and worms, a larger collective will have more skills, knowledge, and financial resources to develop more advanced capabilities.

The next point on the Y axis represents groups, which would be more of a collective than a fully operational organization. The example would be a group like Anonymous where members choose to participate, but where there is not control over the group with a full hierarchical structure (Uitermark 2016). The *ad hoc* structure of these groups have shown that they can have an impact on the infosphere, but their ability to sustain an attack is limited because of the nature of the collective (Uitermark 2016). *Wikileaks* would also be an example where there is somewhat of an organizational structure, but most of its support is from self-affiliating individuals. The long-term viability of groups like these is limited, which limits the level of cyber attacks they can engage in.

The third waypoint would be a group which has a hierarchical basis and formalized membership. These types of groups could be environmental or animals-rights activists, terrorist, or criminal groups. These groups could be more effective in the longer term with regard to a cyber war because of their organizational structure, and their focused goals. These attributes allow such groups to engage in a more involved campaign because they can generate resources and marshal skilled operatives that could result in an increased warfighting capacity.

Another actor that will be positioned on the spectrum is that of private industry. These organizations have for years engaged in corporate espionage against each other, and one assumes that they are continuing with this activity to remain competitive in the system. Additionally, some corporations will possess more effective cyber warfare capabilities given their nature, especially tech companies.

The final level would be that of the nation-state/state. Nation-states are still the primary actor in the international system with the capacity to generate a level of resources that no other actor in the system can marshal. While there have been observers who have argued that through globalization nation-states are becoming less relevant, these class of actors are still dominant in the infosphere. The United States, China, and Russia have all shown a significant capacity to engage in cyber war that no other actor can match. The actions of Russia, and its "patriotic" hackers, in allegedly trying to influence the 2016 American presidential election (New York Times Archive 2016/17), and it also appears the French presidential election in 2017 (Auchard and Bate 2017). The "revelation" of China's of cyber element to its military was a surprise to no one given the cyber probing that has come from China over the years (Knake and Segal 2016). Nation-states have the resources to generate very specific types of cyber weapons that others cannot. For example, many have argued that the Stuxnet attack on Iran could only have come from a nation-state given the precision and sophistication of the attack (Lindsay 2013; Kerr et al. 2010).

5.7   Z Axis

Lastly, the Z axis examines the outcome of cyber warfare on the target. The level of disruption is an important consideration for assessing the impact of cyber war. Any cyber-attack, just like a kinetic attack, can be more or less successful, but that success is measured in the results. In terms of a kinetic attack, the damage to the target is assessed with the most successful attacks removing the target completely. Given the disruptive nature of cyber war, it is not simply about destruction, but in the effectiveness of the cyber weapons to undermine the effectiveness of a target. Kallber and Cook (2017) argued that traditional measures of effectiveness cannot be used, however as disruption is the focus, not destruction, that can be assessed. A cyber-attack that cannot disrupt the target at any level is a failure. Therefore, as the level of disruption increases, whether measured in being a nuisance, to stealing data, or to undermining the capability of computer networks to operate properly the impact on the target increases. The reason for looking at the ability of an attacker to disrupt a target was laid out by Colarisk and Janczewski (2012: 34), "so dependent on technology have modern nations become that they are fundamentally weakened when such systems and processes are disrupted for any meaningful time. This vulnerability, of course, continues to have national security implications."

The second point on this axis would be an attack that has a limited disruptive impact. While *limited* is a general term, a broad approach to disruption makes sense given the wide variety of options available to attackers. A website being defaced or a limited denial of service attack would fall within this category. These types of attacks are more annoying that a threat to society and may have an effect on individuals. Some elements of cyber-crime could be classified at this level, for example individuals who have had their identities stolen.

The third waypoint has a moderate effect in terms of disruption of the target. At this level, the impact of the attack's effects are felt throughout the target rather than being restricted to a smaller group of individuals. Examples of this outcome include an act of cyber-crime that had broader impacts than just among a limited number of individuals—the hack on the retail chain Target is one where much of the company's customer American database was compromised (McMullen et al. 2016). Another example would be the 2015 hacks, allegedly by China, of the US Office of Personal Management. This attack exposed information on over 20 million federal employees, including security clearance files (Nakashima 2015). This type of attack is an example of cyber espionage, but given the nature of the data taken, the national security ramifications were much broader even though the data was not exposed on the Internet. The damage this hack did was wider than just individuals whose data was exposed. It potentially created a US Government wide disruption by limiting the Government's ability to engage in action within the infosphere (and physical world), especially with regard to undercover intelligence operatives. Another example involved the state of Georgia. Russia, through the use of cyber capabilities, was able to disrupt Georgia's ability to effectively respond to the Russian invasion in 2008 (Tikk et al. 2010).

The final waypoint on this scale would be an attack that has a high or catastrophic impact on the targeted actor. Cyber war is about disruption of the target whether it is a person, company, group, or state. This level is somewhat of a hypothetical level because there does not exist an example of such a catastrophic impact. If executed, this level of cyber disruption would be characterized by a complete paralysis of the target for an extended period of time, or significantly reduced the capacity of the actor to operate. An example would be an attacker being able to shut-down the electrical grid, halt all telecommunications, or cause other critical infrastructure components to stop working. This type of warfare, if carried-out, would threaten the viability of the target to operate.

5.8   Conclusion

In trying to understand cyber war, the complexity of the topic is rooted in the issue of information. Most of the subject literature examines issues like stealing information or crashing a system, however as has been shown in recent cyber-attacks having too much information may be as much if not more of a problem. As Clausewitz (1984) argued, information whether too little or too much can be a problem as it creates problems for making decisions. Information overload is now a feasible goal for an attacker who wants to overwhelm the target's ability to process the data and be able to make a decision. This aspect combined with the potential to manipulate data means that an information dependent actor is at risk. Cyber war may in fact be a more significant problem than has been discussed, not in a cyber Pearl Harbor sense, but in a broader aspect that could significantly disrupt *any* target.

Given this development the importance of building a viable framework to understand cyber war has been proposed. This revamped X, Y, Z framework provides more nuance than previous typologies, but can be elaborated as new developments occur and new research is published. The important shift is to focus more strongly on the disruption aspect of cyber war. Cyber warfare does not reap the physical destruction of other forms of warfare, but the disruptive element needs to be better addressed within the context of the literature. This typology should help with classification, so that more can be done in the future.

5.9   Principal Concepts

The principal concepts associated with this chapter are listed below. Demonstrate your understanding of each by writing a short definition or explanation in one or two short sentences.

- Fog-of-war;
- Infosphere;
- Misinformation; and
- Cyber espionage.

5.10   Study Questions

1. Explain what is meant by *cyber war*.
2. In the context of making important decision, explain why having too much information can be as limiting as not having enough information.

5.11 Learning Activity

Wikileaks release of information over the years has impacted many states. Using one of the Five-Eyes countries (Australia, Canada, New Zealand, the United Kingdom, and the United States), research the type of information that *Wikileaks* has released about this country's confidential international/security affairs. Then, using the typology discussed in this chapter, assess the impact this unauthorized release is likely to have had.

References

Auchard E, Bate F (2017) French candidate Macron claims massive hack as emails leaked. Reuters. http://www.reuters.com/article/us-france-election-macron-leaks-idUSKBN1812AZ

Betts RK (1978) Analysis, war, and decision: why intelligence failures are inevitable. World Polit 31(1):61–89

Cetron MJ, Davies O (2009) Ten critical trends for cyber security. Futurist 43(5):40–49

Clarke RA, Knake RK (2010) Cyber war: the next threat to national security and what to do about it. Ecco, New York

Clausewitz C (1984) On war. Howard M, Paret P (eds). Princeton University Press, Princeton

Colarisk A, Janczewski L (2012) Establishing cyber warfare doctrine. J Strat Sec 5(1):31–48

Danadio R (2017) Why the Macron Hacking Attack Landed with a Thud in France. The New York Times. https://www.nytimes.com/2017/05/08/world/europe/macron-hacking-attack-france.html?smid=fb-nytimes&smtyp=cur&_r=1

Greathouse CB (2014) Cyber war and strategic thought: do the classic theorists still matter? In: Cyberspace and international relations. Springer, Berlin/Heidelberg, pp 21–40

Haggard S, Lindsay JR (2015) North Korea and the Sony Hack: exporting instability through cyberspace, Asia Pacific Issues no. 117. East-West Center, Honolulu. http://hdl.handle.net/10125/36444

Handel M (1989) War, strategy and intelligence. Routledge, London

House of Commons Public Administration and Constitutional Affairs Committee (2017) Lessons learned from the EU Referendum. House of Commons, London

Jervis R (1968) Hypotheses on misperception. World Polit 20(3):454–479

Kallber J, Cook TS (2017) The unfitness of traditional military thinking in cyber: four cyber tenets of undermines conventional strategies. IEEE Access. https://doi.org/10.1109/ACCESS.2017.2693260

Kaplan F (2017) Dark territory: the secret history of cyber war. Simon and Schuster Reprint Edition, New York

Kerr PK, Rollins J, Theohary CA (2010) The Stuxnet computer worm: harbinger of an emerging warfare capability. Congressional Research Service. https://fas.org/sgp/crs/natsec/R41524.pdf

Kiesling EC (2001) On war: without the fog. Mil Rev 81:85–87

Knake R, Segal A (2016) How the next U.S. president can contain china in cyberspace. J Int Aff 70 (1):21–28

Lindsay JR (2013) Stuxnet and the limits of cyber warfare. Secur Stud 22(3):365–404

McMullen DA, Sanchez HM, O'Reilly-Allen M (2016) Target security: a case study of how hackers hit the jackpot at the expense of customers. Rev Bus Financ Stud 7(2):41–50

Miladi N (2016) Social media and social change. Domes 25(1):36–51. Academic Search Complete, EBSCO*host*

Nakashima E (2015) Hacks of OPM databases compromised 22.1 million people, federal authorities say. The Washington Post. https://www.washingtonpost.com/news/federal-eye/wp/2015/07/09/hack-of-security-clearance-system-affected-21-5-million-people-federal-authorities-say/?utm_term=.be8cc4d64af6

New York Times Archive (2016–17) Russian hacking in the U.S. election. https://www.nytimes.com/news-event/russian-election-hacking

Owens B (2001) Lifting the fog of war. Johns Hopkins University Press, Baltimore

Schaap AJ (2009) Cyber warfare operations: development and use under international law. Air Force Law Rev 64:121–174

Shane S, Rosenberg M, Lehren AW (2017) Documents said to reveal hacking secrets of C.I.A. New York Times, 8 March 2017

Syal R (2017) Brexit: foreign states may have interfered in vote, report says. The Guardian. https://www.theguardian.com/politics/2017/apr/12/foreign-states-may-have-interfered-in-brexit-vote-report-says

Tikk E, Kaska K, Vihul L (2010) International cyber incidents: legal considerations. Cooperative Cyber Defence Center of Excellence, Tallinn. NATO. https://ccdcoe.org/publications/books/legalconsiderations.pdf

Uitermark J (2016) Complex contention: analyzing power dynamics within anonymous. Soc Mov Stud. https://doi.org/10.1080/14742837.2016.1184136

Valeriono B, Maness RC (2014) The dynamics of cyber conflict between rival antagonists, 2001–11. J Peace Res 51(3):347–360

Waldman T (2010) Shadows of uncertainty: Clausewitz's timeless analysis of chance in war. Def Stud 10(3):336–368

Chapter 6
Archer's Stakes in Cyber Space: Methods to Analyze Force Advantage

Daniel P. Hughes

6.1 Introduction

A charge of horse-mounted men-at-arms would no doubt be a force to be reckoned with. Cavalry charges were used to overwhelm the enemy by causing confusion; disrupting command-and-control and any possibility of executing an effective response. Military historians have described how in previous centuries armies used *archer's stakes* as a means of combining weapons and tactics to boost the fighting power of troops without increasing their numbers (Hinsley 2015). By positioning archers behind a barrier of spear-like stakes, commanders used this simple strategy to multiply their forces—charging mounted soldiers would risk impaling their horses on the stakes planted in front of the archers.

Combining weapons and tactics, has since, been used in conflicts to accomplish similar results—take for instance, the beach fortifications deployed by the Nazi forces against the Allied armies during the D-Day invasion. But, what about force-multipliers in conflicts in cyber space? Cyber weaponry certainly presents an advantage. Nevertheless, how would a commander assess the likely advantages of using a cyber weapon? Well, it would require some sort of analytic framework to be able to weigh-up the benefits and the disadvantages.

This chapter presents two frameworks that can be used by a nation's commanders to analyse deployments of offensive cyber weapons. Framework One is based on the proposition that the factors that comprise the deployment of cyber weapons can be examined according to a definitional model that establishes four categories of analysis. These categories are:

(a) how the cyber weapon is deployed;
(b) the effects the cyber weapon creates;

D. P. Hughes (✉)
Victoria University of Wellington, Wellington, New Zealand
e-mail: dan.hughes@vuw.ac.nz

© Springer International Publishing AG, part of Springer Nature 2018   71
H. Prunckun (ed.), *Cyber Weaponry*, Advanced Sciences and Technologies for
Security Applications, https://doi.org/10.1007/978-3-319-74107-9_6

(c) the target against which the cyber weapon is launched; and
(d) the objectives that are sought through deployment of cyber weapons.

The utility of Framework One is illustrated through an examination of Operation Orchard—the cyber enabled Israeli strike on a suspected Syrian nuclear facility in 2007. Framework Two provides an alternative means to analyse state cyber weapon deployment. Moreover, it may be used to provide predictive analysis regarding future deployments of cyber weapons. This analysis is derived from an examination of the competing influences that a state must consider when determining whether the deployment of cyber weaponry will be politically advantageous.

The analysis centres on a comparative calculation regarding the benefits and disadvantages (dis-benefits) arising from the use of cyber weaponry. Consideration of benefits focuses on the political value of objectives that can be achieved through the deployment of cyber weaponry, as well as the likelihood that these objectives will successfully be achieved. Analysis of dis-benefits focuses on internal and external political constraints on state deployment of cyber weapons, and the risk and impact of retaliation against the state initiating cyber weapon use. The utility of Framework Two is explored by examining the Stuxnet attack on Iranian nuclear enrichment capabilities.

6.2 Framework One

6.2.1 Analysing State Deployment of Cyber Weapons

Potential and actual deployments of cyber weaponry may be scrutinised according to a definitional model that analyses each element of their use. As shown in Fig. 6.1, this model suggests that the deployment of cyber weaponry is most productively analysed according to the proposition that state-deployed cyber weapons use *Cyber Means* to create *Effects* against *Targets* in order to achieve particular *Objectives*.

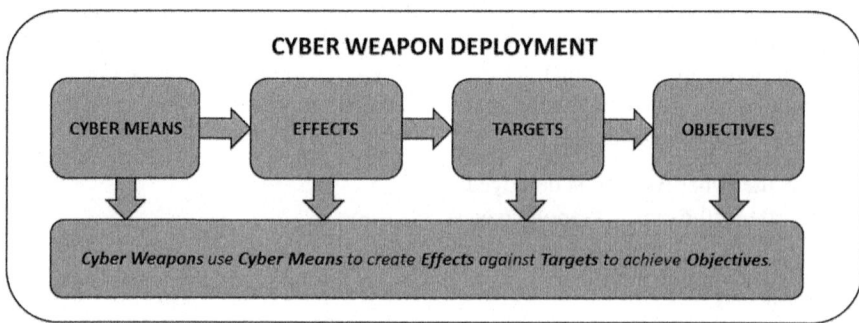

Fig. 6.1 Framework One

Four analytical categories are thus established; each pertaining to a different element of the actions and intent underlying the deployment of cyber weaponry. *Cyber Means* concern the mechanism(s) through which the cyber weapon payload is deployed. Means by which the payload may be delivered include computer network penetration, as well as "Other Than Internet" (OTI) (Dipert 2013) techniques; such as the insertion of compromised or infected devices into a network or device, or the use of various radio frequency transmission protocols. Notably, the commonly used term *computer network attack* (CNA) (US DoD 2010; Kirsch 2011; Turns 2012) is insufficient, because it does not account for OTI delivery mechanisms developed to circumvent the security provided by standalone, "air gapped" networks.

Effects concern the interaction of the cyber weapon payload on targets. In academic literature (Rid 2012; Clarke and Knake 2011; Arquilla and Ronfeldt 1993; Schaap 2009) two categories of effect are evident—direct effects and cascading effects. Key direct effects are *disruption, degradation, manipulation,* and *destruction.* Conversely, cascading effects identified in literature are focused on potential cascading impacts of cyber weapons, such as potentially lethal kinetic violence, casualties and other outcomes synonymous with more conventional modalities of warfare. Direct effects occur logically prior to cascading effects. The latter result from the consequences of the application of direct effects to targets and can only occur through a combination of direct effect and target.

The literature pertaining to cyber weaponry identifies a wide array of targets: from information, to computers and computer networks, through to military systems and infrastructure (Clarke and Knake 2011; Arquilla and Ronfeldt 1993; Schaap 2009; Bachmann 2012). It is proposed, however, that all targets of cyber weaponry can be rationalised into three categories: *information, information based systems and processes*, and *cyber controlled objects*. Information in-and-of-itself is a virtual target; it stands alone as a target category as it is possible to achieve considerable impact by disrupting, degrading, manipulating, or destroying information, without undermining the functional integrity of the information system or cyber controlled object in which the information resides.

Information based systems and processes are considered an appropriate parent category for computers, computer networks and computer systems. These objects are all constituted through an interaction of the virtual (information) with the physical (hardware), and, considering the potential reach of cyber effects, sole reference to computers and computer networks is regarded as unnecessarily restrictive in the consideration of the targets of cyber weaponry. The category of cyber-controlled objects has similar utility, it is sufficiently expansive to encompass the wide array of potential targets, including, but not limited to, critical infrastructure, and military hardware.

The boundaries between these three categories have a degree of fluidity; however, it is possible to articulate the borders between them. Targeting information involves disrupting, degrading, manipulating, or destroying information in a manner that does not undermine the functional integrity of the system the information is located in. In effect, the system the target information is resident in is still functioning correctly, but is operating on false or corrupted data, causing the system to operate in an erratic or damaging manner. Targeting information based systems and processes involves the application of direct effects in a manner that undermines the functional integrity of an information based system or process. The system may be destroyed, or its functions may be compromised to such a degree that they no longer fulfil their purpose. Conversely targeting cyber-controlled objects involves the application of direct effects in a manner that affords direct control of a physical cyber-controlled object. An example would be using a cyber weapon to take control of the weapon systems of a Predator drone.

Objectives concern the goals sought to be achieved via the application of cyber weaponry. In the cyber weaponry literature, an array of objectives are identified; these include: affecting adversary will (Libicki 2014); denying freedom of action in cyberspace (Birdwell and Mills 2011); disrupting and destroying information and communication systems (Arquilla and Ronfeldt 1993); information superiority (Clemmons and Brown 1999); and the support of offensive or defensive military strategy (Taddeo 2012). What unifies these disparate objectives is that they may achieve—or contribute towards achieving—three levels of objectives: tactical, operational, and strategic. Crucially, the use of cyber weapons may achieve multiple types of objectives simultaneously; for example, a successful deployment of cyber weaponry may achieve or contribute towards achieving tactical, operational, and strategic objectives.

The examination of the categories Cyber Means, Effects, Targets, and Objectives provides for the expansion of the conceptual model, presented in Fig. 6.2.

The expanded model details the key analytic components identified under each category. It can now be used as a basis to analyse the characteristics of the deployment of cyber weaponry in the first case study—Operation Orchard.

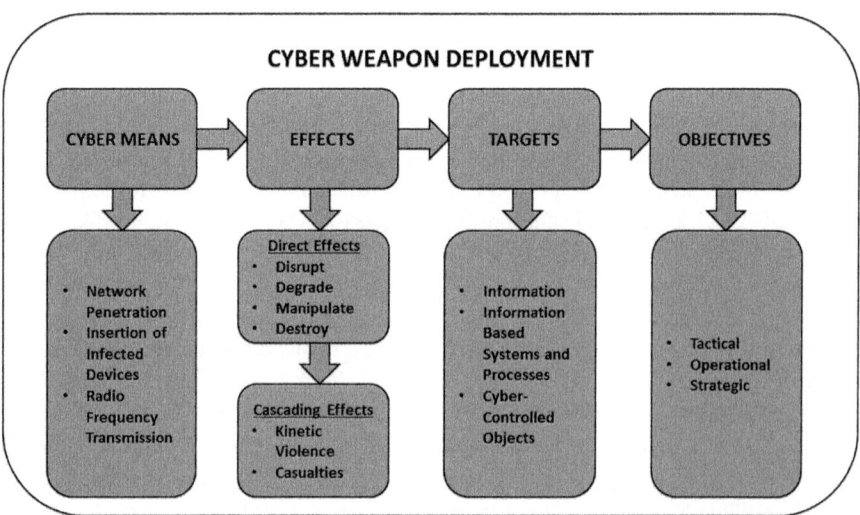

Fig. 6.2 Framework One—expanded

6.2.2 Case Study One—Operation Orchard

The story of Operation Orchard begins with human error. In 2006, a senior Syrian official left a laptop unattended in a London hotel. Israeli intelligence operatives are understood to have taken this opportunity to install covert intelligence software that allowed them access to the contents and any communications sent to or from the device. During analysis of the laptop's contents, one photo was of concern to Israel; it showed Chon Chibu, a lead figure in the North Korean nuclear program, and Ibrahim Othman, director of the Syrian Atomic Energy Commission, standing together in Syria. In conjunction with other documents stolen from the compromised laptop, such as plans and photographs of devices used to create fissile material, Israeli intelligence is reported to have drawn the conclusion that Syria, with aid from North Korea, was secretly constructing a facility to process plutonium. As the processing of plutonium is an essential step in creation of a nuclear bomb, this data was taken as evidence that Syria was developing a nuclear weapons capability (Singer and Friedman 2014).

The existence of a Syrian nuclear program was regarded as an existential threat to Israel by senior members of the Israeli government (Follath and Stark 2009). This position eventually led to the Israeli decision to strike the nascent Syrian nuclear capability. Shortly after midnight on September 6, 2007, seven Israeli F-15I strike fighters flew deep into Syrian airspace and released air-to-ground weapons that struck the fledging nuclear facility. Remarkably, there was no reaction from any Syrian anti-aircraft system. Due to the penetration of the Syrian network by an Israeli cyber weapon, a false-negative was returned to the operators of Syrian anti-aircraft forces—radar showed empty skies, when in fact the Israeli strike force was closing rapidly with its target. Reportedly, the first Syrian forces knew of the strike was when the bombs began to explode at the facility at Kibar. (Singer and Friedman 2014) Due to the deployment of cyber weapons that blinded the Syrian network, Operation Orchard was a success. The Syrian nuclear site was destroyed by a comparatively small Israeli force with no loss of life or materiel.

6.2.3 Analysing Operation Orchard

Through the application of the expanded conceptual model, the key elements of cyber weapon deployment involved in Operation Orchard become apparent. A visual summary of the application of the expanded conceptual model to Operation Orchard is provided at Fig. 6.3.

The *Cyber Means* used to deliver the cyber weapon is held by Dipert (2013) to most likely be some form of OTI delivery mechanism, such as software inserted into the Syrian anti-aircraft defence network by Israeli intelligence operatives via the manipulation of optical cables. The direct *effect* of the cyber-attack was

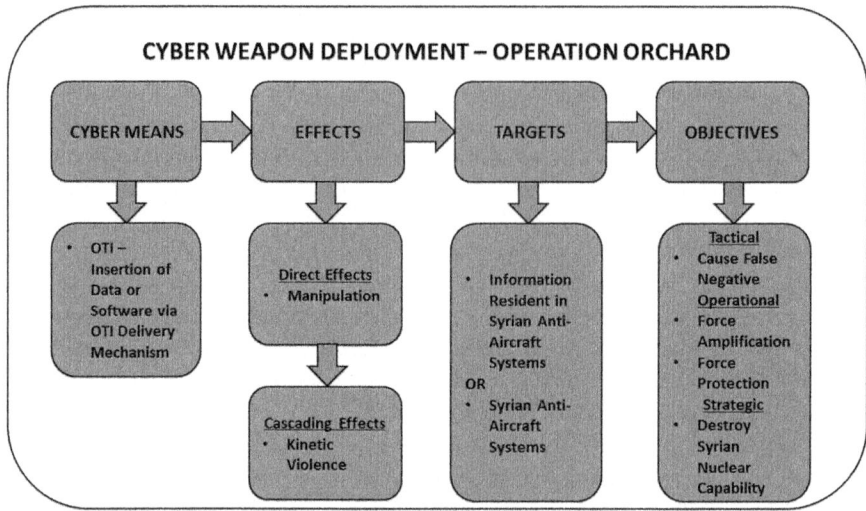

Fig. 6.3 Analysis of Operation Orchard according to framework one

manipulation—to cause the anti-aircraft system to provide a false negative in response to the presence of Israeli jets. When combined with the related air strike, the cascading effect of the cyber-attack was major kinetic violence. Without definitive knowledge regarding the precise actions of the cyber-weapons involved, it is difficult to determine whether Operation Orchard's target was information resident in Syrian anti-aircraft systems, or the anti-aircraft system (an information based system) itself. If the Israeli cyber weapon only affected data then the target is best understood as information. If, however, the cyber weapons acted to fundamentally undermine the processing functions of the anti-aircraft system, then the target is better understood as the anti-aircraft system itself.

The use of cyber weapons achieved both tactical and operational *Objectives*. The tactical objective was to manipulate the Syrian anti-aircraft system so that the incoming Israeli air strike was masked. The operational objective can be understood as both *force amplification* and *force protection*. The operational objective of force amplification was met as cyber weapon deployment allowed maximum conventional force (delivered via air power) to be applied to the fledgling Syrian nuclear site without the diversion of military resource to neutralise Syrian anti-aircraft capability. This allowed for the Israeli strike force to be considerably smaller than would have been the case if full Syrian anti-aircraft capabilities had to be reckoned with. Similarly, the operational objective of force protection was met as cyber weapon deployment mitigated the risk to Israeli forces by disrupting the ability of the Syrian anti-aircraft system to project defensive force. Perhaps most importantly, use of cyber weapons in Operation Orchard directly contributed to the wider Israeli strategic objective of denying the emergence of Syria as a nuclear power.

6.3 Framework Two

6.3.1 *Analysing State Deployments of Cyber Weapons*

Framework One provides a useful mechanism for analysing potential and actual deployments of cyber weaponry. It does not, however, provide a basis for predictive analysis regarding potential uses of cyber weapons. Whether a state elects to deploy cyber weapons—either independently or in conjunction with other coercive measures such as military force—will be dependent on the relative power of that state, compared with the actor that the initiating state intends to take coercive action against. In effect, a state considering the deployment of cyber weapons must first consider the benefits of cyber weapon use; that is, the ability to realize or contribute towards the realization of politically valuable tactical, operational and strategic objectives. Benefits must then be considered against dis-benefits—the degree to which risks arising from the use of cyber weapons are likely to erode benefits provided by cyber weapon deployment. Several factors are relevant to this calculation. These include the cyber dependence of the state and the targeted actor, the coercive capabilities of the state and targeted actor, internal and external constraints, such as national will and international opinion, the strength and support of each actor's allies, the likelihood that the cyber weapon deployment will be attributed to a particular actor, as well as any demands imposed by the strategic landscape against which the deployment of cyber weaponry is being considered.

The potential deployment of cyber weapons is thus a calculation influenced by multi-faceted and mutable considerations. The basic form of the calculation is shown diagrammatically in Fig. 6.4.

The basic form of the calculation—weighing the advantages of benefits versus the disadvantages, is not complex. The factors that contribute to the calculation of benefits and dis-benefits, are, however, complex and contextual. For cyber weapon deployment to reap benefits for the initiating actor the cyber weapon must have a high likelihood of directly achieving strategic objectives. Alternatively, cyber weapon deployment must achieve tactical or operational objectives that make important contributions to broader coercive measures undertaken to achieve strategic objectives, as was the case in Operation Orchard. The calculation concerning benefits is largely dependent on qualitative analysis by the initiating actor on how valuable potential objectives are. This can be considered with reference to tactical and operational concerns, or strategically with reference to security doctrine and policy. Further relevant considerations can be uncovered by in-depth analysis regarding the impact on, or costs to, the initiating actor if the identified objectives are not achieved. Another relevant factor is the comparative efficacy of cyber weapon deployment versus the deployment of a more conventional coercive capacity. The deployment of cyber weapons may create effects that realise objectives in a manner that is superior to traditional weaponry—for example, objectives may be able to be achieved without risk to military personnel or materiel. Alternatively,

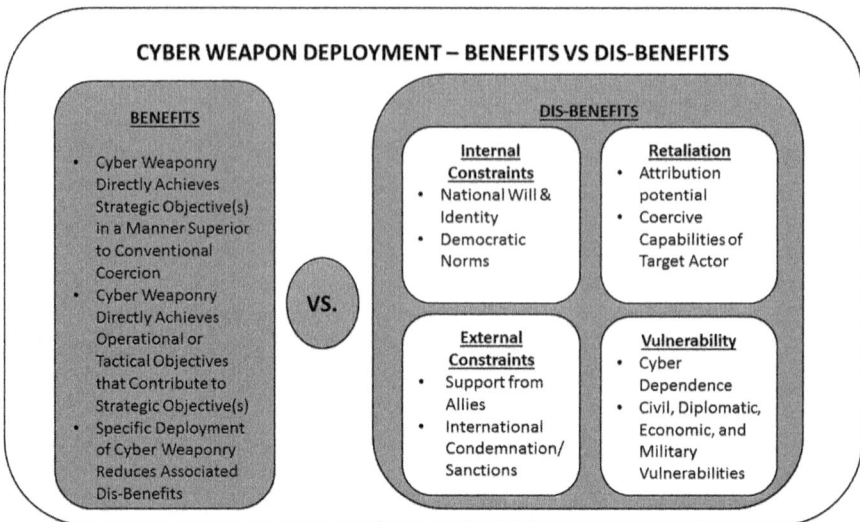

Fig. 6.4 Framework Two: benefits vs. dis-benefits of cyber weapon use

cyber weapons may reach targets that are resistant to traditional weapons due to formidable physical defences.

It is worth emphasising that the likelihood that cyber weapons can successfully achieve or contribute toward achieving objectives is a crucial criterion. If there is any degree of uncertainty regarding the efficacy of the cyber weapon to be deployed, then the calculation of potential benefits to the initiating actor becomes uncertain, weakening the argument for cyber weapon deployment. Similarly, if the deployment of cyber weaponry is tactical or operational, the initiating state needs to possess a certain degree of political or military power to exploit the cyber weapon deployment. Operation Orchard required a powerful aerial strike force to succeed. If Israel did not possess such a capability then its manipulation of Syrian anti-aircraft systems would have been pointless.

The calculation of dis-benefits arising from cyber weapon deployment has similar complexities. The initiating actor must consider any internal constraints that may impede the deployment of cyber weaponry. Democratic states may have to consider national will or appetite for the use deployment of cyber weapons. Similarly, considerations as to whether the self-identity of a state is consistent with first use of cyber weapons may also be pertinent. External constraints are also relevant—will the actor's allies support the use of cyber weapons? This can be a critical constraint if the initiating actor is a weaker actor that may rely on a strong ally for diplomatic or military protection. The reaction of international bodies such as the UN may also be relevant. If the use of cyber weapons can be attributed to the initiating actor then the actor may face international condemnation and even sanctions. Of course, if cyber weapon use is tactical or operational, and in support of a more damaging coercive measure, such as a conventional military strike, then the use of cyber weapons may be considered as incidental or secondary to the destruction caused by the traditional application of military force. In this case, calculations concerning retaliation or condemnation are more likely to be made based on the impact of the conventional military strike, rather than the cyber weapon deployment that enabled it.

Direct retaliation by the targeted actor is another critical consideration. The threat of retaliation is highly dependent on whether the cyber-attack can be attributed to the initiating actor. Much has been written regarding what has been termed the attribution problem (Lin 2012; Dipert 2013), the potential difficulties associated with definitively determining the actor behind a cyber-attack. When, however, cyber weapons form part of a combined armed operation, as was the case with Operation Orchard, the attribution problem all but disappears. Even when cyber weapon deployment is not a component of a combined arms strike, it may still be attributable to a state if it is obvious that a certain state is the recipient of significant strategic advantage as a result of the cyber-attack. In effect, there is a correlation between the political value of objectives and the likelihood that the use of cyber weapons will be attributed to the initiating state. The more obvious the strategic advantages for a state by using a cyber-attack, the more likely it is that the cyber-attack will be attributed to them, with or without indisputable technical evidence.

There is, however, an additional factor that can complicate attribution, even when the effects of an attack are of obvious strategic advantage to certain states. This occurs when the effects of cyber weapons present in a manner that allows them to be mistaken for routine or internal failures, rather than as an attack by a third party. In cases such as this the target may not even realise they are under cyber-attack, thus removing, or at least delaying, attribution considerations entirely.

If a state is attributed with using cyber weapons, the likelihood of retaliation will depend on the coercive capabilities of the targeted actor, and that actor's political and military appetite to use these capabilities. Weaker actors have fewer retaliatory measures than strong actors. Weaker actors are more likely to retaliate using an asymmetric vector, such as cyber-attacks of their own. The effectiveness of such attacks will be contingent on the cyber dependence of the initiating state. Cyber dependence concerns the degree to which a state is dependent on cyberspace for functioning economic, military, and civil infrastructure. The greater the cyber dependence of a state, the more susceptible it is to retaliatory cyber-attacks.

Retaliation to a cyber-attack, nevertheless, need not take the form of a cyber action. Coercive capabilities take many forms; each of which may be used as a basis for retaliation to the deployment of cyber weapons. Militarily powerful actors may choose the path of *escalation dominance* (Mahnken 2011) and elect to retaliate to cyber-attacks with a conventional military strike. Economically powerful actors may impose economic sanctions. Multi-laterally influential actors may also lobby supra-national bodies for diplomatic sanctions. Actors with strong alliances may rely on powerful allied states to take retaliatory action on their behalf. It is possible that certain actors may even elect to retaliate with asymmetric measures, such as state-sponsored terrorism. The effectiveness, and therefore the weight of dis-benefits, associated with retaliatory measures, is directly correlated with the civil, diplomatic, economic, and military vulnerabilities of the state considering use of cyber weapons. These vulnerabilities may be amplified if the state in question has a high degree of cyber dependence.

Considered holistically, all these factors contribute to a framework that provides for the comparative calculation of benefits and dis-benefits associated with a state initiating deployment of cyber weapons. This framework can be applied to hypothetical deployments of cyber weapons to generate predictive analysis regarding their potential use. The framework can also be used to analyze empirical examples of cyber weapon deployment, such as the Stuxnet cyber-attack against Iranian nuclear enrichment facilities.

6.3.2   Case Study Two—Stuxnet

Stuxnet refers to a cyber weapon—specifically a computer worm—that targeted the clandestine Iranian nuclear weapons program. While formal responsibility for the Stuxnet attack has never been acknowledged, it is commonly considered to be a joint Israeli/US operation that sought to delay Iranian acquisition of nuclear weapons (Sanger 2012; Lindsay 2013). Stuxnet targeted a specific type of industrial controller, manufactured by Siemens and designed to control the configuration of nuclear centrifuges found at a specific location—the Natanz nuclear facility, suspected to be part of Iran's nuclear weapon development program (Langner 2011). Stuxnet was not an instrument of brute force, but of subtlety. Rather than causing wholesale destruction to its intended target (like Operation Orchard), it instead enacted gradual "adjustments" to nuclear centrifuges, causing them to speed up or slow down, and occasionally to operate beyond their safety parameters. This had two effects; first, the centrifuges began to fail to produce refined uranium fuel, and second, they began to break-down—due to the damage caused by consistent operation outside their intended speed of operation (Singer and Friedman 2014).

Crucially, Stuxnet also affected the Siemens monitoring software, causing it to provide false records of centrifuge operation (Denning 2012); to the Iranian scientists monitoring the centrifuges there was no apparent reason why the centrifuges were failing. Accordingly, affected centrifuges were presumed to be faulty and were replaced, only for the problem to repeat itself and eventually damage the new centrifuges in the same manner (Singer and Friedman 2014). This created a psychological element to the Stuxnet attack that amplified the impact of the physical damage it caused. Due to the manipulation of the controlling software, Iranian scientists could not explain the failures they were witnessing. It is reported that this led to low morale and difficult questions regarding the competence of scientists tasked with advancing Iran's nuclear ambitions. Eventually, the worm was discovered, not by Iran, but by a German computer specialist—Ralph Langer—who blogged about his discoveries in 2010 (Singer and Friedman 2014). The overall effectiveness of the Stuxnet attack is contested, some estimates suggest that it resulted in the destruction of thousands of centrifuges at the Natanz facility (Denning 2012), setting Iran's nuclear ambitions back several years (Richardson 2011). Other sources have disputed this, suggesting that the Iranian nuclear enrichment capability recovered within a year (Lindsay 2013).

6.3.3 Analysing Stuxnet

A visual representation of the analysis of the Stuxnet attack according to Framework Two shown in Fig. 6.5.

For the purposes of analysis, it is assumed that the United States and Israel were responsible for the Stuxnet attack. Stuxnet enabled both parties to directly achieve a valuable strategic objective—delaying Iranian acquisition of nuclear weapons—through the deployment of a tailored cyber weapon. Crucially, the mechanism of the Stuxnet attack, cumulatively degrading Iranian nuclear infrastructure in a manner that masked the actions of the cyber weapon, reduced the dis-benefits associated with cyber weapon deployment. This was due to the secrecy and subtlety with which Stuxnet functioned, which allowed its effects to be interpreted as a routine or internal failure.

By degrading the Iranian centrifuges in a manner that simulated internal failure, it was not apparent that the Natanz facility was under attack. This significantly reduced the threat of retaliation—if Iran did not realise its nuclear program was being sabotaged using an offensive cyber weapon, then there would be no reason for retaliation. If the target did not realize it was under attack, then neither would the

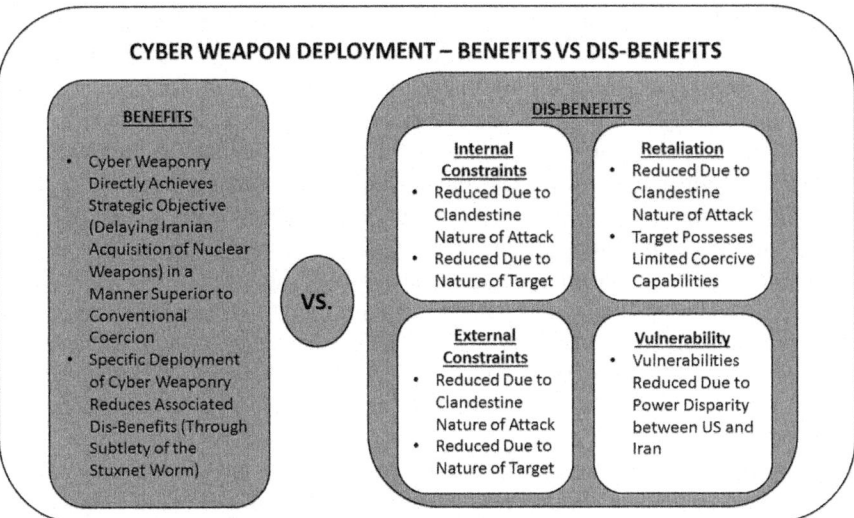

Fig. 6.5 Analysis of Stuxnet according to Framework Two

international community, thereby reducing the chance of widespread political opposition to using a cyber weapon. Similarly, the secrecy that characterized the attack meant there was no immediate domestic opposition to a cyber-attack.

Even when the Stuxnet worm was discovered, the massive power disparity between the United States (and its ally, Israel) and Iran expressively reduced the possibility of retaliation that would pose a threat to the national security of either country. The United States and Israel's comparatively high degree of cyber dependence offered some potential for asymmetric retaliation by Iran, but ultimately Iran's options were limited by the United States' military, economic, and diplomatic might. Likewise, when news of the attack broke, there was limited criticism anywhere on the globe. The target of the attack was a clandestine nuclear program that was widely condemned in the United States and Israel (Waltz 2012) and which was the target of sanctions levelled by the United Nations and European Union (Laub 2015). The fact that Stuxnet was a bloodless attack, one that caused no collateral damage or human casualties, likely further weakened any form of condemnation. Considered in its entirety, these factors made the strategic deployment of a cyber weapon a superior option to the type of cyber-enabled attack that characterized Operation Orchard.

6.3.4 Predictive Analysis

Several conclusions can be drawn from the presentation of Framework Two and the Stuxnet case study. Taken together, these conclusions provide predictive analysis regarding the circumstances under which states may seek to deploy cyber weapons. First, a state is more likely to deploy cyber weapons if the deployment has a high probability of achieving politically valuable objectives. These may be strategic objectives achieved through cyber weapon deployment, such as was the case with Stuxnet. Alternatively, they may be tactical or operational objectives that contribute towards a broader strategic objective, as illustrated by Operation Orchard. Second, a state is more likely to use offensive cyber weapons if these weapons can reduce the dis-benefits associated with coercive action, as was the case with the Stuxnet attack.

Third, as further demonstrated by Stuxnet, the comparative power of the initiating state and the target actor is also an important factor in determining the likelihood of cyber weapons deployment. If the initiating state has the diplomatic power or economic strength to shield itself from international opposition, and the military might to limit the likelihood of retaliatory strikes, then the benefits associated with cyber weapons are more likely to outweigh the dis-benefits. The cyber dependence of the initiating state may be a factor that increases dis-benefits, but the threat of a powerful state's coercive capabilities can act to shield it from cyber-attacks that are significant enough to threaten its national security. The nature of the target of the cyber weapon deployment is also relevant, particularly domestic and international opinion. If the target is undertaking actions that are perceived as a threat to the initiating state, or the wider international order, then opposition to the use of cyber weapons is likely to be muted.

6.4 Conclusion

Two frameworks have been presented use in analysing the potential and actual cyber weapon deployment by nation states. Framework One focused on the analysis of the nature of and relationships between the different elements that comprise the deployment of cyber weapons. Use of the framework can provide for analytical clarity regarding the scope and characteristics of the *Cyber Means*, *Effects*, *Targets*, and *Objectives* that interact to constitute cyber weapon deployment. Conversely, Framework Two analysed the competing factors that may lead a nation state to deploy cyber weapons. This analysis focused on the elicitation of a comparative calculation regarding the benefits and dis-benefits arising from the deployment of offensive cyber weapons.

Analysis of benefits focused on the value of the tactical, operational, and strategic objectives that can be achieved by cyber weapons. In addition, benefit calculations considered how the use of cyber weapons may be superior to other coercive capabilities; such as conventional weapons, or may act to limit the dis-benefits arising from coercive action. Analysis of dis-benefits focused on domestic and international political constraints on state deployment of cyber weapons, and the risk and impact of retaliation against the state initiating cyber weapon use. Unsurprisingly, comparative state power remains the most influential determinant of whether cyber weapon deployment is strategically feasible.

6.5 Principal Concepts

The principal concepts associated with this chapter are listed below. Demonstrate your understanding of each by writing a definition or explanation in one or two sentences.

- Attribution problem;
- Force amplification;
- Direct effects;
- Cascading effects; and
- Cyber dependence.

6.6 Study Questions

1. What are the three categories of targets that cyber weaponry may affect? What are the differences between them?
2. Explain why conventional weaponry may need to be deployed in addition to cyber weaponry in order to achieve a strategic objective.

3. Describe a hypothetical situation where a state could achieve significant strategic objectives through the deployment of cyber weaponry, either through using cyber weapons independently, or as part of a combined operation.

6.7   Learning Activity

As with any analytical method, the two frameworks discussed in this chapter can be considered nascent; they can be iterated or expanded upon to improve their explanative power. So, individually, or in a small group, investigate recent incidences where the press has reported the use of cyber weapons. Using either Framework One or Framework Two, analyse the data. Now, brainstorm a variation to the Framework and apply it to the same data. What are your thoughts? Has the variation improved the Framework?

References

Arquilla J, Ronfeldt D (1993) Cyberwar is coming! Comp Strateg 12(2):141–165

Bachmann SD (2012) Hybrid threats, cyber warfare and NATO's comprehensive approach for countering 21st century threats–mapping the new frontier of global risk and security management

Birdwell MB, Mills R (2011) War fighting in cyberspace: evolving force presentation and command and control. AIR UNIV MAXWELL AFB AL AIR FORCE RESEARCH INST

Clarke RA, Knake RK (2011) Cyber war. HarperCollins, New York

Clemmons BQ, Brown GD (1999) Cyberwarfare: ways, warriors and weapons of mass destruction. Mil Rev 79(5):35

Dipert RR (2013) Other-than-Internet (OTI) cyberwarfare: challenges for ethics, law, and policy. J Mil Ethics 12(1):34–53

DoD US (2010) JP1–02: department of defense dictionary of military and associated terms. DoD, Washington, DC

Follath E, Stark H (2009) How Israel destroyed Syria's Al Kibar nuclear reactor. Spiegel Online, 11. Lin, 2012

Hinsley M (2015) Playing for high stakes: the Archer's stake and the battle of agincourt. Historian, London 127(Autumn):30–34

Kirsch CM (2011) Science fiction no more: cyber warfare and the United States. Denv J Int Law Policy 40:620

Langner R (2011) Stuxnet: dissecting a cyberwarfare weapon. IEEE Secur Priv 9(3):49–51. Denning, 2012

Laub Z (2015) International sanctions on Iran. CFR Backgrounders, Council on Foreign Relations 15

Libicki MC (2014) Why cyber war will not and should not have its grand strategist. Air University Maxwell AFB/Air Force Research Institute

Lindsay JR (2013) Stuxnet and the limits of cyber warfare. Secur Stud 22(3):365–404

Mahnken TG (2011) Cyber war and cyber warfare. Am Cyber Futur Secur Prosp Inf Age 2:53–62

Richardson J (2011) Stuxnet as cyberwarfare: applying the law of war to the virtual battlefield. J Marshall J Comput Inf Law 29:1

Rid T (2012) Cyber war will not take place. J Strateg Stud 35(1):5–32

Sanger DE (2012) Obama order sped up wave of cyberattacks against Iran. New York Times, 1, p
    A1
Schaap AJ (2009) Cyber warfare operations: development and use under international law. AFL
    Rev 64:121
Singer PW, Friedman A (2014) Cybersecurity: what everyone needs to know. Oxford University
    Press, Oxford
Taddeo M (2012) An analysis for a just cyber warfare. NATO CCD COE/IEEE Publication
Turns D (2012) Cyber warfare and the notion of direct participation in hostilities. J Confl Secur Law
    17(2):279–297
Waltz KN (2012) Why Iran should get the bomb: nuclear balancing would mean stability. Foreign
    Aff 91:2

Chapter 7
The Rule of Law: Controlling Cyber Weapons

Henry Prunckun

7.1 Introduction

When computer-based systems or the mechanisms by which their electronic data are transmitted are disrupted, the resulting problems are serious. Losing access to vital records; losing productivity and accountability; and losing revenue are just a few of the tangible results of such a failure. One only needs to turn on the evening news or read a newspaper to know the effect a major ICT (information and communication technology) disruption has—the impact on ordinary life is far-reaching. The consequences of a systems failure are much more than an inconvenience; these events lead to public distrust, fear and confusion—a case in point is Hurricane Katrina in 2005. Disaster response expert David Simpson (2007: 58) said: "We have more available to us, but when systems fail, we have a bigger breakdown." This is because the key to civil societies' strength—a system of processing and distributing information and knowledge—is also its greatest weakness.

When it comes to these natural disasters, there is nothing that can be done to deter the forces of nature that wreak havoc on ICT systems.[1] It is, however, another matter when it comes to human threats. Malware, backdoors, application-specific hacks, phishing schemes are part of the methods used to disrupt ICT systems. It is acknowledged that a layered approach to security is the best stance against interruption. Known as *defense-in-depth*, this approach usually comprises: (1) intrusion preparation; (2) monitoring and response; and (3) a recovery and continuity planning.

---

[1]For the purpose here, ICTs refer to computer-based data systems that include both hardware devices and software applications.

H. Prunckun (✉)
Australian Graduate School of Policing and Security, Charles Sturt University, Sydney, Australia
e-mail: hprunckun@csu.edu.au

© Springer International Publishing AG, part of Springer Nature 2018
H. Prunckun (ed.), *Cyber Weaponry*, Advanced Sciences and Technologies for
Security Applications, https://doi.org/10.1007/978-3-319-74107-9_7

As sound as these emergency management measures are, there is the issue of prevention—"consider[ing] the risk[s] and try[ing] to implement ways that could stop it from happening (Prunckun 2015: 302)." Take the case of gun control. Laws mitigate the hazard firearms pose to society through preventative legislation. These laws regulate the manufacture, sale, distribution and use of guns. These laws also regulate the caliber, capacity and rate of fire these weapons have and who can own and discharge them.[2]

Moreover, in arms-producing countries that export, sell firearms and weapons of warfare[3] is regulated by law—if for no other reason, it is in the country's strategic interest to know what, how many, and where such weapons are being sold (and potentially used). Such concern is easy to understand because these weapons can result in great physical harm. Unregulated proliferation is simply dangerous.

But, should the same concern be expressed for weapons proliferating in the cybersphere, specifically those designed to inflict harm on ICT systems, which are, arguably, society's lifeline? These, too, are not bloodless weapons (Yunos and Zin 2003). Take for instance the 2017 *WannaCry* ransomware that was reported to have infected over 200,000 computers in more than 150 countries and affecting health facilities across Britain:

> Britain's health service was hit Friday by a huge international cyberattack that froze computers at hospitals across the country—an attack that shut down wards, closed emergency rooms and brought medical treatments to a screeching halt. (Associated Press 2017)

7.2 Background

Cyber weapons are essentially software programs that have been weaponized. They are used to target a variety of computer-based systems—their effect can range from disrupting services to the complete destruction of data, data-processing functions, and physical equipment. Cyber weapons also include certain types of computer hardware that enable the launching of these software-based attacks. Perpetrators vary from young cyber vandals to transnational criminals, international terrorists, and hostile governments.

The same ICT-infrastructure that society uses to transmit everyday information also creates unprecedented opportunities for threat-agents: theft, destructive attacks,

---

[2]Although on the surface, one would find it hard to discount the merits of such legislation, there are some dissenting voices that argue along the lines of the American National Rifle Association that there is a constitutional '...right of the people to keep and bear arms...' (*The Amendments to the Constitution of the United States of America*, December 15, 1791). In Australia and some other developed countries, by contrast, there is no such constitutional right, and the Commonwealth of Australia moved to further regulate various aspects of firearms when, in 1996, Martin Bryant murdered 35 people and injured 37 others at Port Arthur, Tasmania.

[3]Typically, *weapons of warfare* are categorized as being over 0.50 caliber. Whereas, weapons of 0.50 caliber or less are categorized as *small arms*. (Mouzos 1999)

industrial espionage, and information warfare are all possibilities. Intent, therefore, can differ from merely causing a nuisance, to one that jeopardizes national security.

The question that presents itself is: Should governments legislate the control of cyber weapons in the same way it has done for nuclear weapons, chemical weapons, biological weapons, and radiological weapons? If this is an exaggerated proposition, then should cyber weapons be treated like weapons of warfare—mortars, rockets, cannon, or fully automatic rifles? If not, should they be treated as the equivalents of sporting rifles and other small arms—revolvers, pistols, and shotguns? Or, should they simply do nothing because the destruction of data is not equal in any sense to the destruction of human life? The answer is not obvious and the response from a policy perspective is obscure.

As Grabosky (2005: 13) once put it: "Predicting precisely what the next big cyber-crime will be in a given country is not easy. What is easier is the identification of vulnerabilities." Therefore, to identify how society is vulnerable (and to what extent), cyber weapons need to be understood in their criminogenic context and from the perspective of the risk they pose. Then, if necessary, relief can be crafted in the form of the rule of law.

7.3   Criminogenic Risk

In recent years, information and communications technologies have been the subject of crime, the object of crime, as well as the devices for planning and committing crime. ICTs have even become an emblem for crime—deception and intimidation (Grabosky and Smith 2007).

In its criminogenic context, information and communications technologies facilitates a range of anti-social behaviors from inconveniences, such as e-mail spam, to more serious activities, such as fraud, theft, stalking, money laundering, and pornography. More serious still are those activities that fall into the categories of espionage, arms, and drug trafficking, sabotage, terrorism, and other forms of ethnic extremism (Arquilla and Ronfeldt 2001). At the pinnacle of hostile intent is the use of ICT to enable cyber warfare—that is, waging hostilities in cyberspace.

If a shipment of arms arrived on a nation's soil, that cargo would pose a clear danger. Yet, cyber weapons have entered most countries via the cybersphere, unnoticed, undeclared, and reside in the hands of people unknown (Fig. 7.1).

Denning (2000: 43–53) pointed-out that cyber weapons are easy to obtain and use, and becoming more powerful. What is available on the Internet to download can penetrate most networks' firewalls and routers. Some weapons can launch attacks simply by typing the Internet address directly into the attack-enabling website. "It's cheap and easy to put together a credible attack capability either in-house, or for hire (Campbell: 1999)."

Fig. 7.1 Information and communications technologies have become one of the chief centers of crime activity (Photograph by Jhi Scott and courtesy of the U.S. Department of Defense)

By way of example, take the case of Operation Ababil. It's alleged to have involved a series of denial of service attacks in 2012 by a group called the Cyber Fighters of Izz Ad-Din Al Qassam (or, Qassassm Cyber Fighters). The cyber-attacks targeted the New York Stock Exchange and JP Morgan Bank in what was claimed to have been retaliation to an anti-Islamic video that was posted to *YouTube*. This is not a theoretical problem. How the world's political leadership treats these dangers is a question of substantial importance.

Even though cyber weapons share similarities with kinetic weapons (e.g. Stuxnet), they occupy a new position simply by their character. "Their uniqueness requires well-considered policy for their use (Bayles 2001: 44–58)." Because of their volume, frequency and ubiquity, governments cannot realistically continue to solve the problems individual attacks cause on a case-by-case basis; they need to address the over-arching problem—cyber weapons themselves. These developments should be the "alarm bell" for governments to consider legislation that could prevent uncontrolled access to cyber weapons. If we look at how behaviors that are unsafe, harmful, and socially undesirable are addressed, we see that it is to seek this relief in the rule of law. Could this avenue offer reprieve from the danger of cyber weapons as it does with firearms?

7.4 The Law as Protection

Laws are normative constructs by which governments establish principles for the societies they govern. If citizens do not conform to these standards of behaviour, laws direct administrators to enforce the prescribed norms upon the wrong doers (Quinney 1970). Through this process, citizens either obey the rule of law, or are subject to official enforcement (e.g. police, regulatory or compliance action; and in the international sphere, military interdiction or intervention).

Therefore, legislating the control of cyber weapons would provide law enforcers with the ability to actively target those with ill intent—those who are not merely an anti-social nuisance, but those who purposely design to undermine or destroy the fabric from which society's well-being is woven. Legislative controls for cyber weapons provide not only a practical basis for prevention (through enforcement), but also a symbolic springboard for related policies.

Denning (2000: 1) wrote in her watershed paper on the topic—*Reflections on Cyberweapons Control*—"The general sentiment seems to be that strong controls are not desirable, enforceable, or cost-effective, and careful study may confirm that." Denning's judgment may be correct from a strictly technical point of view—*strong* controls may not be the best policy option, if one looks at the problem from an executive government's administrative perspective (for instance, how does a government enforce laws against multiple offenders who operate in jurisdictions that are hard to determine based on the rules of the physical world—e.g. extraterritorial issues).

But what about legislation that is more *balanced*? What about laws that reflect the realities of the cybersphere rather than geographical boundaries? Wouldn't such measured laws project a government's concern on the issue regardless of the difficulties inherent in enforcement? The current stance is one that could be interpreted as governments turning a "blind-eye" to the issue because it may not be cost-effective administratively (or as some may more bluntly argue—laws have never and will never effect change).

If the analogue of drug control is used, one could suggest that because the current legislative framework for illicit drugs has failed to manage the distribution and use of these harmful substances, legal controls are immaterial. It would be inconceivable that any responsible government would deregulate drugs, let alone abolish all laws to regulate it. Even jurisdictions that have discriminated cannabis still have laws that control this substance (alcohol, as another example, is legal in some jurisdictions, but nevertheless regulated by law). So, why would governments want *every* Internet user in their jurisdiction to have "bullet-proof" defensive cyber weapons, including terrorists, organized criminals, embezzlers, drug dealers, and pedophiles? This, and like questions, have policy implications for the world's lawmakers.

7.5 Hazard Identification

As a list of cyber weapons is potentially long, the first issue to be addressed is which weapons would be considered in such a definition? Like firearms, there are offensive and defensive cyber weapons, and some weapons that function as both.

Purely offensive cyber weapons include the thousands of computer viruses that circulate across the Internet each year as well as worms, Trojan horses, logic bombs,[4] programs that execute denial of service attacks, exploit scripts, and programs that take advantage of vulnerabilities in operating systems (or how they are configured operationally).

Like their physical world cousins, offensive cyber weapons intend to strike at ICTs to inflict damage or limit performance in the same way kinetic weapons can kill, wound, or destroy an object or construction.[5]

Cyber weapons for defence include anti-virus programs, anti-spam programs, anti-spyware programs, firewalls (both software and hardware), e-data shredders, system log cleaners, cookie cleaners, and encryption programs. (Strauss 2007a: 8).

Dual-purpose cyber weapons include system log cleaners (these can be to either cover hackers' tracks as they maneuver through a computer system and/or deleted data that could be exploited by hackers who are mounting an offensive attack), vulnerability scanners[6] (these are programs that search a network for weaknesses that could be exploited for either good or malice), and network monitoring software (i.e. software that automatically monitors the network and servers for failures—they allow for the identification of issues and fix unexpected conditions before users report them). (Strauss 2007a: 8).

---

[4]A virus is a program that contains instructions that allow it to replicate itself by attaching itself to other programs. The 'infection' is spread once the program is executed (i.e. *run*). Viruses can simply replicate themselves or cause damage by performing some harmful action. A worm is a program that replicates itself throughout a network (including the Internet) without the aid of a host program—like a virus. When a worm replicates, it overloads the network creating performance issues—usually with memory, hard drives, and bandwidth. A Trojan horse is like a worm in that it does not require a host program to execute, but rather it substitutes itself for a legitimate program hence its name. A logic bomb is dormant computer code added to software and activated at a predetermined time or by a predetermined event. For example, a cyber vandal might insert code into a program that will destroy important files should an event occur, or not occur. Although discussed as individual cyber weapons, viruses, worms, Trojan horses, and logic bombs can be created as combination weapon. For instance, a virus could gain access to a network through a Trojan horse. This virus could then install a logic bomb within a software application that is running on that network which in turn initiates a worm when that application executes.

[5]Note the difference between a *weapon* and a *tool*; the latter being an implement to help perform a piece of work. (Australian Institute of Criminology & Australian High-Tech Crime Centre, 'Acquiring High Tech Crime Tools,' *High-Tech Crime Brief*, no. 13, Canberra 2006).

[6]Defensive scanners would be expected to stop at the point where vulnerabilities are found. Offensive scanners would then take this information and go one step further—try to determine how to exploit the vulnerability(s).

7.5.1 Scalable Regulatory Framework

Although the issue of cyber weapons has been on the policy horizon for some time, the issue has not made it to a prominent political agenda for discussion (Strauss 2007b: 2). If this was because cyber weapons posed no hazard to society, then one would expect some justification in the literature to this effect. However, the literature is barren of such a position. In contrast, the literature abounds with references such as the comments from Joel Brenner (2007), a US counterintelligence executive, who stated: "We've got to rethink the adequacy of our legal authorities to deal with the cyber thieves and the vandals who I call the Barbary pirates of the twenty-first century."

Other references to electronic security and the need to secure the information technology infrastructure are plentiful. To demonstrate this, one need only look at the private sector that is awash with businesses that specialize in providing electronic security risk management, cybersecurity advice, and cybersecurity hardware and software installation, testing, system configuration, and more. The same applies to government organizations. Whole departments have been set-up to manage the risk to civil service sector ICT-infrastructure.

The striking feature of cybersecurity is that these measures focus firmly on what would have been termed in the physical world "locks, fences, and doors." These security measures overlook the fact that existing jurisdictional laws do not provide an adequate legal foundation for control.

As the Australian Institute of Criminology (Choo et al. 2007) stated: "There is no single all-encompassing answer to responding to technology-enabled crime." The question that then presents itself is whether legislation is needed to prohibit, restrict, or contain the creation, possession, sale, distribution and use of cyber weapons?

If the analogy of firearms is used—take for instance, sub-machine guns—there are legitimate users (e.g. the military and police), and those whom governments do not want to have such weapons (e.g. motorcycle gangs and illicit drug dealers). If the volume of cyber weapons in circulation is so great, then it follows that governments should want to be able to define in legislation those who are to have access to them (and under what circumstances), and those who should not. To illustrate, it could be desirable for the military and law enforcement agencies to have access to cyber weapons to, respectively, protect national security and combat organized crime. There may be other people who should have legitimate access to the source code of such weapons (e.g. anti-virus software developers), but prohibit others from possessing, selling, or distributing them (e.g. ranging from cyber vandals to terrorists).

To describe a policy towards cyber weapons as a choice between *laisser-faire* and total prohibition would be simplistic. These two policy options are often seen in political circles as the "Rivers of Blood" positions—both are characterized by vivid scenarios of what would happen if a government adopts a position at one-or-other end of this policy spectrum. As such, these two options should be seen for what they are—extremes. However, in practical terms, there are three middle-ground (*balanced*) options that could be added to these two polarizing situations. Described in real-world terms, these three strategies are listed below and form part of a taxonomy for what could be a scalable regulatory framework.

Prohibition

- Criminalization of the creation, possession, distribution, sale, transfer or use of all or some software- and hardware-based cyber weapons by anyone other than those with government approval.

Regulation

- Restricting the use of software-based cyber weapons for illegal acts defined in existing criminal statutes by enacting amendments to current laws or regulations.
- Licensing (or another approval mechanism) the creation, possession, distribution, sale, transfer or use of all or some software-based cyber weapons through a governmental regulatory framework, similar in nature to that which regulates firearms, explosives or other dangerous goods (e.g. ammonium nitrate fertilizer that is used in improvised explosives).
- Licensing the creation, possession, distribution, sale, transfer or use of all or some hardware-based cyber weapons as per software cyber weapons described above.

Laissez-faire

- An unregulated system where government does not interference in the creation, possession, distribution, sale, transfer or use of all software- and hardware-based cyber weapons.

7.5.2   Regulatory Options

In addition to the *strategic* regulatory positions above, there are several *tactical* options that could be added, which would avoid the "strong controls" that Denning (2000: 43) saw as undesirable, unenforceable, and lacking cost-effectiveness. The options presented below do not imply that it is an exhaustive list, nor should it seen as an inclusive "package" that requires all (or most) to be implemented. The options are simply choices that could be considered as part of a flexible approach to cyber weapons control.

Licensing

- Setting of eligibility requirements for a person or body corporate before being able to code, compile, test, distribute, or sell a cyber weapon.

- Licensing could be for "life" or for a specific period of time (with the option of making the license renewable).
- Licensing options could be introduced for industry sectors—virus software developers, firewall manufactures, users of encryption, and so on.

Penalties

- Both criminal sanctions could apply—fines and imprisonment—as well as civil penalty-expiation fees. Quantum for each of these types of penalties could vary from trivial to severe depending on the need for deterrence.

Absolute ban on certain categories of cyber weapons

- There are several cyber weapons that should be subject to a total ban for members of the public. One clear example is that of a *botnet*—a collection of computers covertly controlled through a Trojan software program by a hacker to command the machines' processor for unauthorized/illegal use. (Choo 2007).

Storage and Transmission

- Regulation could proscribe how certain categories of cyber weapons, if licensed, needed to be stored and transmitted—as with software developers working on antivirus applications. This would add a high degree of protection against inadvertent release "into the wild."

Training

- There could be provision for a minimum standard of training for citizens who request to develop or use a cyber weapon.

Amnesty

- There could be a cyber weapon amnesty to encourage people who possess cyber weapons to surrender or destroy them before bringing in criminal sanctions, or expiated civil penalties.

Complicity

- Provision could be included for instances where individuals act jointly.

7.6 Discussion

Weapons such as rifles, handguns, shotguns, explosives, as well as materials and devices used in chemical, biological, and nuclear weapons, are governed by national laws, and in some cases, international treaties, because their kinetic effects present a clear danger. But, so do cyber weapons. Therefore, regardless of whether the weapons are tangible or virtual, the fact that they have a physical impact should be the determinate for their control.

Until the Internet, attacks on computer-based systems were isolated and relatively few. Internet-connected computer systems now support governments, commerce, and industry, banking and finance, passenger transport and cargo (including land, air and sea), education, health, telecommunications (including satellite), critical infra-structure (e.g. water, gas, electricity, and waste treatment), as well as police, emer-gency services, and military. A cyber-attack on any one of these key systems would not only impact on the target, but are likely to have flow-on effect to systems and organizations that are joined in some way with the target; resulting in cascading national, or even international, disruptions.

If a police investigation were to discover specimen viruses on a seized computer, password crackers, and lists of operating system vulnerabilities (i.e. *exploits*[7]), there would be no crime to charge the suspect with. As such, police would be hard pressed to remove these programs or otherwise confiscate them and thereby prevent future malicious usage. If, however, there were provision in the criminal law that could distinguish between classes of cyber weapons and between legitimate users and those with mal-intent, law enforcers could take decisive action.

If, for example, an age limit is specified, as is with alcoholic drinks, cigarettes, driving a motor vehicle, or the possession of spray paints, anyone caught in possession of, say a port scanner, would be viewed in the same way as a youth roaming the streets with aerosol paint would be—a vandal. The port scanner could be confiscated and the matter dealt with by way of the courts, or an expiation notice on a case-by-case basis as it is in the kinetic world.

Using such an approach would afford police and regulatory agencies the ability to differentiate between cyber weapons that could cause grievous harm—that is to say, placing lives at peril or the ability to cause economic damage to an industry sector—and those that merely produce a nuisance.[8] It would also allow them to identify cyber weapons that are, in the main, used purely for defensive reasons and form part of a legitimate cyber-crime prevention strategy (and take no action).

7.6.1 Classes of Weapons

A useful way of classifying cyber weapons is according to their use—offensive, defensive, and dual-use. Conceptualizing cyber weapons in this way aids in classi-fying them according to statute. As there are many dozens, if not hundreds, of types

---

[7]In fact, there is a *white market* for system exploits where software researchers can sell zero-day vulnerabilities that they discover back to software developers so that the developer can patch the flaw.

[8]For instance, there is what seems like and endless stream of emails circulating that promote some form of hoax.

of cyber weapons in circulation, it would be impracticable to try to define them on an individual basis. It would be far more practical to define them according to a set of attributes—like *sporting rifles*. By way of example, it would be futile to define a sporting rifle based on an individual examination. This would require the arms maker to submit a sample at, say, the design stage to be categorized, and then again at manufacture stage to assure that what was intended was reflected in the manufactured product. This process also does not consider the underground arms trade, including homemade guns (e.g. through metalwork and 3D printing). If this model were applied to cyber weapons, then a large percentage of weapons would slip through the legal net set to catch them because they are created by anonymous programmers.

Alternatively, a descriptive classification system could be used (defined in *Regulations*[9] so that such definitions can be amended easily by an administrative unit of executive government—for example, an attorney-general's department, or the police—as opposed to the more cumbersome process of a parliament or congress), as the need arises. Such a construction can then be used to assess whether a cyber weapon is captured by the law and if so what category it falls into. If we look at how this currently works with firearms, we see that a firearm means "(A) any weapon (including a starter gun) which will or is designed to or may readily be converted to expel a projectile by the action of an explosive; (B) the frame or receiver of any such weapon; (C) any firearm muffler or firearm silencer; or (D) any destructive device" (United States 2010).

Rather than divert this discussion to what could be a debate as to how such a definition should be crafted, suffice to say that a nation's legislators would have that debate after public consultation. And, like most laws, it might be imperfect, but it will be the best result given the competing interests that are in existence at the time. The only point that needs to be made here is that through a system of classifying, cyber weapons can be managed in an orderly and systemic way.

The features of this type of system would include the enactment of a specific piece of legislation (say, for instance, a hypothetical *Cyber Weapons Control Act*, or internationally via a Treaty) that sets out how issues arising out of the Act will be administered (e.g. perhaps, through a consultative committee comprising a range of interested parties), the terms under which a person (or body corporate) can possess and use a cyber weapon, how a cyber weapon can be acquired, transferred, and who can deal in cyber weapons.

---

[9]A *regulation* is a legal requirement created by an administrative unit of government which carries the threat of sanction or fine if the provisions are not complied.

7.7 Conclusion

Certain critical information and communication technologies permit criminals to have anonymity, a broad pool of potential victims (individuals, organisations, corporations and governments) and an inexpensive and accessible set of devices and applications for committing crimes. "Measures thus far adopted by the private and public sectors have not provided an adequate level of security. While new methods of attack have been accurately predicted by experts and some large attacks have been detected in early stages, efforts to prevent or deter them have been largely unsuccessful, with increasingly damaging consequences (Sofaer et al. 2000)."

Computers and software are now used in such ways that they have become cyber weapons. Like kinetic weapons that are controlled by legislation, regulation, and other forms of legal doctrine, is it not timely for policymakers to consider controlling the creation, availability, distribution, possession, and use of cyber weapons?

Control of cyber weapons is integral to protecting information and communications technology infrastructure. ICT-infrastructure in turn is vital to national security because of the essential services it provides to a nation's social and economic well-being as well as its defence and internal security. An important aspect of ensuring the stability of ICT-infrastructure is electronic security, or as it is often referred, *cyber-security* (previously termed *e-security*). Cybersecurity is arguably the most important enabler of all forms of e-commerce, knowledge development, and communication on the globe.

The issues for formulating legislative policy to address the depth and breadth of possible cyber weapon control options are large—because there is no one way to deal with this question. In fact, although the issue of controlling cyber weapons has been on the policy agenda for some years, the literature is relatively silent as are examples of how legislators have addressed this issue in practice; that is, translating policy into law.

Restricting the use of software-based cyber weapons to existing criminal statutes would most likely require some amendments. If this were being contemplated, legislators would be better advised to consider enacting new laws tailored for a licensing regime. In this regard, several licensing options suggest themselves for consideration.

If licensing was enacted provisions could be fashioned to regulate the creation, possession, distribution, sale, transfer, or use of all or some software-based cyber weapons through a governmental regulatory framework. The same could apply for hardware-based cyber weapons. The regulatory options are numerous and offer lawmakers great flexibility in enacting legislation that suits that nation's needs, yet conforms to an international model (which would be the desirable strategic goal of such laws).

The need for international cooperation for pursuing cyber criminals is undisputable. Converting this imperative to control the spread of cyber weapons before their proliferation reaches "wild-west" proportions is the challenge for civil societies the world over. By its nature, cyber-crime—including the weaponization of computer software and hardware—can only be tackled at the global level.

7.8   Principal Concepts

The principal concepts associated with this chapter are listed below. Demonstrate your understanding of each by writing a short definition or explanation in one or two sentences:

- critical information and communication technology;
- defense-in-depth;
- policy options; and
- regulatory framework.

7.9   Study Questions

1. Explain the difference between a law (i.e. a statute) and a regulation.
2. List four types of cyber weapons that are in circulation—two software weapons and two hardware weapons.
3. Explain how a person who builds a computer that is more powerful than the typical commercially marketed hardware could be used as a cyber weapon; for example, in breaking passwords?
4. Explain why cyber weapons need to be addressed at a global level?

7.10   Learning Activity

Individually, or in a small group, brainstorm a list of cyber weapons that could be used by a person, business, or government's legitimate computer defensive plan. Argue why these software applications and/or hardware devices could be used in a cyber-crime prevention strategy. Describe what your strategy might look like.

Acknowledgement   The author would like to thank the editor of the *Global Crime* for permission to use his previously published paper (Prunckun 2008).

References

Arquilla J, Ronfeldt D (eds) (2001) Networks and netwars: the future of terrorism, crime and militancy. Rand Corp, Santa Monica
Associated Press (2017) World cyberattack cripples UK hospitals, demands ransoms. The New York Times, 12 May, available at: https://www.nytimes.com/aponline/2017/05/12/world/europe/ap-eu-britain-hospital-problems.html?_r=0. Accessed 16 May 2017
Bayles WJ (2001) The ethics of computer network attack. Parameters, Spring, pp 44–58

Brenner J (2007), quoted in Jeanne Meserve, Official: international hackers going after US networks. CNN Washington Bureau, 19 Oct [online]. Available at http://www.cnn.com/2007/US/10/19/cyber.threats/index.html. Accessed 17 May 2017

Campbell, Major General John H., cited in Stephen Green (1999) Pentagon giving cyberwarfare high priority. Copley News Service, 21 Dec, available at http://www.fas.org/irp/news/1999/12/991221-cyber.htm. Accessed 17 May 2017

Choo K-KR (2007) Zombies and Botnets. In: Trends and issues in crime and criminal justice, No. 337. Australian Institute of Criminology, Canberra

Choo K-KR, Smith RG, McCusker R (2007) The future of technology-enabled crime in Australia. In: Trends and issues in crime and criminal justice, No. 341. Australian Institute of Criminology, Canberra, p 6

Denning D (2000) Reflections on cyber weapons controls. Comput Secur J XVI(4, Fall):43–53

Grabosky PN (2005) Recent trends in cybercrime. 11th United Nations congress on crime prevention and criminal justice, Bangkok, April 22, 13

Grabosky PN, Smith RG (2007) Crime in the digital age: controlling telecommunications and cyberspace illegalities. Transaction Publishers, New Brunswick

Mouzos J (1999) International traffic in small arms: an Australian perspective. In: Trends and issues in crime and criminal justice, No. 104. Australian Institute of Criminology, Canberra

Prunckun H (2008) Bogies in the wire: is there a need for legislative control of cyber weapons. Glob Crime 9(3):262–272

Prunckun H (2015) Scientific methods of inquiry for intelligence analysis, 2nd edn. Rowman & Littlefield, Lanham

Quinney R (1970) The social reality of crime. Little, Brown and Company, Boston

Simpson D (2007) quoted in Logan Ward, Facing down disaster. Popular Mechanics, number 58

Sofaer A, Goodman S, Cuéllar M-F, Drozdova E, Elliott D, Grove G, Lukasik S, Tonya P, Wilson G (2000) A proposal for an international convention on cyber crime and terrorism. Stanford University/The Hoover Institution/The Consortium for Research on Information Security and Policy/The Center for International Security and Cooperation, Stanford. August

Strauss H (2007a) Cyberwarrior: operationalizing cyberwarfare involves challenges across the defense enterprise and beyond. Gartner Inc., Stamford, p 8

Strauss H (2007b) Findings: cyberwarfare matures as a military option. Gartner Inc., Stamford, p 2

United States (2010) US code. Section 921(3)

Yunos Z, Zin ANM (2003) Future cyber weapons. The Star in Tech, November 13

Chapter 8
Double-Edged Sword: Dual-Purpose Cyber Security Methods

Angela S. M. Irwin

8.1 Introduction

In our interconnected world, vast amounts of personal and private data travel around the Internet daily. Although many organizations have taken significant steps to secure their data, the truth is, security breaches are not only more common, but are more devastating. There were many notable security incidents in 2016 and 2017 that revealed that governments are suffering from the same security issues as enterprises and individuals. For example, in 2016, *LinkedIn*, *Tumblr*, *Myspace*, *Yahoo*, and *AdultFriendFinder.com* had the usernames, passwords, and other personal information of millions of customers stolen and sold on the dark marketplace. The US Department of Justice, Department of Homeland Security and the FBI had employees' personal information stolen and made available on public forums and *Twitter*, *Netflix*, *PayPal*, *Pinterest* and the *PlayStation Network* suffered distributed denial of service (DDoS) attacks which resulted in their networks being brought down for extended periods of time. In 2017, the largest ransomware attacks in history hit personal, organizational, and government computers around the world; locking victims out of their devices until a ransom was paid.

Using forensics techniques, organizations can uncover vital evidence and information regarding intrusion methods and techniques, what actions an intruder took when inside the system or network and what information was taken. However, anti-forensic techniques are being used by cyber-criminals to remove the traces which can be used to successfully investigate their intrusion or cover the fact that an intrusion has taken place. Many of the modern cyber-security programs that are used to defend networks, and the data held within them, are being used by those who

A. S. M. Irwin (✉)
Department of Security Studies and Criminology, Macquarie University, Sydney, NSW, Australia
e-mail: angela.irwin@mq.edu.au

© Springer International Publishing AG, part of Springer Nature 2018
H. Prunckun (ed.), *Cyber Weaponry*, Advanced Sciences and Technologies for Security Applications, https://doi.org/10.1007/978-3-319-74107-9_8

would wish to enter these systems without permission—they are a double-edged sword. Cyber-security applications provide important advantages to security professionals. Nevertheless, these advantages are reduced, or lost, when they are used by cyber-criminals in an anti-forensics manner.

This chapter explores how common security techniques and methods, such as system logging, vulnerability scanning, and network monitoring, can be misused by cyber-criminals to hide their presence on the network. It then explores some simple security practices and approaches that can be used by network defenders to reduce the effectiveness of these anti-forensic practices.

8.2   System Logging

System and event logging records events that happen on a computer or network. Examining these logs can assist security professionals trace suspicious activity, respond to important events, and keep their systems secure (van der Aalst and de Medeiros 2005; Mao et al. 2014; Khan et al. 2016). When a network is hit by malicious activity, such as a worm, virus, Trojan horse, or other type of malware—or an intrusion takes place—logs are essential for determining how and when the attack occurred. In effect, system logs provide forensic evidence of activity on the computer or network. If logging is switched off, or the correct events are not logged, obtaining forensic evidence to identify the time and date, or method of unauthorized access or other malicious activity can be extremely difficult, if not impossible. After a security event, it is essential that the root cause of the attack is uncovered, affected systems and machines are cleaned and normal business resumes as quickly as possible. Without knowing the root cause of the attack, it is unlikely that systems are protected any better than they were before the incident occurred.

Most operating systems have auditing and logging functions built-in. For example, *Windows* systems use system, application and security logs and Unix systems provide the general-purpose syslog logging feature. These can audit account logon events such as account lockouts and failed password attempts, directory service access, object access, policy change, privilege use, process tracking and system events. For each of these activities, logging can be set to log success, failure or nothing. If logging was not enabled for object access, there would be no record of when a file or a folder was last accessed. By enabling failure logging only, a record of when someone tried to access a file or folder but failed, due to having improper authorisation, would be recorded. However, there would be no record of when an authorised user accessed the file or folder. This may be extremely important information when attempting to investigate an insider threat or when an intruder has managed to access a cracked username and password.

Logged information gives security personnel a starting point to investigate how the attack or incident occurred. Nonetheless, logged information can be difficult to manage and interpret, due to the sheer volume of logs created on even a modest network. Therefore, many organizations have started to use security information event management (SIEM) systems, like *SolarWinds' Event Log Consolidator/Manger, LogRhythm, ArcSight,* or *Splunk,* to monitor and log various actions on their computers and networks, and collect other security-related data for analysis. Most SIEM systems deploy numerous collection agents to assemble security-related events from network equipment, end-user devices, servers, firewalls, antivirus, and intrusion prevention systems. The collected events are then forwarded to a centralized management console to inspect for anomalies.

SIEMs provide a holistic view of an organization's information technology (IT) security and enable security analysts to look at all data from a single point of view, which makes it much easier to identify trends and see patterns that are out of the ordinary and take defensive action more quickly. Cyber threat intelligence enables organizations to identify potential threats and vulnerabilities to minimize what is known as the *threat attack window* and limits the amount of time that an adversary has in the network before discovery.

Very few organizations have the capacity or capability to anticipate cyber threats and implement preventative strategies. Still, prevention has proven to be more cost effective and customer-focused than reactive strategies. It has been said in the past that the best offence is a good defence. However, it is no longer a viable option to rely on defence. This is because even the best defences will eventually be breached and an adversary will eventually get into the target's system. A more effective strategy is for an organization to know exactly what is going on around them.

At the most basic level, SIEM systems can be rule-based or employ statistical correlation engines to establish associations or relationships between event log entries (Lavrova and Pechenkin 2015). Some systems may do pre-processing at edge collectors, with only certain events being passed through to a centralised management node, to reduce the volume of information being communicated and stored (Mertka 2017). Though, this may result in relevant events being filtered-out too soon.

Payment Card Industry Data Security Standard (PCI DSS) compliance has traditionally driven SIEM adoption in large enterprises. But, concerns over advanced persistent threats (APTs) has led many smaller organizations to look at SIEM technology.

System and event logging can provide valuable clues after an attack has taken place and logs often detect incidents that would not otherwise have been noticed. Logging can also provide indications that at attack is imminent. However, monitoring and logging activities must be balanced with system performance. Logging every event provides a detailed record of everything that goes on in the computer or network, something which would be valuable in a forensic investigation, nevertheless, it severely impacts on system performance because even in a moderately-sized network, the processor is busy recording millions of entries every time users press a button or click a mouse.

Although system performance is a major consideration when deciding on a logging strategy, it should be kept in mind that many hacker methods and Trojan horse programs contain utilities that allow them to alter log files to conceal their actions; hide their intrusion and ensure that no trace of their malicious activity has been left in log files. Examples include remote access Trojans, such as *SubSeven*, *BO2K*, and *The Thing*, which delete and modify files and folders, including log files.

Intruders can also clear event logs using applications such as Metasploits' *Meterpreter*. The *clearev* script in Meterpreter can go into the event logs on a Windows operating system and clear-out the logs, or at least remove evidence of the connections and/or attempted connections made by the intruder.

Another way to clear the security, application or security log files on a Windows system is to use the *clearlogs.exe* file. When the clearlogs.exe *–sec* command is run, the security events in the Event Viewer are cleared leaving no trace that the intruder has been there, unless they carelessly leave the clearlogs.exe file behind.

Unix, Linux and Mac operating systems use the *syslogd daemon* to log system information in the */var/log* directory (Jepson et al. 2008). An intruder can open the log file and delete all entries related to their compromise or delete the contents of the logs using a simple text editor (Skoudis 2007). On a Macintosh system, an attacker is primarily interested in the *system.log* and *secure.log* files. The system.log file contains most of the system notices, kernel debug information, and log-in information. Authentication and authorisation information is also logged to the secure.log file. In addition, several daemons and applications have their own log, such as *mail. log* and *ftp.log*, which may contain information logged during an attack. Also, there are logs for the application firewall (*appfirewall.log*) and BSD firewall (*ipfw.log*) which may need to be edited or deleted (Maintain 2008; Scott 2008). Earlier versions of Mac operating systems had a pruning facility that allowed potential attackers to remove process IDs, host, time, and other keys (Apple 2004). Apple removed the pruning functionality from the syslog application and replaced it with the *asl manager* system log file manager. This program is limited in its functionality, allowing users to delete logs based on the number of days since the logs were created or their size. This limited functionality means that intruders cannot selectively remove certain log entries, limiting their ability to conceal their intrusion.

Another method of potential detection and source of forensic evidence in Unix or Linux operating systems is the *command history*. Analysing the command history can help the system administrator detect and decipher exactly what the intruder did while they were inside the system. An intruder can simply set up a Bash shell script[1] and set the history size to zero, ensuring that none of their commands are stored. Intruders may not always have time to erase the history file or change the history size variable, in these circumstances the intruder can simply shred their history file by entering a simple command that overwrites the history with zeros and deletes the file.

There are several effective ways to block an intruder's ability to alter of delete log files. These include: setting permissions to deny access to anyone who is not the system administrator (Skoudis 2001); password protecting the log files, or the directory where they are stored; backing-up log files to a dedicated computer or

---

[1]Bash shell script is a computer program written in the Bash programming language. A Bash shell script can contain a single command, a very simple list of commands or contain functions, loops, conditional constructs.

server that has unique security settings (Skoudis 2001); hiding log files in an unexpected place; saving log files to write-once media, such as CDs; and encrypting the log files, making them difficult for the intruder to hack or spoof[2] (Skoudis 2001). In addition to encrypting the log files, adding a message authentication code (MAC)[3] to each of the records in the log file makes it difficult to spoof the log records (Jiang et al. 2004). To increase security of the log files, a combination of these protection mechanisms would prove useful as preventing unauthorized access to a network or system is not always possible. Regardless, the ability to swiftly detect an intrusion, patch identified vulnerabilities, close entry points, and resume normal operations as quickly as possible is paramount for the success of an organization. Without the confidence of accurate, unmodified logs, this may not be possible.

8.3 Vulnerability Scanners

As its names implies, a vulnerability scanner scans a network or system for vulnerabilities (Juuso and Takanen 2010). These can include open ports, missing updates, insecure software configurations or misconfigurations, susceptibility to malware infections, active Internet Protocol (IP) addresses and operating systems, software and services that are installed and running, and unknown vulnerabilities, such as zero-day vulnerabilities.[4] The scanner then compares the information that it finds against known vulnerabilities found in its own or a third-party database. Such third-party databases include the Common Vulnerabilities and Exposures (CVE)[5] and Open Vulnerability and Assessment Language (OVAL) databases provided by The MITRE Corporation or the National Vulnerability Database provided by the National Institute of Standards and Technology (NIST).

Vulnerability scanners are used as part of a vulnerability management program by those tasked with protecting the system or network. Vulnerability management is integral to computer and network security and is the "cyclical practice of identifying, classifying, remediating, and mitigating vulnerabilities" (Foreman 2010: 1).

Vulnerability scanners can be used to run pre-scans of a system to uncover the components of that system, to ensure that there are no unknown areas or parts of that system, or can be used to scan the system after patching has taken place to ensure that the patches and/or systems are functioning as expected.

---

[2]Spoofing refers to the act of tricking or deceiving a computer system or computer user by hiding one's identity or pretending to be another user.

[3]MACs are time sensitive, making it difficult to spoof log records from a prior time-period. The MAC is calculated for the first time-period and is then used to calculate the MAC for the next time-period. The first MAC is then permanently deleted (Lantz et al. 2006: 45).

[4]A zero-day vulnerability refers to an exploitable bug in software that is unknown to the vendor. The security hole may be exploited before the vendor can fix it (Symantec 2016).

[5]A CVE is a dictionary of publicly known information about security vulnerabilities and exposures.

Scanners can be passive or active. Passive scanning provides accurate, up-to-date information on the network. Yet, they suffer in terms of overall completeness (Barlett et al. 2007). For example, a passive scanner cannot detect an application that has never been used and, much like the techniques used in counterintelligence, it can easily be fooled by a system intentionally emitting misinformation and disinformation (Prunckun 2012). Active scanners examine the responses they receive to evaluate whether a specific node represents a weak point within the network; they can simulate an attack on the network, uncover weaknesses that a potential hacker could exploit, or examine a node, following an attack, to determine how the hacker breached the system.

Active scanners can autonomously resolve security issues, such as blocking potentially dangerous IP addresses. Although active vulnerability scanners can provide many benefits, they can also have effects on system up-time and reliability. Both types of scanner can co-exist within a network. In fact, they complement each other's capabilities to provide a much more holistic approach to vulnerability identification, classification, remediation and mitigation.

Vulnerability scanners can facilitate network security tasks. Still, they should not replace the expertise and knowledge of trained security personnel. This is because scanners can return false-positives (Type-I errors), indicating a weakness where none exists, and false-negatives (Type-II errors), where a security risk is overlooked. Qualified security personnel must carefully analyse the data provided by scanners to detect erroneous results. A scanner's vulnerability assessment is based solely on its database of known exploits. However, a scanner cannot extrapolate from the data it discovers to conceive of new and novel methods an intruder may use to attack a network (Orrill 2017). Therefore, vulnerability scanners should be combined with active blocking methods, such as anti-virus software and firewalls.

For many years, hackers have used vulnerability scanners to gain knowledge and understanding of a system or network's weak points and exploited these to gain unauthorized access. The exploitation of vulnerabilities is a major route through which intruders' access networks. This is evidenced by results in the *Verizon Data Breach Report* of 2015, where it was reported that 99.9% of exploited vulnerabilities in 2014[6] were disclosed and given a CVE number more than a year prior (Verizon 2015). The results demonstrate that attackers are exploiting vulnerabilities that had solutions and patches developed for them, in many cases, several years earlier. Nevertheless, it also demonstrates that organizations and individuals are not patching their systems quickly enough, thereby, allowing these old vulnerabilities to be exploited.

Research published by Verizon in 2017, that looked at cyberattacks committed in 2016, showed that the exploitation of vulnerabilities decreased in 2016 from

---

[6]The vulnerability dataset came from 200 million + successful exploitations across more than 500 CVEs from over 20,000 enterprises in more than 150 countries. Security incidents were collected from SIEM logs, then analysed for exploit signatures, and paired with vulnerability scans of the same environments to create an aggregated picture of exploited vulnerabilities over time.

previous years, with only 6% of breaches in 2016 involving the exploitation of vulnerabilities (Verizon 2017). Although many organizations have now implemented a good vulnerability and patch management system to fix the exposures in their systems, large attacks are still common. For example, in May 2017 a ransomware attack known as *WannaCry* spread very quickly across the globe. *WannaCry*, hailed as "the biggest ransomware outbreak in history" (F-Secure 2017), affected more than 300,000 computers in 150 countries in a matter of hours. This attack was particularly damaging because it was not just a ransomware program but a worm, which looked for other computers and systems to infect. *WannaCry* encrypted all files on the systems that it infected, making them unavailable to the victim. *WannaCry* exploited a Microsoft operating system vulnerability, which was exposed as part of the leaked NSA hacker applications, and had a patch released for it 2 months earlier. Unfortunately, infected systems had not been updated with the new security patch (F-Secure 2017).

Exploit kits are often used by criminal actors to take advantage of system vulnerabilities to distribute malware or conduct other malicious activities. Typical exploit kits provide a management console and contain add-on functions to make it easier for cyber-criminals to launch attacks. In 2015, exploit kit, *Angler*, started the wave of delivering ransomware to victims' systems. The *Angler Exploit Kit* accounted for 60% of the overall activity in 2015 (Trend Micro 2017) and has proven to be a steadfast threat since then due to it being constantly updated to exploit newly-discovered vulnerabilities.

To mitigate vulnerabilities, there are best practices that organizations can follow, including: promptly patching all endpoints to block known exploits; updating browsers and plug-ins to secure against zero-day browser exploits; and using advanced behaviour monitoring products to protect systems from known and unknown vulnerabilities before security patches can be deployed. Another important method in the defender's arsenal is to educate users about the human element in perpetrating attacks, and the importance of good security hygiene.[7]

8.3.1 Network and Traffic Monitoring

Most organizations rely on their data networks as the lifeblood of their operations. However, it is common for networks to go unnoticed until something goes wrong and the data stops flowing. Security failures can be very damaging, expensive and difficult to fix. Therefore, it is essential that organizations know how many routers,

---

[7]Cyber security hygiene is the establishment and maintenance of an individual's online safety and encapsulates the daily routines, occasional checks and general behaviours required to maintain a user's online security. This would typically include the following best practices: updating virus definitions, using a firewall, running security scans, proper password selection, updating software, securing personal data and backing-up data (InfoSec Institute 2015).

switches and firewalls they have on their network, and whether a system or device is down, not fully-operational or not performing as it should.

Networks have become much more complex than they were in the past (du Toit 2015). Most modern networks have thousands of devices, run hundreds of services and applications, and span vast geographical locations. Some are located on cloud platforms, are virtual private networks (VPNs), and involve Software-Defined Networking (SDN) architectures. Managing the complexity of these networks, as well as trying to keep them safe, secure and running at optimal performance, would be impossible without the aid of a network management system.

Organizations, with large volumes of internal and external users and consumers, would find it extremely challenging to manage their service offerings and networks without the use of automated processes and procedures that facilitate network mapping and real-time monitoring. These applications enable around-the-clock monitoring of network health and security, the gathering of information on network metrics, the creation of reports on the current state of the network, the ability to make forecasts on future requirements of the network, and pre-emptive alerting that signals potential technical or security issues on the network.

Network and traffic monitoring avoids losses caused by undetected system failures, provides peace of mind that systems and applications are running as expected and provides threat awareness and intrusion detection.

At the time of writing, monitoring solutions, such as *FireEye* and *Palo Alto*, have gained popularity for protecting networks from intrusion, but they are expensive and out of the reach of most small to medium sized businesses. It is ironic because it is small and medium sized businesses that are increasingly being targeted by cyber-criminals (Verizon 2015) due to their poor security practices, and their inability to respond to attacks.

Programs such as *Nmap*, *Metasploit* and *Wireshark* are common in the security professionals' "tool box." These applications capture, view, and analyse network traffic and troubleshoot network problems. Alerts can be set based on certain types of event, which notify the system administrator/security analyst before an issue escalates.

Nmap, short for Network Mapper, is a well-known free, open-source hacker program used for network discovery and security auditing. System administrators use *Nmap* for network inventory, checking for open ports, managing service upgrades and updates and monitoring host or service uptime. *Nmap* uses raw IP packets to determine what hosts are available on the network, what services (including the application name and version) those hosts are providing information about, what operating systems are running and what firewalls are being used by the target. This is a valuable network discovery application for a malicious actor who wants to discover important information about their target network.

The Metasploit Project, a collection of hacking programs and frameworks, was developed as an educational approach to assist cyber-security professionals and ethical hackers to developer their skills in a safe environment. *Metasploit* provides the user with vital information regarding known security vulnerabilities and helps them to formulate penetration testing and intrusion detection system testing plans, strategies and methodology for exploitation. Nevertheless, this program has also become popular with the hacking community, allowing them to hone their skills in an environment that reduces their risk of detection and capture.

Wireshark is a freely-available penetration testing and protocol analysis application that captures data packets travelling over a network in real-time and then displays them in a readable format. It is a popular program with Security Operations Centre (SOC) analysts and network forensic investigators because it allows them to dig deep into network traffic and inspect individual data packets. *Wireshark* can detect denial of service attacks, act as a firewall, and secure networks from outside intruders by alerting to hackers or spies on the network. *Wireshark* has also become popular with hackers allowing them to gather information about network traffic, decode different protocols, including encrypted traffic,[8] and hack usernames and passwords travelling across the network.

The reality is, it is difficult to prevent malicious actors scanning a network or analyzing traffic as it moves across the network boundary. Regardless, there are things that organizations can do to detect scanning as it takes place. These include monitoring and documenting existing network traffic flows between all endpoints so that abnormal connections are flagged, monitoring port-level information (for example, TCP port 80, UDP port 53) and setting rules on which networks and other connection boundaries can and cannot communicate with each other. Running sensors on every endpoint and then bringing data together for analysis would be advantageous. However, creating alerts would be problematic and creating traffic flow maps would likely result in analysis paralysis in all but the smallest of networks and organizations.

8.4 Conclusion

Network and device security is a complex and ever-evolving challenge to network defenders. If done correctly, organizations can use security applications and methods to give them a complete and accurate picture of their network, thereby, providing them with valuable, actionable cyber threat intelligence. If done incorrectly, or inadequately, these same application and methods provide cyber-criminals with routes into the network, and once inside, these intruders can perform a number of anti-forensic tactics to frustrate the efforts of security personnel. Many of these anti-forensic techniques are relatively easy to employ, but with some simple counter-measures, security personnel can reduce the likelihood and impact of these double-edged swords.

---

[8]If they have the encryption key.

8.5   Principal Concepts

The principal concepts associated with this chapter are listed below. Demonstrate your understanding of each by writing a short definition or explanation in one or two sentences:

- Dual purpose cyber-security methods;
- Threat intelligence;
- Anti-forensic techniques;
- Network and traffic monitoring;
- System logging; and
- Vulnerability scanning.

8.6   Study Questions

1. Compare a rules-based approach to event log management to the statistical correlation engine-based approach. Explain which approach is likely to be more effective in establishing relationships between event log entries, and why?
2. Explain how intelligence gained from at least one of the programs discussed in this chapter could be used in a tactical, operational, or strategic cyber intelligence program?
3. Describe how the use of sound security design can reduce an organization's threat attack window?

8.7   Learning Activity

Threat intelligence must be "actionable"; it must be possible to use it to affect the various phases of a cyber-attack. If an organisation is not able to map their vulnerabilities to a threat, there will be no risk management, and, as a result, no actionable intelligence. Individually, or in a small group, discuss the properties that cyber intelligence must have to be considered actionable. Think of a recent cyber-attack and explore how actionable intelligence obtained from one or more of the methods and techniques examined in this chapter may have prevented the attack from occurring or reduced the severity of the attack.

References

Apple Inc. (2004) Syslogd.8 [Online]. Available at: https://opensource.apple.com/source/syslog/syslog-64/syslogd.tproj/syslogd.8.auto.html. Accessed 10 July 2017

Bartlett G, Heidemann J, Papadopoulos C (2007) Understanding passive and active service discovery [Online]. Available at: http://conferences.sigcomm.org/imc/2007/papers/imc168.pdf. Accessed 10 July 2017

du Toit J (2015) How network architecture can affect the reliability of your reports [Online]. Available at: https://www.irisns.com/how-network-architecture-can-affect-the-reliability-of-your-reports/. Accessed 10 July 2017

Foreman P (2010) Vulnerability management. Taylor & Francis Group, Boca Raton, p 1

F-Secure (2017) WannaCry, the biggest ransomware outbreak ever [Online]. Available at: https://safeandsavvy.f-secure.com/2017/05/12/wannacry-may-be-the-biggest-cyber-outbreak-since-conficker/. Accessed 10 July 2017

InfoSec Institute (2015) The importance of cyber hygiene in cyberspace [Online]. Available at: http://resources.infosecinstitute.com/the-importance-of-cyber-hygiene-in-cyberspace/#gref. Accessed 10 July 2017

Jepson B, Rothman E, Rosen R (2008) Mac OS X for Unix geeks, 4th edn. O'Reilly Media, Inc, Sebastopol

Jiang T, Liu J, Han Z (2004) Secure audit logs with forward integrity message authentication codes. ICSP'04 proceedings, pp 2655–2658

Juuso A-M, Takanen A (2010) Unknown vulnerability management. Codenomicon whitepaper [Online]. Available at: https://whitepapers.em360tech.com/wp-content/files_mf/white_paper/codenomicon-wp-unknown-vulnerability-management-20101019.pdf. Accessed 10 July 2017

Khan S, Gani A, Wahab AWA, Bagiwa MA, Shiraz M, Khan SU, Buyya R, Zomaya AY (2016) Cloud log forensics: foundations, state of the art, and future directions. ACM Comput Surv 49(1):1–42

Lantz B, Hall R, Couraud J (2006) Locking down log files: enhancing network security by protecting log files. Issues Inf Secur 7(2):45

Lavrova D, Pechenkin A (2015) Applying correlation and regression analysis to detect security incidents in the internet of things. Int J Commun Netw Inf Secur Kohat 7(3):131–137

Maintain (2008) Manage log files [Online]. Available at: http://www.maintain.se/cocktail/help/tiger/files/logs.html. Accessed 10 July 2017

Mao HH, Wu JC, Papalexakis EE, Faloutsos C, Lee KC, Kao TC (2014) MalSpot: Multi2 malicious network behavior patterns analysis. In: Advances in knowledge discovery and data mining. Springer, Berlin, pp 1–14

Mertka B (2017) Security and privacy issues in NG112 [Online]. Available at: http://www.eena.org/download.asp?item_id=234. Accessed 11 July 2017

Orrill J (2017) What is the difference between active & passive vulnerability scanners? [Online]. Available at: http://smallbusiness.chron.com/difference-between-active-passive-vulnerability-scanners-34805.html. Accessed 11 July 2017

Prunckun H (2012) Counterintelligence theory and practice. Rowman & Littlefield, Lanham

Scott C (2008) Covering the tracks on the MAC OS X Leopard. SANS Institute InfoSec Reading Room [Online]. Available at: http://docplayer.net/19125537-Covering-the-tracks-on-mac-os-x-leopard.html. Accessed 11 July 2017

Skoudis E (2001) Defending your log files [Online]. Available at: http://www.phptr.com/articles/article.asp?p=234.64&seqNum=1. Accessed 10 July 2017

Skoudis E (2007) Hacker techniques, exploits, & incident handling. The SANS Institute, Bethesda

Symantec (2016) What is a zero-day vulnerability? [Online]. Available at: http://www.pctools.com/security-news/zero-day-vulnerability/. Accessed 10 June 2017

Trend Micro (2017) Exploit kit [Online]. Available at: http://www.trendmicro.com.au/vinfo/au/security/definition/exploit-kit. Accessed 10 July 2017

Van der Aalst WMP, de Medeiros AKA (2005) Process mining and security: detecting anomalous process executions and checking process conformance. Electron Notes Theor Comput Sci 121:3–21

Verizon (2015) 2015 data breach investigations report [Online]. Available at: http://www.verizonenterprise.com/resources/reports/rp_data-breach-investigation-report_2015_en_xg.pdf. Accessed 10 July 2017

Verizon (2017) 2017 data breach investigation report [Online]. Available at: http://www.verizonenterprise.com/verizon-insights-lab/dbir/2017/. Accessed 10 July 2017

Chapter 9
"Who Was That Masked Man?": System Penetrations—Friend or Foe?

Georg Thomas, Greg Low, and Oliver Burmeister

9.1 Introduction

In the television series, *The Lone Ranger*, the protagonist wore a mask. He wore it not because he was evil, but because he was good. He was a Texas Ranger; the only survivor of a posse that was ambushed by a criminal gang. Once he recovered from his near fatal wounds, he became an avenger who operated on the fringe of the law to pursue justice. His mask hid his Ranger identity, allowing him to remain anonymous.

The term *hacker* has been around since the 1960s when it was originally used in the context for someone who had the ability to understand technology and manipulate it (Morris 2010: 4). It was coined by programmers at MIT in Cambridge, Massachusetts who would manipulate code until it would do exactly what they needed it to do (Granger 1994: 7). Since then, the term has not really evolved, because a hacker still manipulates technology so that it does what they want it to do, but the motives can be very different from what they were in the 1960s. Hackers can be categorized into three types: (1) black hat; (2) white hat; and (3) gray hat. The purpose of this typology is to define some of the motives and activities that hackers engage in (Thomas 2017 and Thomas et al. 2017a).

Some outlaws wear masks to commit crime, but some people, like the Lone Ranger, wear them to do good, anonymously. System penetration is an analogous activity to what the masked man did on television—fighting for justice. The purpose

G. Thomas (✉)
Corrs Chambers Westgarth, Melbourne, VIC, Australia
e-mail: gethomas@csu.edu.au

G. Low
SQL Down Under, Blackburn North, VIC, Australia

O. Burmeister
Charles Sturt University, Bathurst, NSW, Australia

© Springer International Publishing AG, part of Springer Nature 2018   113
H. Prunckun (ed.), *Cyber Weaponry*, Advanced Sciences and Technologies for Security Applications, https://doi.org/10.1007/978-3-319-74107-9_9

of a penetration test is to find vulnerabilities within an organization's computer system so that these weaknesses can be protected from criminals. But like the Lone Ranger, in doing so, the activity can operate on the legal fringe.

9.2 Hacking Typology

9.2.1 Black Hats

Black hats are hackers who exploit systems for illegal purposes; usually for personal gain or to be malicious. These hackers use their knowledge of computer systems to bypass or break-through security controls to gain access to networks. These are the types of hackers that organizations are concern about when protecting their information. Black hat hackers are also known as *crackers*.

An example of one such black hat is Kevin Mitnick, who was known as the most notorious black hat hacker in the world. Mitnick started hacking at a young age, including gaining access to Digital Equipment Corporation's (DEC) and Pacific Bell's systems. He served 5 years in jail and today is a security consultant, operating as a white hat!

9.2.2 White Hats

White hats use the same programs and techniques as black hat hackers, but these hackers are given express permission to use their skills to identify system vulnerabilities to an organization's network. White hat hackers are also known as *ethical hackers* and are also referred to as *penetration testers*. An example of one of the first white hats was Dr. Cliff Stoll, who in 1986 ran an investigation that led to the capture of black hat hacker Markus Hess. Although Dr. Stoll wasn't a hacker, his activities of hunting for a malicious hacker place him as a white hat.

9.2.3 Gray Hats

Gray hats are somewhere in between black hat and white hats. Often described as starting out as black hats, but transitioning to use their skills for good. Gray hats use their talents to identify vulnerabilities much the same as white hats do, but the key difference is that often a gray hat may not have express permission to do, so and after a successful breach will alert the organization they have compromised of the flaw.

According to Graves (2010), gray hats are mostly curious about hacker software and self-proclaimed ethical hackers. Gray hats may want to highlight security problems or educate their target organizations so they secure their systems properly

(Graves 2010: 4). Political activists who hack websites to promote a cause, rather than to cause malicious damage or steal data (these are known as *hacktivists*), can also be categorized as gray hats. Take, for instance, the case of Wikileaks; an organization founded by Julian Assange, who publish secret information. Although it has been argued that Wikileaks was performing a public service, there are more compelling criticisms that leaking classified information has done great harm.

There are two levels of hackers; these are determined by their skills—script kiddies and hackers. *Script kiddies* are inexperienced and use applications available on the Internet, but with little to no understanding of the underpinning systems they are attacking, or the working of the programs they use. The typical script kiddy has been described as being between 14 and 16 years old and still at school (Barber 2001: 15). Hackers are more experienced, and although they use hacking programs, they are capable of developing applications themselves. They will usually have some level of understanding about computer networks and systems.

9.3   Ethical Hacking

Ethical hacking is the practice of attempting to break into an organization's systems for the purpose of identifying vulnerabilities so that they can be remediated. What sets ethical hacking apart and makes it ethical is that the hackers are hired to infiltrate the organization. Because hacking is considered illegal, rules and appropriate agreements, via contracts, need to be in place in order to protect both the ethical hacker and the client. There are generally agreed guidelines about what ethical hackers can and cannot do; there are guidelines for when vulnerabilities are discovered; and what the scope of an engagement will entail, such as the network addresses or systems that are permitted to be tested.

Agreements are drafted to limit liability and to acknowledge that the systems that are to be hacked are in fact owned by the organization. These "rules of engagement" define the scope (Engebretson 2013, p. 3). Additionally, it is common for a non-disclosure agreement (NDA) to be a requirement. This instrument is used to maintain the confidentiality of any information that may be disclosed by either party as part of the engagement.

9.4   Ethical Hacking As a Career

The term *ethical hacker* applies to anyone who is trained in the field. This can include students who have graduated from relevant courses—like university degrees in computer science, cyber-security, or information systems—to seasoned technicians who have been conducting penetration testing for years. It is also common for IT professionals to change careers and engage in ethical hacking, or simply view their roles to evolve to include ethical hacking. For technicians who did not gain their degrees in a cyber-security related field, it is common for them to undertake specialized training or certification in this area; this is part of a global trend to improve IT professionalism through certification (Burmeister 2017).

There is currently a cyber-security skills gap reported by 40.4% of surveyed organizations in Australia and 46.8% of surveyed organizations in Asia (Telstra 2016: 43). American technology conglomerate Cisco estimated a shortage of over one-million cyber-security technicians worldwide (Cisco 2015: 2). Simple economics sees the average wages of cyber-security personnel's rise as demand outweighs the supply. At the time of writing, security consultant and penetration tester roles are attracting six figure salaries in Australia and the United States.

A career as an ethical hacker, or in the cyber security field can be a lucrative one. It comes as no surprise that many are choosing a career in this field and that it is due to the shortage of staff and to the rise in cyber security related crimes during the past decade (Verizon 2016: 8).

9.5   Training and Education

There are several paths to a career in ethical hacking. Courses that focus directly on cyber-security, or another IT related discipline, such as network management or application development, are relevant to the field and will provide an entry point for an ethical hacking career. Just as a store burglar needs to understand locks and physical security devices, so does the ethical hacker. Having an understanding of how networks work; how systems and applications function; and how various devices interact, is necessary to devise methods of breaking into them.

In addition to university degrees, there are a number of certificates that can be obtained through self-study, or instructor-led learning. At the fundamental level, certifications such as CompTIA's A+ and Network+ provide base level knowledge. After obtaining these certifications, more security specific certifications can then be obtained, such as CompTIA's Security+, EC-Councils Certified Ethical Hacker (Cl EH), or GIAC Security Essentials (GSEC).

At an advanced level, certifications such as EC-Council's Licensed Penetration Tester, GIAC's GPEN, GWAPT, and GXPN, and Offensive Security OSCP. Incorporated in 2015, CREST (International) introduced a program for assurance of cyber security professionals and the organizations they work for. With a number of certifications, such as CRT—Registered Tester, CCT—Certified Web Application Tester, and CCT—Certified Infrastructure Tester, CREST is designed to provide a level of assurance that the certified individual has the required skills to effectively conduct penetration testing.

With the appropriate level of experience and certification, ethical hackers typically work for consulting organizations. These are often cyber-security specific (sometimes termed *boutique*) organizations or IT consultancies and auditing firms that have augmented their service offerings to provide cyber-security advice.

9.6 Penetration Testing

Although the terms *ethical hacking* and *penetration testing* are used interchangeably, they refer to two different things. Ethical hacking defines the motive (whether ethical or malicious, for example) and penetration testing, or *pen* testing for short, is one of the tasks that might be undertaken. An ethical hacker is engaged by an organization to conduct a penetration test in relation to a system target to identify security vulnerabilities. These findings are then reported back to the engaging party for remediation.

Because the hackers are commissioned, given explicit permission, not using the findings for personal gain, and are bound by a contract (such as an NDA); they are referred to as an ethical hacker.

9.7 Real-World Pen Testing

There are many real-world applications for penetration testing, and as such there are many different facets to this occupation. Organizations are vulnerable to hacking for different reasons. Often, this is because of the industry they are in: from utility companies and corporations, to government bodies—both large and small. Sometimes there are motives behind the attack; to disrupt electricity supply, or to gain a political edge or expose national secrets, or for financial or personal gain. There are many instances where attacks are not specifically targeted—blanket or random attacks—to see if a vulnerability exists, which can later be exploited.

Attacks can originate externally and internally, involving unknown attackers or trusted insiders (such as disgruntled employees or contractors). These attacks can be the traditional hack attempts where an attacker tries to breach a system, or uses a pretext involving phishing (email), vishing (voice), smishing (SMS), or physical penetration (gaining access to secured areas), or even to stealing corporate information by copying it to a removable drive, or taking-out a physical record.

9.8 Software Programs and Methods

Ethical hackers use a variety of programs and techniques to test systems. Some applications are available free on the Internet, or they can be purchased commercially, cost anywhere from a few dollars to several thousands of dollars. Although programs come-and-go as developers respond to new devices and security procedures, it is worth noting what was available at this writing. The purpose of this survey is not to present a compendium of software and hardware, but to understand this technology to be able to use it to manipulate systems.

9.8.1 Aircrack

When conducting penetration testing of a wireless network, *Aircrack* is a widely used program. Against WEP, WPA, and WPA2 configured networks, *Aircrack* has the ability to "break" the cryptographic shared keys used to protect them. Capturing data such as the initialization vector (IV) in WEP, or the WPA handshake (in WPA or WPA2), it then can be used to either decipher the key, or conduct a brute-force attack to guess the key.

9.8.2 Burpsuite

Burpsuite is a popular program used for web application testing. It can be used to intercept Internet traffic between client and server to identify vulnerabilities. It can also be used to identify vulnerabilities automatically, such as those in the Open Web Application Security Project (OWASP) Top 10 (the top 10 most critical web application security risks as identified by OWASP).

9.8.3 Cain & Abel

Cain & Abel is a password recovery application for *Windows* environments. It has the ability to crack password *hashes*—random strings of characters that have been mathematically constructed to security them—and *sniff* network passwords—that is, a program that looks for, and records passwords send over a network.

9.8.4 Hashcat

Hashcat is another password recovery application, but works across Linux, Mac OSX, and Windows operating systems. Like *Cain & Abel*, *Hashcat* can crack passwords using a variety of attack types, such as brute-force, dictionary, and permutation.

9.8.5 Hydra

Another program for testing passwords is *Hydra*, also known as *thc-Hydra*. *Hydra* has the ability to automate logging onto various systems, and can accept different types of passwords through lists, or from a password generation algorithm, such as

John the Ripper (JTR). *Hydra* can be used to attempt brute-force attacks against many platforms, including Cisco AAA, FTP, HTTP Forms, MS SQL, MySQL, POP3, SIP, SMB, SMTP, SNMP, SSH, Telnet, VNC, and more.

9.8.6   Kali Linux

Based on Debian Linux, the Kali Linux is a free, open-source downloadable penetration testing and ethical hacking environment that was developed by the commercial firm Offensive Security. Kali Linux can be run directly from a DVD or a USB drive in a live environment, or it can be installed onto a system. Once launched, Kali Linux contains over 300 functions, which can be used for information gathering, vulnerability analysis, wireless attacks, web application testing, exploitation, forensics, stress testing, sniffing, spoofing, password attacks, reverse engineering, hardware hacking, and reporting (Kali Tools n.d.).

9.8.7   Metasploit

Metasploit is a penetration testing software application. It is available in several different versions, from the free *Metasploit Framework*, low cost *Metasploit Community*, to the commercial Express and Professional editions. *Metasploit* is used to test exploits against known vulnerabilities, and includes pre-loaded vulnerabilities as well as the ability for a penetration tester to create their own.

9.8.8   Nessus

Nessus is a vulnerability scanner that identifies system weaknesses. It uses a pre-loaded database of vulnerabilities that can be configured for various situations, or compliance requirements. Once a vulnerability is identified, it is ranked in terms of criticality using the Common Vulnerability Scoring System (CVSS)—this is a framework for measuring impact. In CVSS Version 3.0, 0.0-3.9 is considered a low impact vulnerability; 4.0-6.9 is considered medium, 7.0-8.9 is considered high, and 9.0-10.0 is considered critical ("NVD – CVSS" n.d.).

9.8.9   Nmap

Nmap (Network Mapper) is a network scanning program designed to discover hosts on a network. Often used first to perform the scanning phase of a penetration test,

Nmap discovers live hosts, which ports and services are listening, and what operating systems are running. In addition to scanning the network, *Nmap* can also run scripts to perform more advanced tasks, such as identifying vulnerabilities. A *Windows* operating system version, called *Zenmap*, is also available.

9.8.10 Zap

Known as the *OWASP Zed Attack Proxy* (ZAP), or *zaproxy*, Zap is can automate the process of finding vulnerabilities in web applications. Zap allows for the inspection and manipulation of traffic, or for simple validation against the OWASP Top 10 vulnerabilities.

9.9 Hardware Devices

In addition to software, there are devices that have been created for ethical hacking. A few examples of these devices include:

9.9.1 Pwn Phone

The *Pwn Phone*, by Pwnie Express, is a portable smart phone that can be used to test networks. Additional attachments, such as high-gain antennas and USB Ethernet adapters can be attached for testing different types of networks.

9.9.2 Pwn Plug

Also by Pwnie Express, the *Pwn Plug* is an all-in-one hacking device. Preconfigured with the appropriate hardware to run attacks and using a customized Kali Linux distribution called *Pwnix*, the devices can be placed within an organization and remote controlled.

9.9.3 USB Rubber Ducky

The USB *Rubber Ducky*, by Hak5, is a device that resembles a USB drive, but is detected as a human interface device (HID). Because of this, it bypasses the USB mass storage controls that may be in place and can behave as an input device, such as a keyboard. It can be used to send keystrokes via scripts, behaving as if a person were sitting in front of the system.

9.9.4 WiFi Pineapple

Also from Hak5 is the *WiFi Pineapple*. This device is designed for wireless network testing and can be configured to mimic a wireless hotspot. Once an unsuspecting user connects to the device, several attacks, such as man in the middle (MiTM), credential harvesting can occur.

9.10 Other Software and Methods

In addition to software that is designed specifically for penetration testing and hacking, a number of other software packages used for normal day-to-day business are frequently used as part of penetration testing engagements.

9.10.1 OWASP Top 10

The *OWASP Top 10 Project* is a list of the ten most critical web application security risks. Developed by the Open Web Application Security Project, the framework allows ethical hackers to test for these security vulnerabilities.

This program describes the top 10 web application security risks as: (1) injection; (2) broken authentication and session management; (3) cross-site scripting (XSS); (4) insecure direct object references; (5) security misconfigurations; (6) sensitive data exposure; (7) missing function level access control; (8) cross-site request forgery (CSRF); (9) using components with known vulnerabilities; and (10) invalidated redirects and forwards.

9.10.2 Powershell

Included as part of *Windows* operating system since *Windows 7* is *Powershell*. This program can be used as part of a penetration testing software suite to automate tasks and manipulate data. This is especially useful because *Windows* has the greatest market share, and hence, devices running this operating system face larger exposure to black hats.

9.10.3 *Python*

Python is a programming language that can be used for many purposes. Created by Guido van Rossum in 1991, *Python* is easy to use and flexible. Using *Python* allows an ethical hacker to create small applications, either from scratch or by downloading existing libraries. *Python* can be used to perform a variety of automation and testing tasks.

9.11 Friend or Foe?

The programs, techniques, and devices just surveyed are used by a wide variety of hackers—ethical as well as malicious. This raises the question of misuse. Although it is self-evident that black hat hackers use these application for unethical purposes, it is not often thought that ethical hackers could also misuse their knowledge for the wrong reasons.

If an ethical hacker gains access to an organization's data, it is plausible that this data could be misused. Ethical hackers, like other occupations, do not have a requirement to abide by a code of ethics, and any voluntary code is not uniformly applied across the industry. Although there are several accreditation bodies that permute codes of practice, it is not mandatory for ethical hackers to become certified or adhere to such a code.

Given the sensitivity of privately held data the consequences of misuse can be weighty. There are several issues that need to be considered. A data leak can have serious reputational, legal, and compliance ramifications for the client. This is particularly serious in environments that are regulated or have specific laws or requirements for protection in place. These include the health and insurance industries, financial institutions, and industries regulated by privacy legislation.

There is also a reputational impact to the occupation, which could affect the credibility of other ethical hackers. This could result in less organizations being willing to engage their services, and as a result, leaving themselves more exposed to system vulnerabilities.

In sum, there is merit in the use of penetration testers. Experience shows that these white hats assist organizations mitigate cyber threats. Using the offensive methodology of pen testing, can provide a more holistic view of an organizations security posture, and provides thorough testing of software security policies, procedures, and controls. The role of a penetration tester as an integral part of a security program is quickly becoming a prevalent feature of a mature security program.

Nevertheless, there are some risks in engaging ethical hackers. With no current mandated code of conduct there is no guidance on what is or isn't appropriate, and it is up to the ethics of the occupation on how it conducts itself. There also laws around privacy that many countries have that need to be taken into consideration (Thomas et al. 2017b). Organizations need to ensure that they conduct appropriate background checks to minimize the risks of hiring a hacker who has crossed over to the criminal side—they need to be unmasked, to some degree.

A career as an ethical hacker is often seen as an interesting one, with very little repetition and ever-changing environments to work in. It is because of this that penetration testers need to not only have an understanding of how networks and systems work, but they need the ability to think laterally so they can adapt to the changing environment.

9.12 Principal Concepts

The principal concepts associated with this chapter are listed below. Demonstrate your understanding of each by writing a short definition or explanation in one or two sentences:

- Black hat;
- Gray hat;
- Hacker;
- Penetration testing; and
- White hat.

9.13 Study Questions

Discuss how a person could pursue such a career as an ethical hacker?

1. Who "watches the watcher"—discuss how can organizations can ensure that their pen tester is a person of integrity?
2. Discuss how black hat and gray hat hackers can become a white hat?

9.14 Learning Activity

Using a free program, such as *Nmap perform a port scan against your local computer.*

1. Download and install Nmap from https://nmap.org
2. Open a Command Prompt (cmd.exe)
3. Type nmap 127.0.0.1 and press Enter
4. Record the output.

The output displays the ports that are listening on your local computer and attempt to identify the services that are running.

For example, 135/tcp msrpc is interpreted as:

- Port: 135 (of 0-65535 possible ports)
- Protocol: TCP
- Service: msrpc (Microsoft Remote Procedure Call)

A hacker will run the same process against remote systems to identify what services are running and potentially able to be exploited.

Analyze and interpret the other open ports from your port scan. How might a hacker attempt to exploit these services?

References

Barber R (2001) Hackers profiled—who are they and what are their motivations? Comput Fraud Secur 2001:14–17

Burmeister OK (2017) Professional ethics in the information age. J Inf Commun Ethics Soc 15(2)

Cisco (2015) Mitigating the cybersecurity skills shortage: top insights and actions from Cisco Security Advisory Services, 2015, 2. Viewed May 15, 2017. http://www.cisco.com/c/dam/en/us/products/collateral/security/cybersecurity-talent.pdf

Engebretson P (2013) The basics of hacking and penetration testing: ethical hacking and penetration testing made easy. Elsevier, Waltham

Granger S (1994) The hacker ethic. In: Proceedings of the conference on Ethics in the computer age, ACM, pp 7–9

Graves K (2010) CEH: certified ethical hacker study guide. Wiley, Indianapolis

"Kali Tools" (n.d.) Viewed June 5, 2017. http://tools.kali.org/tools-listing

Morris RG (2010) Computer hacking and the techniques of neutralization: an empirical assessment

"NVD – CVSS" (n.d.) Viewed May 19, 2017. https://nvd.nist.gov/vuln-metrics/cvss

Telstra (2016) Telstra cyber security report 2016. Viewed April 28, 2016. http://exchange.telstra.com.au/2016/02/23/telstra-cyber-security-report-2016/

Thomas G (2017) An ethical hacker can help you beat a malicious one. The Conversation. Viewed May 19, 2017. https://theconversation.com/an-ethical-hacker-can-help-you-beat-a-malicious-one-77788

Thomas G, Burmeister OK, Low G (2017a) Issues of Implied Trust in Ethical Hacking. In: Proceedings of The 28th Australasian Conference on Information Systems, December 4–6, Hobart, Australia

Thomas G, Duessel P, Meier M (2017b) Ethical issues of user behavioral analysis through machine learning. J Inf Syst Secur 13(1):11

Verizon (2016) 2016 data breach investigations report. Viewed May 24, 2017. http://www.verizonenterprise.com/verizon-insights-lab/dbir/2016/

Chapter 10
Development and Proliferation of Offensive Weapons in Cyber-Security

Trey Herr

10.1 Introduction

Understanding what might constitute a weapon in cyber-security is slippery. Access to a protected computer system can be malicious in itself, more so if that access is used to deploy a payload that steals data, wipes critical files, or even causes physical damage. This chapter looks at how academics categorize offensive cyber capabilities, including what might constitute a "cyber weapon." Explaining why developing offensive weapons, especially those with destructive effects, can be so challenging, the chapter explains how this code can proliferate between different actors through the malware markets.

This chapter argues that proliferation of cyber weapons is less about destructive payloads and more about the techniques in how attackers can gain and maintain access to targeted computer systems. Moreover, while developing destructive software payloads does not require special resources, making that payload reliable and autonomous takes substantial intelligence collection and testing capabilities. In sum, proliferation of cyber weapons matters, but much more because of the knowledge and software that support these weapons than because of code which causes destruction.

10.2 What Makes a Weapon in Cyberspace?

Defining a cyber weapon is thorny, but important. Software can be malicious or not depending on whose hands it is in, but there is analytical utility in understanding how different groups might characterize a weapon. While the following definitions

T. Herr (✉)
Harvard Kennedy School, Washington, DC, USA
e-mail: trey_herr@hks.harvard.edu

© Springer International Publishing AG, part of Springer Nature 2018   125
H. Prunckun (ed.), *Cyber Weaponry*, Advanced Sciences and Technologies for
Security Applications, https://doi.org/10.1007/978-3-319-74107-9_10

should not be taken as policy recommendations, the discussion around them has been used to bound what can be developed, possessed, and used by non-state groups or individuals, and what might be limited to state use.

There are a variety of definitions and these disagree about the importance of causing versus threatening harm; whether that harm takes the form of physical destruction, and the need for a cyber weapon to be software at all. Weapons definitions could be effects based, architectural, or some combination:

- Architectural—definitions based on the design included components of a piece of software. This is like defining a firearm, which requires the inclusion of certain components, like a barrel, upper receiver, and lower receiver.
- Behavioral—what is done to the target system to produce an effect? Behavioral definitions look between what the weapon is and what effects it can produce to consider how it behaves on a computer system. The 2013 Wassenaar definition of intrusion software falls along these lines with the specification that such code be, "designed or modified to avoid detection by 'monitoring tools', or to defeat 'protective countermeasures'" (Wassenaar Arrangement 2015)
- Effects Based—under an effects-based definition, cyber weapons are categorized by what they do when executed on a target machine. Typically, the effects discussion focuses on physical effects, changing rotor speed or disabling a turbine, or destructive digital effects, wiping a computer hard drive.
- Hybrid—here, weapons are defined as some combination of attributes from the previous three categories. The PrEP model, which combines elements of the Architectural and Effects-Based definitions (three distinct components as well as a payload with destructive effects) (Herr 2014).

For purposes of this chapter, the effects based definition has greatest use in separating the discussion of *weapons* cleanly into code that can cause destructive effects from all other kinds. All malware has a payload of one kind or another, but using this effects-based definition, only that small sub-set that can cause destructive effects are considered weapons. Thus, the remainder of this chapter refers to both cyber weapons and malicious software in the discussion.

10.3   Building Destructive Software

When looking at the effects of a weapon, a key factor is the design of the payload. Malicious software's payload is the code designed to achieve a specific outcome, whether stealing sensitive files or causing physical destruction to machinery. Anyone can write software code, though most may not do it well. The ability to create and employ destructive payloads is not limited to states. Such a payload might require that a developer learn proprietary coding languages or master the arcane functions of a particular piece of hardware, but such information is often available on the Internet. There is no reason to consider that only the most technically advanced states can build destructive malware. However, that does not mean that anyone can build a cyber weapon that is autonomous, reliable, and effective.

Creating destructive effects does not require a secret software sauce. It bears on the discussion to distinguish between digital effects, those taking place within a computer system, and physical, those that impact devices and equipment connected to a computer. Manipulating a computer program to take actions unintended by its developer or owner does not require superhuman feats of engineering. Destroying data, that is deleting it beyond recovery, is the function of any number of quotidian administrative IT programs available for free on the Web. This sort of data destruction or *wiping* has been employed by malware in a variety of attacks (Raiu 2013).

Causing sufficient damage to a computer to render it useless without extensive repair is also feasible with only software, and some know-how—all computers start-up using a small piece of permanent software (firmware) called a BIOS or UEFI.[1] These firmware instructions initiate the user's operating system and associated hardware. Overwriting this firmware makes it impossible for the computer to start and operate normally. It was this sort of attack employed by the malware which disrupted Saudi-Aramco's operations in 2013 and affected more than 30,000 computers (Rashid 2015).

The knowledge required to understand how to manipulate computers is present on the Web and can be applied to most modern operating systems. The sequence of operations required for the Shamoon virus to wipe nearly Saudi-Aramco's computers clean, requiring that they be unplugged and replaced, took advantage of code from a commercial product (the RawDisk administrative application) to wipe the target computers clean (Mackenzie 2012). There are dozens of tutorials online that discuss how to create a keylogger, a program that records keystrokes on a computer looking to capture passwords, or to perform other espionage tasks. Other sites list links to programs that can be used to disrupt the availability of services; so-called distributed denial of service payloads (InfoSec Institute 2017). Equally important is having insight into the inner workings of different software, especially operating systems, including their existing features and defensive technologies. This information can be accessed from online forums that do not have an offensive focus, like *StackExchange*, as well as some of the earliest Hacker zines, such as *Phrack*. These publications provide information on how to gain access to, and manipulate computer systems ("exploit – Stack Overflows – Defeating Canaries, ASLR, DEP, NX" 2013; One 1996).

Destructive physical effects make for a more nuanced story. Again, if the task is simply writing computer code, then there are few special resources required. Ralph Langner, in writing about Stuxnet, offered that, "At the control system level, Stuxnet did not exploit any zero-day vulnerabilities, buffer overflows or other fancy geek stuff, but legitimate product features. In the industrial control system space, the worst

---

[1]Basic Input/Output System or Unified Extensible Firmware Interface—both of which serve a similar purpose.

vulnerabilities are not bugs, they are features" (Langner 2013). Creating physical effects however, different from digital, usually entails manipulating a piece of equipment being controlled, or otherwise interacting with, a computer.

The software for these control systems: industrial, medical, or automotive, are typically written in languages and using techniques less common in the broader commercial software development industry (Allen Bradley 2016; Bacchus et al. 2014; Glisson et al. 2015; Radcliffe 2011). Nevertheless, documentation relating to these are widely available on the Web. Even where such information is accessible, the process of turning ideas into a design to disrupt a control system, then implementing it into code, and making it reliable presents an immense barrier to entry.

The software languages used by many industrial control system (ICS) vendors are proprietary, and so less widely known than those of major commercial operating systems, though there are a bevy of resources available online. For example, the corporate website for Siemens, a large industrial control system vendor, hosts several how-to-write guides for its control language, known as *Graph 5*, as well as an online course (Siemens 2005).

In sum, all embedded systems are not created equal, and the point of this overwhelming variety of educational resources for compromising different types of control devices is not to suggest it is simple or easy. Taking control of a car, even to the point of being able to manipulate the braking system, is a far different challenge from shutting down the power grid. Understanding how to create strategic effects with cyber weapons is more complicated than just writing software that can cause physical destruction.

10.4   Destructive Effects Used for Strategic Ends

Developing malware that is both destructive and precisely targeted, or immensely reliable, does require substantial resources. Immense intelligence gathering and software testing capacity are required to create an autonomous platform like Stuxnet. Thus, the critical limitation in who can build destructive code comes more in designing malware that will work well, repeatedly, and against competent defenders (see McGonagle's Chap. 3, in this volume). These goals demand understanding, intelligence collection capabilities, and testing resources typically found within a small number of countries.[2]

---

[2]This in conjunction with the need for material resources to build test environments for this malware and the precision required of intelligence collected on potential targets are part of the explanation behind why there have been so few destructive attacks.

10.4.1 Knowing What to Hit—Intelligence Infrastructure

While there may be many people who could write software to create destructive effects, writing this code and knowing where to send it are to very different things. The specific layout and attached hardware of industrial control systems (ICS) environments represent substantial complexity and a major intelligence challenge for attackers. This highlights the first challenge to creating strategically useful destructive effects, having timely information about the target systems, their configuration, and relative layout of the environment. The relative difficulty of gaining access to protected systems and networks will vary with the target, but it matters that this information need be both relatively complete—again because this malware will likely need to operate without much developer interaction—and timely. The challenge faced by attackers, generally, is that a single, small change by defenders can wreck a carefully planned attack by rendering a malware payload or exploit functionally useless.

10.4.2 Effects over a System

Using destructive effects to strategic ends requires the attacker know about more than just the target computer or associated pieces of hardware; infrastructure like an electrical grid or nuclear power plant are complex combinations of many dozens of devices. Attackers must also understand how these devices depend on and interact with each other; how these many devices come together to form a larger system. This raises the second issue of strategically useful destructive effects—targeting a system instead of individual devices.

Stuxnet has reached the threshold over-citation usually reserved for international relations theorists' discussion of the First World War, it remains the best understood public domain example of a reliably engineered destructive malware platform that impacted not just singular devices, but entire systems of hardware. While designed to manipulate individual centrifuges, Stuxnet was also able to coordinate its effects across these devices, organized into cascades. By shifting rotor speed and valve pressures to magnify the destructive effect across the enrichment system, this first cyber weapon had strategic effects beyond simple destruction (Falliere et al. 2011).

Understanding a system rather than individual devices requires a design awareness that is certainly likely to depend on direct experience with the sort of industrial control systems being targeted or time consuming, and costly reconnaissance (Langner 2011). Attempting to develop malware to target the power grid, dam infrastructure, petrochemical facilities, or other high consequence targets would likely require similar domain experience. Translating what may be publicly available knowledge on how to program a control system into a design for how to manipulate it towards destructive ends is always going to be a substantial challenge for payload designers.

10.4.3   Making it Dependable—Reliability in Software
Engineering

Once a destructive payload can be accurately targeted and developed to impact a system instead of individual devices, the question remains—will it work? To build a payload and take such a design from theory to practice however, an attacker would still need to test their code to ensure it produces: (a) the desired effects; and (b) works across the various system configurations and defenses it might encounter while acting largely without outside control.

Acquiring the control devices and arranging them into a facsimile of the target system would be costly and time consuming. Identifying and securing the attached hardware may be relatively easy if the device is an insulin pump, but a substantial barrier if the attacker is looking for multi-ton industrial power turbines or complex electrical transmission equipment. Testing these devices and their controllers to destruction only increases this logistical challenge.

A further consideration is trying to keep such a project secret. Testing a payload on a real-world industrial scale increases the potential for information leaks (Prunckun 2012). Take for instance the case of the CIA's Glomar Explorer. In the early-1970s the CIA embarked on building a vessel that could raise from the ocean floor the Soviet nuclear-armed submarine, K-129, that sank in 1968. The size of the vessel needed to do the job was so large that a cover story was required to mask the project's intent. To this end, the eccentric businessman Howard Hughes lent his support. He is reported to have advised the media that he was building the ship to extract rare minerals from the ocean floor. However, the true purpose leaked, and the *Los Angeles Times* published the story (Varner and Collier 1978). Parallels between this example and other projects can be drawn.

10.5   Where the State Might Have an Advantage

One of the legacies of thinking about cyber-security in terms of nuclear weapons, a poor analogy on several fronts, is the assumption that states have a built-in advantage in building destructive malware. This assumption matters, in part, because of the discussion of how this code can proliferation between groups. Before getting to the discussion of proliferation, it is useful to clarify where exactly the state might have an advantage in developing and using cyber weapons.

The idea of a state advantage is largely a flawed idea; there are very low barriers to writing software and few malicious effects through a computer, as discussed above, which require materials or resources outside the reach of the average person. The logic of state's dominance in conventional military affairs, their material resources, and control of nuclear, chemical, and biological technologies, has little application to the development of malicious software (Herr 2017a). Additionally, few states are created equal or alike and so it is difficult to generalize claims of capability between, say, the United States, United Arab Emirates, and Uzbekistan. States can lay taxes and raise armies, but the information security ecosystem, they are often on an equal or inferior plane with other actors, whether non-state or individual.

The arguments for a state advantage in cyberspace tend to boil-down into one of two categories: (a) there is something technically sophisticated required to generate destructive effects; and (b) only states have, so far, mastered the capability to develop and deploy these sophisticated effects. These arguments are problematic because they confuse capabilities with incentives and fail to recognize that using a weapon in cyberspace is about much more than just writing computer code.

The capability to do something is not the same as possessing incentives to do it. There have been few instances of physical destruction from malware, but this is less about who can launch such attacks and more about who is motivated to do so. There is evidence to indicate that many states operate with a set of strategic motivations which are not nearly as sensitive to the cost/benefit guiding most criminal groups behavior (Romanosky and Herr "Understanding Cyber Crime" in Harrison and Herr (2016)). Targeting physical equipment or computer systems for destructive effects has so far proven a poor way to make money and is more likely to draw the attention of law enforcement agencies, so there has been little destructive activity attributed to criminal groups.

Where this idea, that the state as political entity with dedicated intelligence gathering resource and some claim to material superiority over the average citizen, may have purchase is in the resources required to reliably develop and integrate destructive malware and gather the intelligence required to target and deploy these programs. Looking at the most advanced states in the context of operational offensive capabilities like the United States, Russia, Israel, China, and perhaps the UK and France, each has a more capable intelligence collections infrastructure than in the clear majority, if not all, criminal groups. This intelligence capacity, together with the financial and human resources necessary to procure control systems and esoteric industrial hardware create a means of overcoming the barriers to entry for developing destructive effects just outlined.

What states do best is less about writing code and more about the ability to operate at scale, collecting intelligence on a wide range of targets simultaneously; obtaining detailed information on well-defended targets, and designing elaborate software applications to compromise computers. The larger distinction between states and non-state groups lays in targeting and reliably engineering physical effects, where the information required to accurately map a control system and its associated equipment, identify its physical vulnerabilities, and design a sequence of control inputs to obtain the desired outcome is substantial. The reconnaissance and intelligence gathering necessary to develop and deploy the programs necessary to generate destructive physical effects are generally substantial and may, in many cases, be cost or infrastructure prohibitive for a non-state group.

Making these programs reliable, such that the cyber weapon can be deployed on a target system and trusted to operate reliably without substantial user guidance is another area of potentially prohibitive cost. Designing the apparatus required to test a weapon targeting industrial control systems for example, would require very accurate software simulation or physical examples of the targeted hardware. These two factors alone, intelligence infrastructure and the ability to reliably engineer, test, and integrate destructive covert software, may make it impractical for non-state groups to develop truly effective cyber weapons.

There are two brief but important caveats that need to be added to the issues of intelligence gathering and reliable engineering capability. These issues are limited to the discussion of developing physically destructive effects, a very small part of the total malware universe, either in daily incidents or total samples collected. While the ability for hostile actors to gather information about their targets varies, outside of destructive effects this intelligence challenge is mostly a question of capacity to employ and maintain malware, rather than a barrier to its development. In addition, these advantages in intelligence infrastructure and reliability engineering do not prevent even the most advanced states from developing novel techniques and tactics from criminal actors and other non-state groups. Innovation in information security flows from states to non-state groups as well as in reverse. Identifying weapons by what only states can do in as a function of software design is a losing battle as every time a new piece of malware, a cyber weapon or not, is analyzed and the results made even semi-public, the result is a diffusion of the techniques embedded in that software to other actors.[3]

One previous effort to identify the line between the most capable state and lessor malicious methods attempted to look at samples of state and non-state malware and identify common architectural or behavioral features which clustered together (Herr and Armbrust 2015). Using the term *milware* to identify trends found in state samples, the study tried to describe the more developed engineering effort evident behind Russian and American code samples, like Duqu, Turla, or Stuxnet; their persistence and innovative means of compromise, in particular, denote a more specialized and extended development cycle than many non-state examples. The architecture of malicious software, like Duqu, betrays a development process like that for major commercial software. More akin to an operating system than a scratched together program, Duqu had a core software platform complimented by functional modules capable of being updated based on user need rather (Bonfante et al. 2013). This shift towards industrial malware development builds on the rudimentary multi-component design effort found in tools like the Blackhole exploit kit where efforts are made to integrate propagation methods and exploits into a single package (Team Cymru 2011). These differences can be further developed as a means to differentiate code samples and cluster groups by common features and capability levels.

---

[3]The information security community is an interconnected web of researchers, organizations, and for-profit companies. There exists an as-yet not well studied pattern of information sharing, both intentional and not, within this web which makes it difficult to contain knowledge of an offensive security innovation (outside of government) for very long. Some of this is because of the ethos of sharing novel finds and insights between researchers to help others get ahead of the curve while some is also likely due to some espionage by states and more sophisticated criminal groups on the same firms watching them.

The original milware study identified several features of these state samples not present in the non-state code, but the results were out of date less than 18 months later as many of the state features could now be found in criminal malware. This short lifespan of the results from this study underlines how rapid the cycle of innovation in cyber-security is and, more importantly, how effectively non-state groups learn from the most advanced state tools—the proliferation of malicious software and even components of some cyber weapons from one group to another.

10.6 Proliferation in Cyber-Security—Role of the Malware Markets

Proliferation deals with the diffusion of capabilities, often new weapons technologies, between different actors in the international political system. In cyber-security, this proliferation describes how groups learn from and reuse methods and programs developed by others, whether intentionally as through collaboration, or unintentionally. Unintentional proliferation is the process whereby the target of a piece of malicious software takes it apart to learn and reuse it. This unintentional proliferation is an issue not unique to cyber-security, but more prominent than in traditional domains of conflict.

Within cyber-security, intentional proliferation of malware involves direct intelligence support and transfer of software from one party to another. In the regard, states have no monopoly on capabilities. Non-state groups are a constant source of innovation on both offense and defense. Proliferation of malware can include a range of different types of information: from highly valuable software vulnerabilities to complete malicious software programs and the supporting infrastructure to covertly deploy them. The skills and capacity of groups on the receiving end of this proliferation can vary dramatically.

In addition to the deliberate transfer of intentional proliferation, cyber-security raises the possibility of unintentional proliferation, where malware's function or some properties are disclosed to a target or third parties during use. When a nuclear device or chemical weapon it is detonated, it leaves few pieces behind for the target to pick-over and reuse.[4] Malicious software leaves itself open to capture and analysis because it must be placed on the target and run successfully to work. This makes complicated malware designs and capabilities subject to far more effective forensic analysis than the comparable blast residue of a guided munition.[5]

---

[4]There are instances where groups have stolen or recovered spent or improperly disposed of weapons of mass destruction materials. These cases would constitute unintentional proliferation, but are extremely rare.

[5]Note—the last two paragraphs are excerpted from Trey Herr, "Governing Proliferation in Cyber-security," *Global Summitry*, 2, no. 1 (July 2017).

10.6.1 Malware Markets

Much of this proliferation takes place through the malware markets, economic transactions for software and services, like spam email, taking place between non-state and state groups ranging from criminals to small companies to intelligence agencies in the largest states like the NSA (Herr and Ellis, "Disrupting Malware Markets" in Harrison and Herr 2016). The problem with software code is that it's simple to transport, modify, and reuse. Some of these markets are informal social links between trusted parties while others are large online shops with customer feedback and rating systems like those found on *eBbay* or *Amazon*. Malware is bought, sold, leased, and rented, along with all manner of services like web hosting and currency exchange. Specialization has become nearly a de-facto standard with one paper observing that, "The underground economy has evolved into a complex ecosystem with commoditized services..." (Thomas et al. 2015).

The budgetary and human resources of states like Russia, the US, and China outstrip those of most criminal organization. While this disparity has long been focused on the threat of states developing destructive payloads, the resources required to reuse these payloads would likely be a stretch for most non-state groups as discussed above. The vulnerabilities states use to gain access to protected computer systems, packages in small software programs called *exploits*, are much more easily adapted and reused. There are several prominent examples of state authored exploits being discovered or leaked and subsequently reused by criminal groups and other states (Shamir 2014; Wolf 2013).

These markets can provide a means to gain access to malicious software that stymie traditional regulatory and governance approaches (Herr 2016). The malware markets can shed light on two kinds of proliferation; intentional, where access to highly capable malware lowers the barrier to entry for new malicious actors, and unintentional, when the markets function as a distribution mechanism for leaked state malware like the Equation Group tools (Schneier 2017a, b). The presence of a market also means that the actions of some buyers directly impact other actors; the price a state is willing to pay for a certain vulnerability, for example, may set the market for other players thereby encouraging new sellers to develop exploits for the vulnerability and potentially price out relatively friendly actors like the vendor responsible for the affected software. Understanding the rules of this market, the guiding framework for transactions, can help researchers understand the network through which code is purchased an exchanged—a roadmap for much of the proliferation in cyber-security.

10.6.2 High-End Cluster

This is a more difficult to research, but likely small ensemble of buyers and sellers focused on the sale of working exploits and well-developed services where communications are handled over encrypted email and chat programs and marketing is accomplished by word of mouth (Radianti 2010; Tsyrklevich 2015). Sellers in the high-end cluster are a fragmented network of skilled individuals who focus on the development and sale of new exploits for common or high value targets, acting at the front end of the market to distribute malware components directly to some buyers, but often to intermediaries who combine components and related services and then sell the assembled package. Reputation is a major determinant of connections between individuals and tends to rely on common points of contact and acquired prestige (Miller 2007).

Intermediaries include both buyers and sellers. Some purchase working exploits and integrate them into existing payloads and propagation programs to create more complete method to sell to government intelligence and law enforcement agencies. Hacking Team, a prominent Italian firm whose internal email and documentation was leaked in May 2015 uses a regular stream of new exploits to support its core malware called *Galileo RCS*, or Remote Control System (Anderson 2015). This malware can be used to spy on a variety of desktop and mobile phone operating systems. Customers can then purchase a license to increase the number of computers and telephones they collect information from at any given time. Companies even offering training, customization, and maintenance features for more developed users (Currier and Marquis-Boire 2015).

Other groups act as brokers between exploit developers and states or groups, like, at the time of this writing, Hacking Team. Firms selling exploits like ReVuln and Exodus Intelligence, generally operate on a subscription service model like the data plan for a cellphone; governments and other intermediaries pay a certain amount every year in exchange for a fixed number of exploits. By one estimate, there are at least half a dozen such firms capable of selling more than 100 new exploits a year to both governments and non-state actors, with an average list price between US $40,000 and US$160,000 (Frei 2013). These prices have potentially grown even higher in recent years; recently leaked emails between the American exploit broker Netragard and Hacking Team indicate prices as high as US$2 million for a single exploit (Ragan 2015).

In the high-end cluster, buyers include a mix of firms, states, and possibly some criminal groups –a mix of high capability groups who select services to supplement their internal resources and less well equipped national police forces and law enforcement organizations. Products are intended largely for states but may also involve some more sophisticated criminal groups. This mix of buyers is interesting as some state organizations may be less capable than certain criminal organizations. While the canonical state threat, America's NSA or Israel's Unit 8200, is generally accorded a high degree of technical capability others, like intelligence bodies for the Republic of Sudan and Ethiopia appear to be lacking even the skillset required to operate Hacking Team's products without potentially glaring errors and remedial training (Currier and Marquis-Boire 2015). There is also cottage industry of companies who, for a fee, will conduct mock attacks on organizations networks to pinpoint weaknesses; these penetration testing firms employ exploits in the same manner as a criminal or state attacker to help identify and improve the security of their clients. These companies often have an interest in the latest research to be most effective, but can purchase exploits more cheaply since they don't require exclusive access (Ellsmore 2013).

10.6.3 Low-End Cluster

The second, much larger and slightly more public low market, exists over a network of web forums and internet relay chat (IRC) channels much like (and sometimes together with) the clandestine online bazaars that sell narcotics and other illicit paraphernalia (Radianti et al. 2007). This low-end cluster is focused more on the sale of malicious payloads and services for criminal users, like botnets. Within both tiers, the demand for previously unknown and yet unpatched exploits has grown substantially in recent years (Frei 2013). Sellers in the low-end cluster are generally hawking both malware components like payloads and propagation methods as well as exploits. A key difference in this market is the absence of high value vulnerabilities, or zero days, because these command a substantially higher price than those that are known to vendors or for which patches are available (Böhme 2005). Interaction takes place via Internet chat with advertising over a shifting collection of forums, like Darkode (Krebs 2015).

The high/low-end clusters are tied to some degree through the vulnerability life cycle; as vulnerabilities are discovered and patched, they move from zero-day (unknown to the vendor) to N-day (N being the number of days since discovery or patch). As this happens, the exploit's value their generally decreases and sellers are motivated to unload them for some fraction of their original worth (Ozment 2004). As in the high-end cluster, intermediaries act as both buyers and sellers but their offerings are rarely as developed. The low-end cluster is less likely to see new or high value exploits but intermediaries can build value by combining less useful exploits together with other malware components to create offerings like the increasingly prolific exploit kit. (Herley and Florêncio 2010) Some of the most popular are exploit kits, such as Angler or Blackhole, where a propagation method and exploits are combined for customers to rent.

These kits can then be used with different payloads of customer's own design or even offered with select payloads ready made to create fully functioning malware. The Angler exploit kit, for example, appears to have integrated the Cryptowall payload with great success (Mimoso 2015). Buyers in the low-end cluster appear less particular about their targets but are far more numerous, ranging from spammers, to criminal groups, to low skill individuals (Radianti and Gonzalez 2007). This category may include groups with a political or otherwise ideological agenda (see Whitford's Chap. 4, in this volume), but more common buyers include criminal organization attempting to steal personally identifying information or banking credentials in order to sell them to other groups in this marketplace (Levchenko et al. 2011).

10.7   Conclusion

Proliferation of malicious software is a challenge for the international security community, but understanding the generative process of malware and what it takes to create a weapon in cyberspace can help shed light on new solutions. Understanding the various paths that program code can take between actors, including the important role of the malware markets, is important to grapple with the policy issue of proliferation. As governments begin to move past their initial responses, which have largely emphasized export controls, offensive malware's dependency on good intelligence information and, in many cases, software vulnerabilities will become critical (Herr 2017a).

The malware market provides a basis to study the development of malicious software and its proliferation between actors. Understanding the basis of this exchange, where actors decide to reuse of code or try to develop independently will require further work but there is a conceptual map and starting point provided in this chapter. Proliferation in cyber-security is a complex topic, but hopefully this chapter serves as a useful starting point.

10.8   Principal Concepts

Some of the principal concepts associated with this chapter are listed below. Demonstrate your understanding of each by writing a definition or explanation in one or two sentences;

- Destructive software;
- Malware markets;
- Reliability and specificity in malware engineering; and
- Malware used for strategic ends

10.9   Study Questions

1. Explain what distinguishes the architectural definition of cyber weapons from the effects-based definition?
2. Describe what makes it difficult to build destructive malware?
3. Discuss why might states have an advantage over other groups in building destructive malware?
4. Explain the different kinds of proliferation that are possible with malicious software?

5. Describe how the different clusters of malware markets are different?
6. List three different companies that sell malicious software and services?
7. Compare what makes nuclear weapons and cyber weapons different?

10.10   Learning Activities

1. Working with in a small group, discuss why criminal and others group might reuse malicious software built by others. Given what you now know about what is required to build destructive malware payloads, what can you identify that might cause an organization to prefer reusing code from someone else instead of writing their own?
2. Make a list of all destructive attacks using malicious software, for instance, Stuxnet. As a group, split into two sections and debate the following—"Resolved: There have been few destructive cyber-attacks because 'weapons' in cyberspace are less useful than once believed."

References

Ablon L, Libicki MC, Golay AA (2014) Markets for cybercrime tools and stolen data: Hackers' bazaar, Rand Corporation. Available at: http://www.rand.org/content/dam/rand/pubs/research_reports/RR600/RR610/RAND_RR610.pdf. Accessed 29 November 2015

Allen Bradley (2016) Logix5000 controllers generals instructions reference manual. Available at: http://literature.rockwellautomation.com/idc/groups/literature/documents/rm/1756-rm003_-en-p.pdf

Anderson C (2015) Considerations on Wassenaar arrangement control list additions for surveillance technologies, Access. Available at: https://cda.io/r/ConsiderationsonWassenaarArrangement ProposalsforSurveillanceTechnologies.pdf. Accessed 7 July 2015

Bacchus M, Coronado A, Gutierrez MA (2014) The insights into car hacking. Available at: http://web.eng.fiu.edu/~aperezpo/DHS/Std_Research/Car%20Hacking%20-%20eel%206931%20final.pdf. Accessed 20 Feb 2017

Böhme R (2005) Vulnerability markets. In: Proceedings of 22C3, vol 27, p 30

Bonfante G, Marion J-Y, Sabatier F, Thierry A (2013) Analysis and diversion of Duqu's driver. In: Colon Osorio FC (ed) Proceedings of the 2013 8th international conference on malicious and unwanted software, presented at the international conference on malicious and unwanted software, IEEE, Fajardo, Puerto RIco, USA, pp 109–115

Currier C, Marquis-Boire M (2015) A detailed look at hacking team's emails about its repressive clients. The Intercept, 7 July. Available at: https://theintercept.com/2015/07/07/leaked-documents-confirm-hacking-team-sells-spyware-repressive-countries/. Accessed 5 Jan 2016

Ellsmore N (2013) Penetration testing market analysis: where is all the revenue? Delling Advisory, 5 April. Available at: http://www.dellingadvisory.com/blog/2013/4/5/penetration-testing-market-analysis-where-is-all-the-revenue. Accessed 9 Jan 2016

"Exploit – Stack Overflows – Defeating Canaries, ASLR, DEP, NX" (2013) Security stack exchange. Available at: http://security.stackexchange.com/questions/20497/stack-overflows-defeating-canaries-aslr-dep-nx. Accessed 20 Feb 2017

Falliere N, Murchu LO, Chien E (2011) W32. Stuxnet Dossier, Symantec. Available at: http://www.h4ckr.us/library/Documents/ICS_Events/Stuxnet%20Dossier%20(Symantec)%20v1.4.pdf. Accessed 21 Oct 2013

Frei S (2013) The known unknowns, NSS Labs. Available at: https://library.nsslabs.com/reports/known-unknowns-0

Glisson WB, Andel T, McDonald T, Jacobs M, Campbell M, Mayr J (2015) Compromising a medical mannequin, arXiv Preprint arXiv:1509.00065. Available at: https://arxiv.org/abs/1509.00065. Accessed 20 Feb 2017

Harrison R, Herr T (eds) (2016) Cyber insecurity: navigating the perils of the next information age. Rowman & Littlefield, Lanham. Available at: https://books.google.com/books?id=NAp7DQAAQBAJ&source. Accessed 6 Jan 2017

Herley C, Florêncio D (2010) Nobody sells gold for the price of silver: dishonesty, uncertainty and the underground economy. In: Moore T, Pym D, Ioannidis C (eds) Economics of information security and privacy. Springer, Boston, pp 33–53

Herr T (2014) PrEP: a framework for malware & cyber weapons. J Inf Warf 13(1):87–106

Herr T (2016) Malware counter-proliferation and the Wassenaar arrangement. In: 2016 8th international conference on cyber conflict: cyber power. Presented at the CyCon, IEEE, Tallinn, Estonia. pp 175–190

Herr T (2017a) Countering the proliferation of malware – targeting the vulnerability lifecycle. Belfer Center, Harvard Kennedy School, Cambridge, MA

Herr T (2017b) Governing proliferation in cybersecurity. Global Summitry, vol 2, no 1. Available at: https://academic.oup.com/globalsummitry/article/doi/10.1093/global/gux006/3920644/Governing-Proliferation-in-Cybersecurity?guestAccessKey=f88e2727-737a-4be2-991e-a3696624b420

Herr T, Armbrust E (2015) Milware: identification and implications of state authored malicious software. NSPW '15 proceedings of the 2015 new security paradigms workshop, ACM, Twente, Netherlands, pp 29–43

InfoSec Institute (2017) Best DOS attacks and free DOS attacking tools, InfoSec Institute

Krebs B (2015) The Darkode cybercrime forum, up close. Krebs on Security, 15 July. Available at: http://krebsonsecurity.com/2015/07/the-darkode-cybercrime-forum-up-close/. Accessed 9 Jan 2016

Langner R (2011) Stuxnet: dissecting a cyberwarfare weapon. Secur Priv IEEE 9(3):49–51

Langner R (2013) Langner – to kill a Centrifuge.pdf, The Langner Group, p 36

Levchenko K, Pitsillidis A, Chachra N, Enright B, Félegyházi M, Grier C, Halvorson T et al (2011) Click trajectories: end-to-end analysis of the spam value chain. Security and Privacy (SP), 2011 I.E. symposium on, IEEE, pp 431–446

Mackenzie H (2012) Shamoon malware and SCADA security – what are the impacts? I Tofino industrial security solution. Tofino Security, 25 October. Available at: https://www.tofinosecurity.com/blog/shamoon-malware-and-scada-security-%E2%80%93-what-are-impacts. Accessed 20 Feb 2017

Miller C (2007) The legitimate vulnerability market: inside the secretive world of 0-day exploit sales. In sixth workshop on the economics of information security, Citeseer. Available at: http://citeseerx.ist.psu.edu/viewdoc/summary?doi=10.1.1.139.5718. Accessed 5 Jan 2016

Mimoso M (2015) Evasion techniques keep angler EK's cryptowall business thriving. Threatpost, 2 July. Available at: https://threatpost.com/evasion-techniques-keep-angler-eks-cryptowall-business-thriving/113596/. Accessed 5 Jan 2016

One A (1996) Smashing the stack for fun and profit. Phrack Magazine, November, vol 49, no 14. Available at: http://phrack.org/issues/49/14.html

Ozment A (2004) Bug auctions: vulnerability markets reconsidered. Third workshop on the economics of information security, pp 19–26

Prunckun H (2012) Counterintelligence theory and practice. Rowman & Littlefield Publishers, Lanham

Radcliffe J (2011) Hacking medical devices for fun and insulin: breaking the human SCADA system. Black Hat conference presentation slides, vol 2011. Available at: http://www.aicas.com/cms/sites/default/files/BH_US_11_Radcliffe_Hacking_Medical_Devices_WP.pdf. Accessed 20 Feb 2017

Radianti J (2010) Eliciting information on the vulnerability black market from interviews. Presented at the fourth international conference on emerging security information, systems and technologies, IEEE, pp 93–96

Radianti J, Gonzalez JJ (2007) A preliminary model of the vulnerability black market. The 25th international system dynamics conference, Boston, USA. Available at: http://www.systemdynamics.org/conferences/2007/proceed/papers/RADIA352.pdf. Accessed 30 Nov 2015

Radianti J, Rich E, Gonzalez J (2007) Using a mixed data collection strategy to uncover vulnerability black markets. Second pre-ICIS workshop on information security and privacy, vol 42, Citeseer. Available at: http://citeseerx.ist.psu.edu/viewdoc/download?doi=10.1.1.94.2652&rep=rep1&type=pdf. Accessed 30 Nov 2015

Ragan S (2015) Hacking team vendor calls breach a 'blessing in disguise'. CSO Online, 9 July. Available at: http://www.csoonline.com/article/2946193/data-protection/hacking-team-vendor-calls-breach-a-blessing-in-disguise.html. Accessed 9 Jan 2016

Raiu C (2013) Destructive malware – five wipers in the spotlight. SecureList, 18 December. Available at: https://securelist.com/blog/incidents/58194/destructive-malware-five-wipers-in-the-spotlight/. Accessed 20 Feb 2017

Rashid F (2015) Inside the aftermath of the Saudi Aramco Breach. Dark Reading, 8 August. Available at: http://www.darkreading.com/attacks-breaches/inside-the-aftermath-of-the-saudi-aramco-breach/d/d-id/1321676. Accessed 20 Feb 2017

Schneier B (2017a) Who are the shadow brokers? The Atlantic, 23 May. Available at: https://www.theatlantic.com/technology/archive/2017/05/shadow-brokers/527778/

Schneier B (2017b) Why the NSA makes us more vulnerable to cyberattacks. Foreign Affairs, 20 May. Available at: https://www.foreignaffairs.com/articles/2017-05-30/why-nsa-makes-us-more-vulnerable-cyberattacks. Accessed 29 June 2017

Shamir U (2014) The case of Gyges, the invisible malware government-grade now in the hands of cybercriminals, Sentinel Labs. Available at: http://graphics8.nytimes.com/packages/pdf/technology/sentinel-labs-intelligence-report-04.pdf

Siemens (2005) GRAPH 5 – graphically programming sequence controllers under SS-DOS operating system. Available at: https://cache.industry.siemens.com/dl/files/689/19374689/att_81661/v1/Graph5_v30_e_OCR.pdf

Siemens. Introduction to control programming – building technologies. Siemens US. Available at: http://w3.usa.siemens.com/buildingtechnologies/us/en/education-services/building-automation/building-automation-self-study/pages/introduction-to-control-programming.aspx. Accessed 20 Feb 2017

Team Cymru (2011) A criminal perspective on exploit packs. Available at: https://blog.qualys.com/wp-content/uploads/2011/05/team_cymru_exploitkits.pdf

Thomas K, Huang D, Wang D, Bursztein E, Grier C, Holt TJ, Kruegel C et al (2015) Framing dependencies introduced by underground commoditization. Presented at the workshop on the economics of information security. Available at: http://damonmccoy.com/papers/WEIS15.pdf. Accessed 29 Nov 2015

Tsyrklevich V (2015) Hacking team: a zero-day market case study, 22 July. Available at: https://tsyrklevich.net/2015/07/22/hacking-team-0day-market/

Varner R, Collier W (1978) A matter of risk. Random House, New York

Wassenaar Arrangement (2015) The Wassenaar arrangement on export controls for conventional arms and dual-use goods and technologies, 12 March. Available at: http://www.wassenaar.org/

wp-content/uploads/2015/08/WA-LIST-15-1-2015-List-of-DU-Goods-and-Technologies-and-Munitions-List.pdf. Accessed 19 Sept 2015

Wolf J (2013) CVE-2011-3402 – Windows Kernel TrueType Font Engine Vulnerability (MS11–087). Presented at the CanSecWest, 8 March. Available at: https://cansecwest.com/slides/2013/Analysis%20of%20a%20Windows%20Kernel%20Vuln.pdf

Chapter 11
No Smoking Gun: Cyber Weapons and Drug Traffickers

Henry Prunckun

11.1 Introduction

In mid-April 2016, heads of state, senior diplomats, and government officials from around the world gathered at the United Nations headquarters in New York to discuss the global drug problem. The reason for this meeting, is because international drug trafficking is a criminal enterprise billion-dollar proportions. It has been estimated that drug-related money laundering accounts for between 0.4% and 0.6% of global GDP (UNODC 2011: 7). The profits of which can be turned into political influence, and in turn, used against law enforcement agencies to undermine their efforts to bring traffickers to heal (Prunckun 2016). Even after decades of concentrated anti-drug efforts, the problem is so great that some Central and South American countries have tittered on becoming failed states because of the illicit drug trade (Wyler 2008: 7).

During 4 days of consultation, the United Nations General Assembly Special Session (UNGASS 2016) concluded that the UN would strengthen its approach to waging a war-on-drugs. In its *Outcome Document*, the UN General Assembly confirmed its commitment to targeting "illicit drug cultivation, production, manufacturing, trafficking and other illicit drug-related activities in order to prevent, reduce or eliminate them" (UNGASS 2016: 26). It also reaffirmed the UN's "unwavering commitment" to "supply reduction and related measures" (UNGASS 2016: 2).

Nonetheless, policymakers have faced the conundrum of what to do in face of growing evidence that the so-called *war-on-drugs* has failed. Treating the demand side of the problem using an evidence-based approach is showing promising results, but what about the supply side? An objective evaluate of the risks and benefits of the

H. Prunckun (✉)
Australian Graduate School of Policing and Security, Charles Sturt University, Sydney, Australia
e-mail: hprunckun@csu.edu.au

© Springer International Publishing AG, part of Springer Nature 2018　　　143
H. Prunckun (ed.), *Cyber Weaponry*, Advanced Sciences and Technologies for
Security Applications, https://doi.org/10.1007/978-3-319-74107-9_11

range of responses to the drug problem cannot ignore the problems created by drug cartels and other organized crime groups when their illicit profits are leveraged against civil society.

If evidence-based legal and policy reform are required, which few would argue against, why don't policymakers reconsider the framework on which current supply side strategies have relied? If the efforts to deal with drug trafficking are referred to as the war-on-drugs, then it makes sense to explore a war-like approach using cyber weapons to defeat drug-trafficking organizations' information processes, which are vital to supporting their worldwide financial networks, as well as their command and control arrangements. This chapter argues that counter-drug policy could benefit from focusing on attacking the command and control aspects of the illicit drug problem using offensive cyber weapons, as Hughes (2018) argues, as a way of gaining a the "force advantage."

11.2   Context

The subject literature on illicit drug use is replete with studies that demonstrate how and why drugs are a global concern. Although drugs have been used for centuries, abuse is at the center of the issue and that phenomenon has grown over the past six decades:

> It is estimated that 1 in 20 adults, or a quarter of a billion-people aged 15–64 years, used at least one drug in 2014. . . . Almost 12 per cent of the total number of people who use drugs, or over 29 million people, are estimated to suffer from drug use disorders (UN 2016: 1).

Apart from the impact drugs have on people's health, livelihoods and relationships, their association with crime has been established to have causal as well as consequential effects on societies worldwide. Without entering the debate as to how drugs and crime are intertwined, it is obvious that criminal enterprises that traffic drugs are of most concern to law enforcers (Oberweis and Petrocelli 2015). Organized crime syndicates that range from just a few conspirators, up to elaborate networks of compartmentalized groups, or autonomous cliques that come together as a collective for an operation(s), are the chief threat. That is because the large profits a successful importation yields can be used to buy political influence (Jordan 1999: 6–7). Once political leaders and law enforcement commanders are corrupted by organized crime, the moral fabric of society begins to disintegrate (Naylor 2004).

To address drug trafficking, the world community has developed several international conventions. These counter-drug conventions are in turn supported by national and state legislation, thus forming a policy framework of prohibition. The aim of drug prohibition is to make drugs scarce, expensive, and risky to supply and obtain. There are other methods that compliment the approach—demand reduction and harm reduction, with police forces working with the health sector to manage these programs—but arguably, it is supply reduction that is assigned the keystone role in the strategy.

11.3 Strategy Options

The supply reduction element of prohibition includes law enforcement measures that criminalize importing drugs and offering them for sale. The risk of apprehension causes drugs to become limited and has added effect of reducing demand by driving users into treatment (Weatherburn and Lind 1999).

The demand reduction component of law enforcement includes measures that criminalize the purchase, possession and use of illegal drugs, and if these measures were successful, would result in a decrease in the illicit drug trade. Both the supply and demand components of supply reduction are intended to impact on user demand—law enforcement supply strategies attempt to drive-up prices and the demand reduction strategies try to make buying and possessing illicit drugs riskier.

> Ultimately, the main emphasis of the war-on-drugs, and the logic of criminalization from which it flows, is placed on the suppliers of illicit drugs; the basic premise is that availability is at the heart of the problem. By stopping the flow of illicit drugs into and within [a country] the problem will disappear (Boyd and Lowman 1991: 116).

11.4 War Metaphor

Beginning with the then-US President, the late-Richard's Nixon's 1971 proclamation that America was embarking on a *war-on-drugs*, other nations have since followed suit. It is rae that any country with an advanced economy does not have some form of a national drug control strategy. But, in 2011 the Geneva-based Global Commission on Drug Policy (2011: 2) questioned the effectiveness of this so-called war, stating, "The global war-on-drugs has failed, with devastating consequences for individuals and societies around the world. Fifty years after the initiation of the UN Single Convention on Narcotic Drugs, and years after President Nixon launched the US government's war-on-drugs, fundamental reforms in national and global drug control policies are urgently needed." (Global Commission on Drug Policy 2011: 2).

This war image is more than just a political ploy; it is a way people can visualise both the seriousness and enormity of the problem. If one accepts this metaphor, it then makes sense to explore war-like policy options. Hypothetically, these options include direct intervention using military forces to carry out crop eradication-type programs, or the use of smaller numbers of special forces to carry out secret operations (i.e. unconventional warfare) against the production, infrastructure and transportation networks of drug-trafficking organizations in source and transhipment countries. But, these options assume that such operations would be approved in some way by the source countries' government, or carried out with their cooperation.

This is not a situation that readily comes to mind as being politically straightforward. But, if such a political hurtle could be overcome, research shows that as "...victories in eliminating one source or trafficking organization are negated almost instantly by the emergence of other sources and traffickers" (Global Commission on Drug Policy 2011: 2).

Although demand and harm reduction programs show a great deal of promise, the discounting of supply reduction programs would not be a wise policy position. Nevertheless, the evidence that the options that have been used so far for enforcing the prohibition are unlikely to win a great deal of future support. However, there is the option of using information warfare techniques in what is now seen as key in fighting today's wars—fourth generation warfare (4GW). 4GW uses methods that differ substantially from the usual modes of operating. 4GW is characterised by forces (that can be other than military) that attack the infrastructure that allows an enemy to plan and execute their strategies rather than destroying actual enemy combatants (Lind 2004).[1]

If applied to the war-on-drugs, an information warfare approach could include attacking drug-trafficking organizations' IT-based systems and the systems of their financial facilitators (i.e. money laundering arrangements). Arguably, these are vital to the command and control function of this stateless collective of organized criminals. Information warfare could also include engaging in psychological operations (psyops) against key organisational personnel (both horizontally, across its operations, and vertically, within its operations) and third-party supporters (i.e. those who aid and abet drug traffickers). The range of potential targets is very wide, indeed.

11.5 Drug Trafficking

Historically, illicit drug trafficking has been popularised by the media in such films as *The French Connection* (based on Moore's 1969 factual book). Such accounts show large amounts of drugs being smuggled into various countries in cargo ships by "Mr Bigs." In the 1960s, the efforts of the New York Police Department's Detectives Eddie Egan and Sonny Grosso (who were responsible for discovering *The French Connection*) resulted in what were at the time some of the largest heroin seizures in US history. This criminally organized operation formed what could be described as a "pipeline" for opiates from major narcotic-producing countries (McCoy 1991: 65–70).

However, the global illicit drug trafficking is different to the pipeline metaphor of *The French Connection*. McCoy, who pioneered scholarship in this area some 35 years ago, argued that the "... drug supply systems are many and complex"

---

[1]First generation warfare was characterised by the Age-of-Napoleon; forces armed with guns operating in close-order formations to defeat cavalry and infantry who were armed with swords and bayonets. Second generation warfare was the age of firepower, managed in such a way that enabled an army to win through attrition. Third generation warfare saw the advent of decentralised attacks based on manoeuvrability and strategy. Fourth generation warfare is much more irregular. In the main, it comprises asymmetric operations that are characterized by mismatch between the combatants' resources with an emphasis is on bypassing the stronger force by the weaker (Lind 2004).

(McCoy 1980: 255). At that time, he observed that rather than a pipeline, there existed a "reservoir" fed continuously "...by streams of varying size and regularity, [the world's] reservoir of heroin supply is kept at a constant level by sources ranging from the kilogram 'body packs' to the multi-kilo lot brought in through private aircraft or concealed in commercial cargo" (McCoy 1980: 255).

According to the UN (2016), there is little reason to doubt that the same does not apply to drugs such as cannabis, cocaine, and amphetamine-type stimulants. But what has changed since McCoy watershed research took place in the distribution of drugs via the Internet, particularly what is termed the *dark net*.[2] Because this virtual market cannot be accessed by using conventional web search software and methods, it allows identities of buyers and sellers to remain anonymous. This means that buyers are not in direct contact with traffickers and as such, outsider the direct observations of law enforcement authorities. The impact of this new reservoir has the potential "...to attract new populations of users by facilitating access to drugs... [and] ...are typically paid for in bitcoins or in other crypto-currencies and are most often delivered via postal services (UN 2016: 24)."

Decades on from McCoy's watershed study, drug detections (approximately 95.2%) still involve numerous small weights (Australian Crime Commission 2005: 4). In practical terms, this drug reservoir has makes it very difficult for law enforcement agencies to control. Like previous studies (Bevan 1991), the UN (2016) found that there was still no Mr. Big. This is because these are independent enterprises—cartels—that operate in competition to one another. There is no credible evidence to suggest that they have formed into a unified body like OPEC (Knox and Gray 2014; Natarajan et al. 2015).

11.6 International Relations

Combating these multiple streams of illicit drugs has presented endless problems for policymakers and law enforcers. Ideally, the control of illegal drugs requires cooperation beyond national boundaries. Though, not all countries have the same political persuasion to attempt to eliminate, or even reduce, the size of, say, the South East Asian opium crop. This approach would require them to adopt an interventionist strategy.

An interventionist approach would be characterised by striking at the source of the illicit drug production—in terms of heroin, that would mean the poppy fields, clandestine laboratories, transport and transhipment arrangements, and money management and laundering arrangements of drug traffickers, rather than attempting to combat supply by police-work once the drugs have entered in the country.

---

[2]An obscure area of the Internet that is distinguished by special search engine access, "password protect pages, unlinked websites and hidden content accessible only to those in the know" (Bartlett 2014: 3).

Most countries have been prevented from challenging governments in drug growing countries, not because they lack political will, but because they lack the superpower "clout" that, for instance, the United States possesses. Lacking the power of America, other countries can only request cooperation of these source countries even though, it could be argued, some source nations' drug policies are influenced (directly and indirectly) by global drug traffickers (Malbry 1994; UN 2016).

Even if a country was in such a commanding political position internationally, the experience of the US Drug Enforcement Administration (DEA) in South America indicates that large-scale counter-drug operations are not *completely* effective. Not because the strategy of eliminating drug laboratories and crops is somehow ineffective, but because strategies that are intended to promote favourable international relations sometimes take a higher priority than anti-drug strategies (Malbry 1994).

By way of example, take the 1991 case of the Central Intelligence Agency (CIA) when it advised then-President Bush that the Syrian government was directly involved in the production of opium and hashish in Lebanon's Bekaa Valley. The CIA estimated that these crops were worth approximately US$1 billion per annum, or around 20% of Syria's GNP. Rather than jeopardise Syria's support for the 1991 Gulf War to liberate Kuwait, the Bush Administration "turned a blind eye" to this, thus over-riding US drug policies (Booth 1996: 348–349). This phenomenon is best explained by Wardlaw et al. (1991: 133–134):

> There will clearly be times when an actual or potential clash could arise between [domestic] drug policy and foreign policy goals … It will sometimes be important, therefore, for the …[governments]… to view supply reduction efforts in terms of their impact on foreign policy concerns. In some situations, it will be the judgment of government that reduced performance in terms of drug-control objectives is a price that must be paid for the advancement of foreign policy objectives.

11.7 Repercussions of Military Intervention

If any country could strike at the poppy fields using military force, such intervention would likely have complicating side effects that would adversely impact on domestic policy as well as clash with foreign policy goals. First, there would be the cost of financing the scale of such an operation. To carry out a credible overseas counter-drug operation, any nation would need to spend, perhaps, several hundred million dollars, if not more. Earmarking this amount of funds for such tactics as drug crop elimination programs (in the case of growing countries) would no doubt prove problematic for governments that would have to find ways of raising the money.

Even if a government was successful in finding a large amount of public money, it is debatable whether such funds would accomplish much even if it were channelled into an "aid package." Could a nation really convince subsistence farmers to shift from growing opium, coca, or cannabis to growing substitute crops unless there was a market for the produce and it would pay as much as it does for their drug crops? Providing such a large amount of aid is likely to be met with a great deal of scepticism by elected representatives and taxpayers, especially if those source countries have had difficulties in the past demonstrating their capability to responsibility account for aid money, or use it to violate human-rights.

The second concern involves the military aspect of such an interventionist approach. To attack drugs at the source would likely require military hardware and equipment to be dispatched to the producer country to dismantle drug traffickers' production infrastructure and distribution networks. This is likely to mean uniformed troops, armoured vehicles, helicopters, transport aircraft, logistic support equipment, barracks, and more. Experience has shown that the presence of combat troops operating openly on foreign soil is a sensitive issue at home as well as abroad. In addition, military personnel could be at great risk—the presence of troops, not to mention by-stander civilian nationals travelling in-country, could present as soft targets for narco-terrorists (LoC 2002) and criminal gangs (Wigginton et al. 2014).

The third point to be made in terms of large-scale intervention is one of corruption. For example, drug traffickers are known to pay off corrupt officials in drug production countries in exchange for secure smuggling routes and weapons (Rose-Ackerman and Palifka 2016). When this type of intervention has been used by the United States in South America, the practical benefits for the Americans were less than expected (LoC 2002).

11.7.1 Covert Operations

Unconventional warfare techniques, such as small-scale covert military operations, may be an alternative to military forces operating in the open, especially if aimed at specific targets that are based on high-grade intelligence (Colby and Forbath 1978). But these operations would be controversial too. This approach would entail, for instance, a country's special forces backed by assets from its intelligence services to identify and then neutralize the most critical and vulnerable parts of a drug-trafficking organization's management, production, transportation and transhipment networks.

The CIA successfully conducted covert operations of this type against guerrilla groups operating in what was Military Region 3 during the Vietnam War (Colby and Forbath 1978; DeForest and Chanoff 1990). Although the intent of the CIA's use of this technique was different, the principles employed were the same.

Small-scale covert military operations, conducted in cooperation with source countries, such as *targeted interception*[3] could impact on the flow feeding the illicit drug reservoir. Such secret operations may have a greater degree of success in deterring those engaged in drug trafficking than increasing domestic law enforcement efforts. Police action can only realistically target drug traffickers' agents for

---

[3]John T. Stark (1990: 6) in his study *Selective Assassination as an Instrument of National Policy* argues that *interception* is a refined tactic of unconventional warfare.

arrest, many of whom are simply *mules* or users engaged in trafficking to fund their own drug habit or an opportunity for quick cash (Fleetwood 2014).

There are instances where some governments have successfully used this type of policy to curb international terrorism. Prominent cases include the use of the British SAS to target IRA terrorists in Ireland (Rivers 1985) and US Special Forces to target terrorists in Beirut (Rivers 1985). Israel is well known for its use of Mossad whose agents selectively targeted members of the Black September terrorist organization throughout Europe in the 1970s, effectively neutralizing that organization (Katz 1990). Israel also called on these same assets to target the terrorists responsible for the November 2002 bombing of an Israeli-owned hotel and the attempted shooting-down of an Israel commercial airliner in Kenya (Kerin 2002). And, in 2010 an un-named intelligence service(s) targeted "...Mahmoud al-Mabhouh while he was visiting Dubai, United Arabs Emirates. Al-Mabhouh was reported to have been a co-founder of the Izz ad-Din al-Qassam Brigades, the military wing of the Islamist Palestinian organization, Hamas (Prunckun 2015: 42)."

Nevertheless, there are concerns with conducting this type of covert operation. These include the ethical question of targeted killings (Cooper 2009; Pratt 2011; Prunckun 2012), and the practical consideration of having an operation compromised, which would leave the responsible government to deal with an international relations debacle.

11.7.2 Offensive Information Warfare

Offensive information warfare, or *cyber-war*, "...is the use of all available electronic and computer tools to shut down the enemy's electronics and communications..." (Dunnigan 1996: 266). Unlike the other military ops discussed, there are few reasons why offensive information warfare tactics could not be adopted to target drug traffickers' management and decision-making systems, especially their informal money transfer systems (i.e. underground banking/money laundering) as well as using psyops to target drug manufactures and key suppliers/supporters as a means of protecting a nation's security from this criminal threat.

Information warfare is an unquestionably remote form of confrontation—it is more acceptable to destroy a drug trafficker's information infrastructure, than to bomb their production facilities or target them personally for interception. Information attacks avoid human casualties as there are no corpses when a logic bomb obliterates all the business data contained in a drug trafficker's computer system. If executed properly, it would permit a country to avoid deciding between competing international and domestic interests— the saying goes, it would allow the government to "have its cake and eat it too."

In the broad sense, information warfare is analogous to that of a naval blockade. Historically, countries imposed sanctions upon an adversary by instituting a cordon. A country could, in effect, isolate its enemy from the world by keeping all ships from reaching the targeted country's ports. With computer technology, a country could impose a blockade on drug traffickers by, for instance, unleashing a denial of service attack against their computers, or turning all their financial data to "electronic confetti" through the introduction of a virus or Trojan, the same way legitimate commercial networks are attacked regularly by hackers. This approach pits a nation's strengths against drug traffickers' weaknesses in an unconventional manner—one in which there is no effective response by drug traffickers.

The National Commission on Terrorist Attacks Upon the United States' (2004) inquiry into the now infamous September 11 attacks recommended a strategy to fight terrorism that parallels what is being suggested here for fighting drug traffickers. It stated that intelligence has enabled law enforcers to identify the financial facilitators whose efforts allowed al-Qaeda to operate. With these key players removed (i.e. arrested or killed) there was a decrease in the money available to finance future al-Qaeda operations and an increase in the cost of carrying out the operations it could organize, making it less effective. Most importantly, it rendered some planned operations totally impossible (US 2004: 382). If the same could be done to the cyber infrastructure that is essential to the financing of illicit drug operations, a similar result could surely be expected.

But to do this, a cyber warfare unit is needed to engage in 4GW. That is, a unit of information warriors who can conduct covert operations in cyberspace. This requires a well-trained cadre of men and women who can attack information infrastructure remotely. These warriors would need to possess high-order intellectual skills and an in-depth understanding of computer architectures, programming languages, tele-communications, IT-security, and data encryption. They need to be aided by a small number of colleagues who are expert in financial intelligence—analysts who can locate and track illicit drug money as it makes its way through the maze of front companies and shell organizations that often provide "cover" for drug traffickers.

Additionally, there is a role for legal counsel in this type of operation. Just as there are lawyers in war-rooms, legal advisers play a vital part in cyber warfare. Take for instance the Stuxnet malware that destroyed Iran's nuclear centrifuges in 2010. It is a matter of public record that this software program was designed to target industrial control systems at the Natanz nuclear facility. Although the combination worm/virus (Zetter 2015) was found to have spread to systems outside this facility, there is no evidence that the program affected them. This, it is argued, was due to the role of lawyers in designing the software—they would have insisted that programmers write the source code so that it would only work at the targeted facility, and not in *the wild*, should be migrate elsewhere, as it did.

These personnel might be soldiers trained as computer engineers or computer engineers trained as soldiers, or some combination thereof. But whatever the com-position of units like this, there is little doubt that the environment in which a counter-drug cyber unit needs to operate is under a military command, or an intelligence agency's clandestine service (Helms and Hood 2003), but not that of the police force or regulatory agency. This is because law enforcement and financial compliance work is focused on collecting and safeguarding evidence for admission in a court of law. In contrast, the military's function is to "...unbalance, counter, dislodge and defeat the enemy" (Australian Army 1993: 19). In an information war-on-drugs, the goal is to defeat drug-trafficking organizations' decision-support and money laundering systems that are critical to their operations; not the seizure and preservation for evidence.

Initial consideration might lead policy-maker to assume that such an option would be complicated. But, it is entirely possible for even a small nation to achieve to, at the very least, develop a menacing capability. Using existing financial intelligence, military and IT experts, a modestly equipped country could wage a raider-style campaign that could cause significant disruption to international illicit drug operations targeting it. Such a strategy would look "...to shatter the [drug traffickers'] cohesion through a series of actions orchestrated to a single purpose, creating a turbulent and rapidly deteriorating situation with which the [drug traffickers] cannot cope" (Australian Army 2002: Chap 4). A more developed country with a military cyber command would be expected to be able to do far more. Taking this proposition further, if a joint international cyber command operation, or intelligence alliance project was undertaken—for instance, by the Five Eyes intelligence partners—this kind of leverage could result in increased strike efficiency, as well impact effectiveness (Fig. 11.1).

Rand Corporation reported that: "Waging information war is relatively cheap. Unlike traditional weapon technologies, acquiring cyber information weapons does not require vast financial resources... Computer expertise and access to major networks may be the only prerequisites" (Rand 1995). For instance, French Resistance fighters during World War II used very modest resources to cut telegraph and

Fig. 11.1 With modest equipment, a raider-style campaign could be carried-out (Photograph by Master Sgt. Barry Loo and courtesy of the U.S. Department of Defense)

telephone lines thus helping prevent Nazi troops from being sent to reinforce costal forces during the Allied invasion on D-Day—undermining the enemy's centre of gravity (Stafford 2000: 197). The equivalent could be done in cyberspace.

In a Stuxnet-esque attack, drug trafficking organizations' computerized resources could be subjected to a well created piece of malware that inflicts a costly impact on their illegal enterprise. Using sophisticated worms, for instance, their systems could be brought down, halting the transhipment of drugs and therefore jeopardising the organization's profitability. Ultimately, these attacks are intended to confront their ability to function freely. The fact that drug traffickers' business systems are connected to the Internet makes them as vulnerable as anyone else (Meinel 2002, 2003). Drug traffickers would be hard pressed to counter a concentrated, sustained attack by a dedicated team of information warriors—and there would be no "smoking gun."

These examples are only part of what information warfare is capable of delivering in relation to the war-on-drugs. Another tactic that has great potential is that of psyops and disinformation. Briefly, drawing on an example from history, American agents were reported to have used disinformation when they inserted forged documents into British diplomatic pouches to try to convince the British that George Washington's army was larger than it was. Although this example might seem dated, it nevertheless demonstrates the parallel of how a disinformation campaign could be waged against drug traffickers, their key operating personnel, and/or third-party supporters, with relative ease via e-mails and social media. As Sun Tzu (1963: 66) wrote: "All warfare is based on deception."

11.8 Conclusion

Drug trafficking organizations have transformed what was at one stage a cottage industry into a global business that now rivals the GNP of some countries. The open borders that exist between some countries facilitates the movement of illicit drugs to transhipment points around the world. Money laundering is accomplished easily through a maze of financial transactions that is facilitated by modern telecommunications and the Internet. These factors have defied traditional law enforcement countermeasures.

If there is a war-on-drugs, then the statistics contained in reports like the United Nations Office for Drugs and Crime's *World Drug Report, 2016* (UNODC 2016), the US State Department's *International Narcotic Control Strategy Report* (USDoS 2016), and the Australian Criminal Intelligence Commission's *Illicit Drug Data Report, 2014–2015* (2015), suggest that it is the drug traffickers who are winning. Therefore, is it not imperative that policy-makers rethink supply-side strategies and realign their approach so that it plays an *offensive* role?

Rather than only chipping-away at the continuous stream of drugs feeding the reservoir using traditional policework, why shouldn't nations embrace war-like tactics that attack the drug problem in front of the customs barrier. Although strategies that use the formal legal system should be employed at every opportunity, the option of using intelligence–led cyber warriors to wage information attacks on drug traffickers' financial infrastructure and their command and control arrangements, deserves consideration.

Acknowledgements The author thanks the editors of the *Australian Defence Force Journal* (Prunckun 2005) and the *Journal of the Institute of Professional Intelligence Officers* (Prunckun 2007) for permission to use his previously published material.

Principal Concepts The principal concepts associated with this chapter are listed below. Demonstrate your understanding of each by writing a short definition or explanation in one or two sentences:

- dark net;
- drug-trafficking organizations;
- fourth-generation warfare; and
- war-on-drugs.

Study Questions

1. Explain why organized criminal enterprises, in general, are a threat to civil society, and specifically, why are those that deal in illicit drugs?
2. Explain why IT-based systems are important to drug-trafficking organizations' illicit operations.

Learning Activity Research the military term *psyops* and read about what it is and how it is used in warfare—both historically and in a contemporary setting. Then, using these examples as an ideas springboard, brainstorm parallel ideas that could be used in cyberspace; particularly, how disinformation could be used to undermine the confidence of drug traffickers' personnel, partners, and/or third-party supporters in the legitimate world. List potential ethical implications of such a campaign and how, perhaps using legal advisors, you could keep the psycop within the restraints expected in law.

References

Australian Army (1993) The fundamentals of land warfare. Department of Defence, Canberra
Australian Army (2002) The fundamentals of land warfare. Defence Publishing Service, Canberra
Australian Crime Commission (2005) Illicit Drug Data Report, 2003–04. Commonwealth of Australia, Canberra
Australian Criminal Intelligence Commission (2015) Illicit Drug Data Report, 2014–15. Commonwealth Government, Canberra
Bartlett J (2014) The dark net: inside the digital underworld. William Heinemann, London
Bevan D (1991) NCA to reveal Italian influence, Adelaide advertiser, 15 July
Booth M (1996) Opium: a history. Simon and Schuster, Ltd., London
Boyd N, Lowman J (1991) The politics of prostitution and drug control. In: Stenson K, Cowell D (eds) The politics of crime control. Sage Publications, London
Colby W, Forbath P (1978) Honorable men: my life in the CIA. Hutchinson, London
Cooper HHA (2009) Ethics and assassination. J Appl Sec Res 4(3):224–244

DeForest O, Chanoff D (1990) Slow burn: the rise and fall of American intelligence in Vietnam. Simon and Schuster, New York

Dunnigan JF (1996) Digital soldiers: the evolution of high-tech weaponry and tomorrow's battlefield. St. Martin's Press, New York

Fleetwood J (2014) Drug mules: women in the international cocaine trade. Palgrave Macmillan, London

Global Commission on Drug Policy (2011) War on drugs. Global Commission on Drug Policy, Geneva

Helms R, with Hood W (2003) A look over my shoulder: a life in the central intelligence agency. Random House, New York

Hughes DP (2018) Archer's stakes in cyber space: methods to analyze force advantage. In: Prunckun H (ed) Cyber weaponry: issues and implications of digital arms. Dordrecht, Springer

Jordan DC (1999) Dirty Money and Democracies. University of Oklahoma Press, Norman

Katz SM (1990) Guards without frontiers: Israel's war against terrorism. Arms and Armour, London

Kerin J (2002) Vengeance will be swift, says Sharon, The Weekend Australian, 30 November–1 December

Knox J, Gray DH (2014) The national and international threat of drug trafficking organizations. Glob Secur Stud 5(3)

Library of Congress, Federal Research Division (2002) A global overview of narcotics-funded terrorist and other extremist groups. Federal Research Division, Washington, DC

Lind WS (2004) Understanding fourth generation war. Mil Rev 84(5):15–17

Malbry DJ (1994) The role of the military. In: Perl RF (ed) Drugs and foreign policy: a critical review. Westview Press, Boulder

McCoy AW (1980) Drug traffic: narcotics and organized crime in Australia. Harper and Row, Sydney

McCoy AW (1991) The politics of heroin. Lawrence Hill Books, Brooklyn

Meinel C (2002) The happy hacker: a guide to (mostly) harmless computer hacking, 4th edn. American Eagle Publications, Inc., Sun City West

Meinel C (2003) Uberhacker II: more ways to break into a computer. Loompanics Unlimited, Port Townsend

Moore R (1969) The French connection: the world's most crucial narcotics investigation. Little, Brown and Company, Boston

Natarajan M, Zanella M, Yu C (2015) Classifying the variety of drug trafficking organizations. J Drug Issues 45(4):409

Naylor RT (2004) Hot money and the politics of debt, 3rd edn. McGill-Queen's University Press, Montreal

Oberweis T, Petrocelli M (2015) Drug enforcement administration. In: The encyclopedia of crime and punishment. Wiley, New York

Pratt SF (2011) Crossing off the names: the logic of military assassination. J Small Wars Insurg 26 (1):3–34

Prunckun H (2005) Information warfare: can the concept be applied to the war-on-drugs? Aust Def Force J 169:52–62

Prunckun H (2007) Could the war-on-drugs be fought using intelligence-led cyber soldiers? J Aust Inst Prof Intell Off 15(1):2–13

Prunckun H (2012) Assassination: targeted killing of terrorists. In: Shanty F (ed) Counterterrorism: from the cold war to the war on terror, vol 1. Praeger, Santa Barbara, pp 359–362

Prunckun H (2015) How to undertake surveillance and reconnaissance. Pen & Sword Books, South Yorkshire

Prunckun H (2016) The paradox of fiction and terrorism's overshadowing of organised crime as a law enforcement target. Salus J 4(2):62–81

Rand Corporation (1995) Information warfare: a two-edged sword. Rand Review 19:2. www.rand.org/publications/randreview/issues/RRR.fall95.cyber/infor_war.html. Accessed 10 Dec 2004

Rivers G (1985) The specialist: revelations of a counterterrorist. Stein and Day, Briarcliff Manor

Rose-Ackerman S, Palifka B (2016) Corruption and government: causes, consequences, and reform. Cambridge University Press, New York

Stafford D (2000) Secret agent: the true story of the special operations executive. BBC Worldwide Ltd., London

Stark JT (1990) Selective assassination as an instrument of National Policy. Loompanics Unlimited, Port Townsend

Sun Tzu (1963) The art of war (trans: Griffith SB). Oxford and Clarendon Press, London

United Nations (2016) World drug report, 2016. Office of Drugs and Crime, Vienna

United Nations, General Assembly Special Session (2016) Outcome document of the 2016 United Nations general assembly special session on the world drug problem: our joint commitment to effectively addressing and countering the world drug problem. United Nations Office on Drugs and Crime, New York

United Nations Office on Drugs and Crime (2011) Estimating illicit financial flows resulting from drug trafficking and other transnational organized crimes. United Nations, Vienna

United States, Department of State (2016) International narcotic control strategy report, vol 1. Bureau for International Narcotic and Law Enforcement Affairs, Washington, DC

United States, National Commission on Terrorist Attacks Upon the United States (2004) 9/11 commission report: final report of the national commission on terrorist attacks upon the United States. US Government Printing Office, Washington, DC

UNODC (2016) World drug report, 2016. United Nations, New York

Wardlaw G, McDowell D, Schmidt J (1991) Australia's illegal drug problem: a strategic intelligence assessment. Attorney-General's Department, Canberra

Weatherburn D, Lind B (1999) Heroin harm minimisation: do we really have to choose between law enforcement and treatment? Crime and Justice Bulletin, Number 46, New South Wales Bureau of Crime Statistics and Research, Sydney

Wigginton M, Jensen C, Vinson J, Graves M (2014) Kidnapping for ransom and social learning theory. Homel Sec Rev 8(2):179–194

Wyler LS (2008) Weak and falling states: evolving security threats and US policy. Congressional Research Service, Washington, DC

Zetter K (2015) Countdown to zero day: Stuxnet and the launch of the World's first digital weapon. Broadway Books, New York

Chapter 12
Autonomous Weapons: Terminator-Esque Software Design

Seumas Miller

12.1 Introduction

Autonomous robots can perform many tasks for more efficiently than humans, for instance, tasks performed in factory assembly lines, auto-pilots, driverless cars; moreover, they can perform tasks dangerous for humans to perform, say, defuse bombs. However, autonomous robots can also be weaponized, and in a manner, such that the robots control their targets (and, possibly, the selection of their weapons). As Sarah Connor, the character in the 1984 Hollywood movie, *The Terminator*, discovered, autonomous weapons are utterly fearless; they don't have emotions, and care nothing for life over death. Further, by virtue of developments in artificial intelligence programming, robots will have superior calculative and memory capacity—this is not just a fantasy limited to the fictitious company, Cyberdyne Systems.

New and emerging (so-called) autonomous robotic weapons can replace some military roles performed by humans and enhance others.[1] Consider, for example, the Samsung stationary robot that functions as a sentry in the demilitarized zone between North and South Korea. Once programmed and activated, it has the capability to identify, track and fire its machine guns at human targets without the further intervention of a human operator. Although, not humanoid, they are "Terminators."

---

[1]For an earlier account of these issues, see Seumas Miller "Robopocolypse?: Autonomous Weapons, Military Necessity and Collective Moral Responsibility" in (ed.) Jai Galliott and M Lotze, *Super Soldiers: The Ethical, Legal and Social Implications* (Ashgate 2015), pp. 153–166.

S. Miller (✉)
Australian Graduate School of Policing and Security, Charles Sturt University, Canberra, Australia

Delft University of Technology and the University of Oxford, Delft, The Netherlands
e-mail: semiller@csu.edu.au

© Springer International Publishing AG, part of Springer Nature 2018
H. Prunckun (ed.), *Cyber Weaponry*, Advanced Sciences and Technologies for Security Applications, https://doi.org/10.1007/978-3-319-74107-9_12

Fig. 12.1 An MQ-1 Predator on its return to Bagram Air Base, Afghanistan, after an Operation Enduring Freedom mission. Predators have been used for armed interdiction, as well as intelligence, surveillance, and reconnaissance (Photograph by U.S. Air Force Master Sgt. Demetrius Lester and courtesy of the U.S. Air Force)

Predator drones are used in Afghanistan and the tribal areas of Pakistan to kill suspected terrorists. While the ones currently in use are not autonomous weapons they could be given this capability in which case, once programmed and activated, they could track, identify and destroy human and other targets without the further intervention of a human operator. Additionally, more advanced autonomous weapons systems, including robotic devices, are being planned.

In this chapter, the moral implications of autonomous robotic weapons are explored. This will be done by addressing several questions. Firstly, in what sense are such weapons really autonomous? Secondly, do such weapons necessarily compromise the moral responsibility of their human designers, computer programmers and/or operators and, if so, in what manner and to what extent? Finally, should certain forms of autonomous weapons be prohibited? (Fig. 12.1)

12.2 Autonomous Weapons

Autonomous weapons are weapons system which, once programed and activated by a human operator, can—and, if used, do in fact—identify, track and deliver lethal force without further intervention by a human operator. By *programmed* I mean, at least, that the individual target, or type of target, has been selected and coded into the weapon system. By *activated* it is meant, at least, that the process culminating in the already programmed weapon delivering lethal force has been initiated. This weaponry includes weapons used in non-targeted killing, such as autonomous anti-aircraft weapons systems used against multiple attacking aircraft or, more futuristically, against swarm technology (for example, multiple lethal miniature attack drones operating as a swarm so as to inhibit effective defensive measures); and ones used or, at least, capable of being used in targeted killing (for example, a predator drone with face-recognition technology and no human operator to confirm a match).

We need to distinguish between what are termed the *human in-the-loop, human on-the-loop,* and *human out-of-the-loop* weaponry. It is only human out-of-the-loop weapons that are autonomous in the required sense. In the case of human-in-the-loop weapons the final delivery of lethal force (for example, by a Predator drone), cannot be done without the decision to do so by the human operator. In the case of human on-the-loop weapons, the final delivery of lethal force can be done without the decision to do so by the human operator; however, the human operator can override the weapon system's triggering mechanism. In the case of human out-of-the-loop weapons, the human operator cannot override the weapon system's triggering mechanism; so, once the weapon system is programmed and activated there is, and cannot be, any further human intervention.

The lethal use of a human-in-the-loop weapon is a standard case of killing by a human combatant and, as such, is presumably, at least in principle, morally permissible. Moreover, other things being equal, the combatant is morally responsible for the killing. The lethal use of a human-on-the-loop weapon is also in principle morally permissible. Also, the human operator is, perhaps jointly with others (such as his or her commander—see discussion below on collective responsibility as joint responsibility), morally responsible, at least in principle, for the use of lethal force and its foreseeable consequences. However, these two propositions concerning human on-the-loop weaponry rely on the following assumptions:

(1) The weapon system is programmed and activated by its human operator and either;
(2) (a) On any and all occasions of use, the delivery of lethal force can be overridden by the human operator; and, (b) this operator has sufficient time and sufficient information to make a morally informed, reasonably reliable judgement whether or not to deliver lethal force or;
(3) (a) On any one occasion of use, but not all, occasions of use, the final delivery of lethal force can be overridden by the human operator; and, (b) there is no moral requirement for a morally informed, reasonably reliable judgement on each and every occasion of the final delivery of force.

A scenario illustrating (3)(b) might be an anti-aircraft weapons system being used on a naval vessel under attack from a squadron of manned aircraft in a theatre of war at sea in which there are no civilians present.

There are various other possible such scenarios. Consider a scenario in which there is a single attacker on a single occasion in which there is insufficient time for a reasonably reliable, morally informed judgment. Such scenarios might include ones involving a kamikaze pilot or suicide bomber. If autonomous weapons were to be morally permissible the following conditions at least would need to be met: (i) prior clear-cut criteria for identification/delivery of lethal force to be designed-into the weapon and used only in narrowly circumscribed circumstances; (ii) prior morally informed judgment regarding criteria and circumstances, and; (iii) ability of operator to override system. Here, there is also the implicit assumption that the weapon system can be switched off, as is not the case with, for instance, biological agents released by a bioweapon.

What of human out-of-the-loop weapons, i.e. autonomous weapons? These are weapons systems that once programmed and activated can identify, track and deliver lethal force without further intervention by human operator. They might be used for non-targeted killing in which case there is no uniquely identified individual target such as in the above described cases of incoming aircraft and swarm technology. Alternatively, they might be used for targeted killing. An example of this would be a Predator drone with face-recognition technology and no human operator to confirm match. However, the crucial point to be made here is that there is no human on-the-loop to intervene once the weapons system has been programmed and activated. Three questions now arise. Firstly, are these weapons systems autonomous in the full-blooded sense of moral autonomy in common use in relation to many, if not most, freely performed, morally informed human actions? (They are "morally informed" because taking someone's life is a morally significant action and, therefore, the person taking this life ought to be making a morally informed decision.) Secondly, are humans fully morally responsible for the killings done by autonomous weapons or is there a so-called responsibility gap? Thirdly, should such weapons be prohibited? Let us begin by getting a better understanding of the notion of moral autonomy.

12.3 Moral Autonomy

In respect of the notion of an autonomous agent, whether human, Martian or otherwise, two sets of distinctions need to be kept in mind.[2] The first is between rationality and morality. An autonomous agent is a rational agent. However, arguably, being rational is not a sufficient condition for autonomy. Rather an autonomous agent needs also to be a moral agent.

The second distinction pertains to sources of potential domination. An autonomous agent is one whose decisions are not externally imposed; he or she is not dominated by external forces or other persons. Nevertheless, an autonomous person is also possessed of self-mastery; he or she is not dominated by internal forces, for instance, addictions.

Evidently, an autonomous person is both rational and moral. So, what is it to be a rational person? Evidently a rational person is possessed of a continuing, rationally integrated structure of mental attitudes, such as intentions, beliefs and desires. Moreover,

---

[2]Stanley Benn, *A Theory of Freedom* (Cambridge: Cambridge University Press, 1988) and Seumas Miller "Individual Autonomy and Sociality" in (ed.) F Schmitt *Socialising Metaphysics: Nature of Social Reality* (Lanham: Rowman & Littlefield, 2003), pp.269–300.

the attitudes in question, notably beliefs, are evidence-based. In short, the mental attitudes of a rational person are both rationally coherent and based on evidence.

Second, a rational person's actions and dispositions to action are based on such coherent and evidence-based attitudes. So their actions are rational in the light of their mental attitudes (which are themselves rational).

Third, for a person's attitudes and actions to be rational in this sense the person must surely engage in both practical (action-oriented) and theoretical (knowledge-oriented) reasoning that makes use of objectively valid procedures; such as deriving valid conclusions from evidence and selecting means on the basis of their efficacy in respect of relevant ends, and so on.

Fourth, the concept of a rational person or being needs to be relativized to empirical circumstances; including inherent properties of the kind of rational beings in question. And, it is possible that there are rational persons who are not human beings, for example Martians or creatures from a far-flung and yet undiscovered planet. If so, then such non-human rational beings might not have all the inherent properties that human beings have. For example, human beings, but not necessarily other rational beings, have emotions, are highly social, live for a finite number of years, and so on. Naturally, a rational being will act rationally in the light of such additional inherent properties (as well as contingent external features of their environment).

Fifth, a rational being can engage in rational scrutiny of their extant higher order attitudes, such as beliefs about their own beliefs. If, for example, a rational person is engaged in self-deception (and, as a consequence, has false beliefs about one's own motives) then, at least in principle, such a person can come to recognize and eliminate this self-deception.

Sixth, evidently, rationality in the sense in question admits of degrees; some people, for example, are better than others at drawing true conclusions from the evidence presented to them.

Seventh, rational beings or, at least, fully rational beings are able to choose their ultimate ends, i.e. those ends that are not simply the means to further ends. Perhaps one's own personal happiness is an ultimate end chosen by many in individualistic social groups, although human beings can choose different ultimate ends, e.g. high social status, great political power, justice for the poor and downtrodden, the survival of future generations threatened by climate change etc. If it is argued that the ability to choose ultimate ends is not a necessary condition for rationality it can be replied that it is certainly a necessary condition for autonomy. For if a creature did not choose its ultimate ends then those ends must surely have been brought about either by the intervention of some other creature, or by some inanimate causal process. Either way, the autonomy of the creature in question is compromised.

Even if it is held that robots could, at least in principle, be possessed of the first six features of rational agency, it is not the case that they could be possessed of the seventh feature; robots cannot choose their ultimate ends since these are programmed, or otherwise designed, into them.

So, much for rationality; what of morality? Someone can be rational, up to a point, without necessarily being moral. Consider, for example, a highly intelligent psychopath. Such a person may well pursue their goals efficiently and effectively and make sophisticated evidence-based judgments in doing so. Accordingly, psychopaths can be highly rational. However, psychopaths do not care about other people and are happy to do them great harm if it suits. Likewise, psychopaths, even if they recognise in some sense the constraints of morality and pay lip-service to them, do not feel the moral force of moral principles and ends. In short, psychopaths can be rational and yet are not moral agents. Therefore, rationality and morality seem to be different, albeit related, concepts.

To return to an earlier point, perhaps rationality is relativised to inherent properties. If so, since psychopaths lack some of the inherent properties of other human beings; for instance, concern for the welfare of others, a moral sense, their rationality is more restrictive and, to this extent, they are less rational than their fellow human moral agents. If this is correct then arguably psychopaths are not simply non-moral or less than fully moral, they are also less than fully rational. At any rate, roughly speaking, a human moral agent is a rational agent who is disposed to make true judgments and valid inferences in relation to the moral worth of human actions, principles, ends, and so on, and to act on those judgments and inferences where appropriate. More generally, moral agents are rational agents who are sensitive to moral properties in the sense that they recognise moral properties as such and respond appropriately to them. While robots are sensitive to physical properties, e.g. heat and light, they are not sensitive to moral properties. Accordingly, robots are not moral agents.

Here it is worth noting the distinction between non-rational and irrational agents, and between non-moral and immoral agents. A non-rational agent *cannot* make judgments or inferences. An irrational agent has the capacity to make such judgments and inferences, but has some significant deficit in their rationality, and thus makes a significant number of false judgments and/or invalid inferences, or often fails to act on the results of their practical reasoning. Similarly, a non-moral agent lacks the capacity to make moral judgments and act on them; an immoral agent, by contrast, is merely (significantly) deficient in their moral judgment-making, or often fails to act on their correct moral judgments. That said, sometimes it is not clear whether we should think of a person as non-moral (or non-rational) or as immoral (or irrational).

Given that a human life involves sensitivity to moral properties and, relatedly, responsiveness to moral reasons, an autonomous human being will be both rational and moral. Understood in the way outlined here, rationality and morality imply independence and self-mastery. Someone who is dominated by the overriding desire to please an authority figure, and who only acts in accordance with that aim, will not count as autonomous. Similarly, the autonomous human being must be able not only to make good judgments about what to believe and how to act, they must be capable of acting in conformity with those judgments. A drug addict, for example, may know perfectly well that it is unwise to keep injecting drugs, but find themselves unable to act on that knowledge; their lack of self-mastery in respect of their desire for the drug means that they lack autonomy, at least in this area of their life.

To say that an autonomous human being is independent and possesses self-mastery, does not, of course, imply that autonomy is incompatible with all forms of constraint. The autonomous person cannot infringe the laws of physics or the laws of logic. The fact that a human agent cannot hope to fly when they jump off a tall building, or cannot both walk and not walk at the same time, does not undermine their autonomy. Further, an autonomous person can choose to comply with the law without comprising their autonomy. Specifically, when human beings choose to comply with laws because these laws embody their moral beliefs, principles and ends, then they may well be acting autonomously; the laws in question being in effect self-imposed.

In light of the above we can now see that autonomous human beings are ones who decide for themselves what is important and valuable to them, and possess the capacity to make reason-based choices on the basis of recognising, assessing and responding to relevant considerations, including non-moral facts, moral principles and ultimate moral ends. When we call an act autonomous, we mean that it is something done by such a person, on the basis of such a response. As we have seen, robots are not autonomous beings in this sense.

Moreover we can also now see that autonomy admits of degree and is in part constituted by various moral features, including freedom of thought and action None of us, presumably, is completely autonomous, since we all fall short of full rationality, perfect morality, absolute self-mastery and so on. And since these things vary from person to person, some people are more autonomous than others. Moreover, someone might be autonomous in one area of their life, but not another. Nevertheless, we achieve the status of an autonomous human being – someone who is entitled to decide for themselves how they wish to live – when we are sufficiently autonomous. Further, autonomy can be undermined if one or more of its constitutive moral features are compromised, e.g. if a person is imprisoned.

There is a presumption that all human adults, at least, have achieved that status. This presumption is defeasible. We may be able to show that a person is so deficient in various conditions of autonomy, such as rationality or self-mastery, that they should not be counted as autonomous, and that others might be justified in making decisions on their behalf. But, absent such defeat, we all possess the status of autonomous human beings. By contrast, there is no such presumption to be defeated in the case of robots.

12.4 Moral Responsibility and Autonomous Weapons

Let us now return to *so-called* autonomous weapons—that is human out-of-the-loop weapons.[3] We have seen that autonomous robots and, therefore, autonomous weapons are not autonomous in the sense in which human beings are since they do not choose their ultimate ends and are not sensitive to moral properties. However,

---

[3]This section is an abridged version of Seumas Miller Chap. 10 in his *Shooting to Kill: The Ethics of Military and Police Use of Military Force* (Oxford University Press, 2016).

the question that now arises concerns the moral responsibility for killings done by autonomous weapons. Specifically, do they involve a responsibility gap such that their human programmers and operators are not morally responsible or, at least, not fully morally responsible for the killings done by the use of these weapons?[4]

Consider the following scenario, which, I contend, is analogous to the use of human out-of-the-loop weaponry. There is a villain who has trained his dogs to kill on his command and an innocent victim on the run from the villain. The villain gives the scent of the victim to the killer-dogs by way of an item of the victim's clothing and then commands the dogs to kill. The killer-dogs pursue the victim deep into the forest and now the villain is unable to intervene. The killer-dogs kill the victim. The villain is legally and morally responsible for murder. However, the killer-dogs are not, albeit they may need to be destroyed on the grounds of the risk they pose to human life. So, the villain is morally responsible for murdering the victim, notwithstanding the indirect nature of the causal chain from the villain to the dead victim; the chain is indirect since it crucially depends on the killer-dogs doing the actual physical killing. Moreover, the villain would also have been legally and morally responsible for the killing if the 'scent' was generic and, therefore, carried by a whole class of potential victims, and if the dogs had killed one of these. In this second version of the scenario, the villain does not intend to kill a uniquely identifiable individual,[5] but rather one (or perhaps multiple) members of a class of individuals.[6]

By analogy, human out-of-the-loop weapons—*killer-robots*—are not morally responsible for any killings they cause.[7] Consider the case of a human in-the-loop or human-on-the-loop weapon. Assume that the programmer/activator of the weapon and the operator of the weapon at the point of delivery are two different human agents. If so, then other things being equal they are jointly (that is, collectively) morally responsible for the killing done by the weapon (whether it be of a uniquely identified individual or an individual qua member of a class).[8] No-one thinks the weapon is morally or other than causally responsible for the killing. Now assume this weapon is converted to a human out-of-the-loop weapon by the human programmer-activator. Surely this human programmer-activator now has full individual moral responsibility for the killing, as the villain does in (both versions of) our

---

[4]Ronald Arkin ("The Case for Ethical Autonomy in Unmanned Systems" *Journal of Military Ethics* vol. 9 2010 pp. 332–341) has argued in favour of the use of such weapons.

[5]It is not a targeted killing.

[6]Further, the villain is legally and morally responsible for foreseeable but unintended killing done by the killer-dogs in the forest, if they had happened upon one of the birdwatchers well-known to frequent the forest and mistakenly killed him instead of the intended victim. (Perhaps the birdwatcher carried the scent of birds often attacked by the killer-dogs.)

[7]See R. Sparrow "Killer Robots" *Journal of Applied Philosophy* vol. 24 2007 pp. 63–77. For criticisms see Uwe Steinhoff "Killing them safely: Extreme asymmetry and its discontents" in B. J. Strawser (ed.) *Killing by Remote Control: The Ethics of an Unmanned Military* (Oxford: Oxford University Press, 2013).

[8]Each is fully morally responsible; not all cases of collective moral responsibility involve a distribution of the quantum (so-to-speak) of responsibility.

killer-dog scenario. To be sure there is no human intervention in the causal process after programming-activation. But the weapon has not been magically transformed from an entity only with causal responsibility to one which now has moral or other than causal responsibility for the killing.

It might be argued that the analogy does not work because killer-dogs are unlike killer-robots in the relevant respects. Certainly, dogs are minded creatures whereas computers are not; dogs have some degree of consciousness and can experience, for example, pain. However, this difference would not favor ascribing moral responsibility to computers rather than dogs; rather, if anything, the reverse is true.

Clearly, computers do not have consciousness, cannot experience pain or pleasure, do not care about anyone or anything (including themselves) and, as we saw above, do not choose their ultimate ends and, more specifically, cannot recognize moral properties, such as courage, moral innocence, moral responsibility, sympathy or justice. Therefore, they cannot act for the sake of principles or ends understood as moral in character, such as the principle of discrimination.

Given the apparent non-reducibility of moral concepts and properties to non-moral ones and, specifically, physical ones,[9] at best computers can be programmed to comply with some non-moral proxy for moral requirements.[10] For example, "Do not intentionally kill morally innocent human beings" might be rendered as "Do not fire at bipeds if they are not carrying a weapon or they are not wearing a uniform of the following description." However, here as elsewhere, the problem for such non-moral proxies for moral properties is that when they diverge from moral properties, as they inevitably will in some circumstances, the wrong person will be killed or not killed (as the case may be)—as an example, the innocent civilian wearing camouflage clothing to escape detection by combatants on either side and carrying a weapon for personal protection is killed while the female terrorist concealing a bomb under her dress is not.

Notwithstanding the above, some have insisted that robots are minded agents; after all, it is argued, they can detect and respond to features of their environment and in many cases they have impressive storage/retrieval and calculative capacities. However, this argument relies essentially on two moves that should be resisted and are, in any case, highly controversial. Firstly, rational human thought, notably rational decisions and judgments, are down-graded to the status of mere causally connected states or causal roles, for example via functionalist theories of mental states. Secondly, and simultaneously, the workings of computers are upgraded to the status of mental states, for example via the same functionalist theories of mental states. For reasons of space I cannot here pursue this issue further. Rather I simply note that this simultaneous down-grade/up-grade faces prodigious problems when it comes to the ascription of autonomous agency. For one thing, autonomous agency

---

[9]The physical properties in question would not only be detectable in the environment but also be able to be subjected to various formal processes of quantification and so on.

[10]See, for instance, Arkin "The Case for Ethical Autonomy in Unmanned Systems," op. cit. and the reply in Miller *Shooting to Kill,* Chap. 10, op. cit.

involves the capacity for non-algorithmic inferential thinking, for example the generation of novel ideas. For another, to reiterate, computers do not choose their own ultimate ends. At best, they can select between different means to the ends programmed into them. Accordingly, they are not autonomous agents, even non-moral ones. So, while killer robots are morally problematic this is not for the reason that they are autonomous agents in their own right but this brings us to our third and final question.

12.5   Prohibition of Autonomous Weapons

Our final question concerns the prohibition of autonomous weapons in the sense of human out-of-the-loop weapons. This question should be seen in the light of our conclusions that such weapons are not morally sensitive agents and their use does not involve a responsibility gap. Rather there are multiple human actors implicated in the use of autonomous weapons: there is collective moral responsibility in the sense of joint individual moral responsibility.[11] The members of the design team are collectively—that is, jointly—morally responsible for providing the means to harm (the weapon). The political and military leaders and those who follow their orders are collectively (i.e. jointly), responsible for these weapons being used against a certain group/individual. Take, for example, intelligence personnel who are responsible for providing the means to identify targets, and the operators who are responsible for its use on a given occasion since they programmed/activated the weapons system. Moreover, all the above individuals are collectively—in the sense of jointly—morally responsible for the deaths resulting from the use of the weapon, but they are responsible to varying degrees and in different ways; for instance, some provided the means (designed the weapon), others gave the order to kill a given individual, still others pulled the trigger, etc. These varying degrees and varying ways are reflected in the different but overlapping collective end content of their cooperative or joint activity. Thus, a designer has the collective end to kill some combatants in some war (this being the purpose of his design-work); a military leader has the collective end (in issuing orders to subordinates) to kill enemy combatants in this theatre of war; and an operator the collective end to kill enemy combatants A, B & C, here and now.

It is important to note that each contributor to such a joint lethal action is individually morally responsible for his/her own individual action contribution—an individual weapons operator who chose to deliver lethal force on some occasion or perhaps, in the case of an on-the-loop weapon, not to override the delivery of lethal force by the weapon on this occasion. This is consistent with there being collective, that is, joint, moral responsibility for the outcome—the death of an enemy combatant, the death of innocent civilians.

---

[11]Seumas Miller "Collective Moral Responsibility: An Individualist Account," in Peter A. French (ed), *Midwest Studies in Philosophy*, vol. XXX, 2006, pp.176–193

It is also important to note the problem of accountability that arises for morally unacceptable outcomes involving "many hands", that is, joint action, and indirect causal chains. Consider, for example, an out-of-the-loop weapon system that kills an innocent civilian rather than a terrorist because of mistaken identity and the absence of an override function when the mistaken identity is discovered at the last minute. The response to this accountability problem should be to design-in institutional accountability. Thus, in our example the weapons designers ought to be held jointly institutionally and, therefore, jointly morally responsible for failing to design-in an override function, that is, for failing to ensure the safety of the weapon system; likewise, the intelligence personnel ought to be held jointly institutionally and, therefore, jointly morally responsible for the mistaken identity. Analogous points can be made with respect to the political and military leaders and the operators.

As we have seen, human-*out*-of-the-loop weapons can be designed to have an override function and an on/off switch controlled by a human operator. Moreover, in the light of our above example and like cases, in general autonomous weapons ought to have an override function and on/off switch. Indeed, to fail to do so would be tantamount to an abnegation of moral responsibility. However, against this it might be argued that there are *some* situations in which there ought not to be a human on-the-loop (or in-the-loop).

Let us consider some candidate situations involving human *out*-of-the-loop weapons that might be thought not to require a human in or on the loop.

(1) Situations in which the selection of targets and delivery of force cannot in practice be overridden on all occasions and in which there is no requirement for a context dependent, morally informed judgement on all occasions e.g. there is insufficient time to make the decision to repulse an imminent attack from incoming manned aircraft and there is no need to do so since the aircraft in a theatre of war are clearly identifiable as enemy aircraft.

(2) Situations in which there is a need only for a computer-based mechanical application of a clear-cut procedure (e.g. deliver lethal force), under precisely specified input conditions (e.g. identified as an enemy submarine by virtue of its design etc.) in which there is no prospect of collateral damage (e.g. in open seas in the Arctic).

However, even in these cases it is difficult to see why there would be an objection to having a human on the loop (as distinct from in the loop) especially since there might still be a need for a human on the loop to accommodate the problems arising from false information or unusual contingencies. For instance, the 'enemy' aircraft or submarines in question might turn out to be ones captured and operated by members of one's own forces. Alternatively, one's own aircraft and submarines might now be under the control of the enemy (e.g. via a sophisticated process of computer hacking) and, therefore, should be fired upon.

A further argument in favour of autonomous weapons concerns human emotion. It is argued that machines in conditions of war are superior to humans by virtue of not having emotions since stress/emotions lead to error. Against this it can be pointed out that human emotions inform moral judgment and moral judgment is called for in war. For instance, the duty of care with respect to innocent civilians relies on the emotion of caring; a property not possessed by robots. Moreover, human stress/emotions can be controlled to a considerable extent, e.g. combatants should not be combatants if not appropriately selected/trained, and the influence of stressors can be reduced, e.g. by requiring some decisions to be made by personnel at some distance from the action.

The upshot of this discussion is that human out-of-the-loop weapons are neither necessary nor desirable. Rather autonomous weapons should always have a human on-the-loop (if not in-the-loop). Furthermore, not to do so would be an abnegation of responsibility. Accordingly, autonomous weapons in the sense of human out-of-the-loop weapons should be prohibited.

12.6   Summary

In this chapter, certain aspects of the morality of autonomous weapons has been discussed. Specifically, autonomous weapons have been described and the sense in which such weapons are autonomous specified. Autonomy was defined as it applies to human beings and it has been argued that autonomous weapons are not autonomous in this sense. The claim that there is a responsibility gap in the use of autonomous weapons has been discussed and it has been concluded that in fact there is no such gap. Human beings are fully morally responsible for the killings involving the use of autonomous weapons. Finally, it was suggested that human out-of-the-loop weapons are not desirable, indeed they are inherently morally problematic; as such, they should be prohibited.

Principal Concepts

The principal concepts associated with this chapter are listed below. Demonstrate your understanding of each by writing a short definition or explanation in one or two sentences:

- Autonomous weapons;
- Moral autonomy;
- Human in-the-loop;
- Human on-the-loop;
- Human out-of-the-loop; and
- The responsibility gap.

Study Questions

1. Explain what is meant by a rational being.
2. Describe the seven principles of rational agency.
3. Explain what is meant by moral autonomy.

Learning Activity

In some scholarly circles, it has been argued that human out-of-the-loop autonomous weapons should be prohibited. Reflecting on the discussion in this chapter, debate the reasoning for-and-against such a proposition. In particular, is a blanket band on such weapons warranted? Could ethical safeguards for out-of-the-loop weapons be developed; or is the issue so problematic that it is not worth pursuing from a policy point of view?

Chapter 13
Warfare of the Future

Sara M. Smyth

13.1 Introduction

The then-Republican Presidential Nominee Donald Trump remarked during a campaign speech in October 2016 at a Retired American Warriors town hall in Virginia that:

> This is the warfare of the future. America's dominance in this arena must be unquestioned, and today it's totally questioned (Newman 2016).

He went on to tell the room full of veterans that, "[a]s a deterrent against attacks on our critical resources the United States must possess...the unquestioned capacity to launch crippling cyber counter attacks...I mean crippling. *Crippling* (Swoyer 2016)."

President Trump's remarks indicate that the wars of the future will be fought online. At the same time, they echo the hawkish rhetoric of "massive retaliation" to deter Soviet aggression in the Cold War era. They suggest that the Trump administration could be preparing for a cyber arms race, or worse—another Cold War (Newman 2016). This policy approach should leave us both concerned and confused. The rationale behind it is outdated and, more importantly, virtual wars fought to achieve virtual victories are likely to be unworkable and even self-destructive in the long-term (Ignatieff 2000).

13.2 Background

Not long ago, only a few very powerful states could contemplate crippling their rivals with catastrophic attacks. Now, for the first time in history, just about anyone can perpetrate attacks against the United States, or any other nation (Wittes and

S. M. Smyth (✉)
La Trobe University Law School, Melbourne, Australia
e-mail: s.smyth@latrobe.edu.au

© Springer International Publishing AG, part of Springer Nature 2018
H. Prunckun (ed.), *Cyber Weaponry*, Advanced Sciences and Technologies for
Security Applications, https://doi.org/10.1007/978-3-319-74107-9_13

Blum 2015: 24). This reality—which mainly owes itself to widespread Internet penetration and diminishing technology prices through the world—has made us increasingly vulnerable to exploitation and attack from almost anyone, anywhere, at any time. And, as technologies evolve, this situation is likely to worsen.

This means that any military advantage that currently exists in the cybersphere will be gradually diminished, driving a relentless effort on the part of American government, intelligence, and military communities to sustain any sort of workable competitive advantage (Ignatieff 2000: 211). Besides, even if virtual victories can be realized in cyberspace, they are unlikely to produce the same kinds of concrete and lasting results that can be achieved in real-space (Ignatieff 2000: 208). The outcome of cyber conflicts can be expected to be unclear, and they will almost certainly not provide long-term peace and security in either the online or offline worlds.

Of course, the story behind the impending cyber arms race did not begin with the Trump Presidential campaign. Top brass within the Obama administration previously warned that the United States was on the brink of a virtual Pearl Harbour—a devastating cyber-attack that could cripple the nation's power grid, financial sector, and public safety systems, to name a few. In a statement that foreshadowed President Trump's concerns regarding the nation's preparedness for cyber-attacks, the then CIA director Leon Panetta stated in a June 2011 speech that the United States would need to adopt "both defensive measures as well as aggressive measures" to counter those threats (Lee 2011).

Even though the reality behind these assertions has been nowhere near that disastrous—a devastating cyber-attack on US soil has, fortunately, not occurred— the United States has been rapidly increasing its capacity to dominate cyberspace, which it now calls the "fifth domain" of warfare. In 2009, the United States established the Cyber Command, the chief objective of which was to integrate defense operations across the military through its aim to "direct the operations and defense of specified Department of Defense information networks" and conduct offensive operations in cyberspace (Walker, 342). Thus, it should come as no surprise that the US military and intelligence agencies have been using computer networks to spy on foreign adversaries, steal data, and cripple facilities that support critical infrastructure in rival states. And, the US views its success in this realm as significant as victories in the physical world, if not more so (Harris 2015: xxi).

Yet, an important contradiction rests at the heart of American national security policy in this so-called fifth domain. On the one hand, US officials paint a picture of themselves as noble cyber-warriors and talk openly about defending the nation's computer networks from hostile invaders. On the other hand, they secretly use the same approaches to attack and spy on other countries (Harris, xxiii). As much as senior leaders are quick to sound the alarm about potential threats to critical sectors of the American economy, they are also keen to use them against others—the very same sorts of "crippling" attacks that they claim they must take extraordinary and aggressive measures to prevent (Harris 2015: xxi).

This point is not only about cyber-warfare. Not only are conventional military weapons now guided and monitored by computer systems, computers have become weapons themselves (Pool 2013: 299). These tactics are the by-product of an evolution in military affairs that began several decades ago, whose purpose was to make warfare more remote, technological, and less bloody (Ignatieff 2000: 164). Just as governments, including the United States, already target their enemies with lethal forces that allow them to shield their own military personnel from harm—primarily drones—cyberspace is another arena that is being exploited in much the same way. Yet, the notion of victory in cyberspace may be little more than an illusion.

Recall that during the Cold War, two superpowers amassed nuclear weapons that they could neither morally, nor politically justify using. It was also helpful that during this period, almost no one wanted there to be an *actual* nuclear war (Wittes and Blum 2015: 83). The stockpiles of nuclear weapons effectively cancelled each other out, preventing the Soviet Union from launching a nuclear attack against the West—and vice versa—producing a stalemate that rendered each side essentially invulnerable to attack from the other (Ignatieff 2000: 165).

Similarly, today, few people—even those in the upper echelons of the world's most powerful governments—want to experience a devastating cyber-attack. Yet, unlike the Cold War, where the technologies used were exclusively military, those needed for a cyber-attack are now widely disbursed and readily accessible (Wittes and Blum 2015: 37). This means that they can be used by non-state actors on behalf of rogue states, such as to retain plausible deniability with respect to the state's role in the attack, or on behalf of an organized group involved in non-international armed conflict, or a criminal gang (Padmanabhan 2013: 291). In contrast, nuclear weapons were primarily developed in classified settings, in top-secret government laboratories, which maintained exclusive control over the facilities, materials, and expertise (Joy 2000).

But, unlike the physical battlefield where America's adversaries are still largely unable to match its military superiority, the US's monopoly over the technologies of the Internet has been all but lost.[1] More and more states have been creating computer network operations or cyber-command units, including China, India, Russia, Iran, North Korea, South Korea, Israel, the United Kingdom, Germany, and others (Walker 2013: 343). Various sub-state groups have also been engaged in producing and deploying cyber-weapons, and this has made Americans vulnerable to attack.

As for those with the technical means and incentive to exploit weaknesses in networked systems, their power is likely to increase over time. Consider, for example, the fact that it is tremendously difficult to build a conventional weapon of mass destruction, such as a nuclear bomb; and, even if that could be done, only a small number can be built at any one time, and each can be used only once (Lessig

---

[1]The Internet was created in the late-1960s from a project started by the Defense Advanced Research Projects Agency (DARPA), as part of the American military infrastructure, which was part of a larger experiment to connect computers across the United States. The founding engineers created a network built of many nodes, each connected to other nodes, so that it would be possible to use various routes without any degradation in the quality of the transmission. From this modest beginning, the Internet has grown into an enormous global network, with most of the supporting infrastructure in the hands of private commercial entities.

2004). The same is not true in cyberspace where networked armies of widely distributed computer robots, or *bots*, can be employed to repeatedly carry out denial-of-service attacks against all sorts of computerized systems. Similarly, self-replicating threats from malicious software now pose an even greater risk to national security than large-scale weapons of the past. They can easily be duplicated and once this happens, they can fall into the hands of rogue states or criminal groups; and, they can replicate out of control, causing substantial harm to individuals in the physical world (Joy 2000).

Our first response to these threats has been to declare it a *war*. But, there is no connection between the call to cyber-arms and any ongoing or impending war in either kinetic world or in cyberspace (Dinstein 2013: 277). Also, note that very notion of dominating cyberspace as a battlefield conflicts with international law principles governing the use of force. *Jus ad bellum* is the Latin maxim for the law governing when it is permissible to use force within the bounds of the United Nations Charter[2] framework and customary international law.

Article 2(4) of the Charter generally prohibits the use of force by one state "...against the territorial integrity or political independence of any State..." However, the Charter provides for three exceptions to the prohibition on the use of force, each of which is relevant to cyber-attacks from both state and non-state actors (Blank 2013: 411). First, a state may use force with the consent of the host state, such as when a state fighting a rebel group requests assistance from other states (Blank 2013: 411). Second, a state can use force when it has been authorized by the UN Security Council.[3] And, third, a state may use force in accordance with the inherent right of self-defence if it has been the victim of an "armed attack."[4]

Since no international treaty governs cyber-attacks, cyber-warfare can only be considered by analogy—equating it to traditional armed conflict and responding either according to the law of war or domestic criminal law (Carr 2010: 47). In assessing whether a hostile act directed at a state rises to the level of an armed attack sufficient to trigger the right of self-defence under Article 51, the International Court of Justice (ICJ) has said we must consider the scale and effects of the act itself (O'Connell 2012: 201). To date, with the possible limited exception of the *Stuxnet* virus—which caused material damage and disruption to state infrastructure—no incidents of cyber-attack have ever been recognized by the international community as an armed attack (Padmanabhan 2013: 289).

There is also controversy over the question of whether a non-state actor—as opposed to a state—can be the source of an armed attack sufficient to justify the use of force in self-defense (Blank 2013: 413). This raises yet another aspect of the limitation of resorting to cyber-war, which is that the Internet respects no geographical boundaries or barriers. Indeed, cyberspace is a virtual domain over which no

---

[2]United Nations, *Charter of the United Nations*, 24 October 1945 [hereinafter "the Charter"].

[3]United Nations, *Charter of the United Nations*, 24 October 1945, art. 42.

[4]United Nations, *Charter of the United Nations*, 24 October 1945, art. 51.

single state can exercise territorial sovereignty (Buchan 2012: 222). National borders, jurisdictional barriers, citizenship, and the distinction between the domestic and international, all have a diminished relevance in cyberspace, making it difficult to definitively identify the source of an attack—much harder, in fact, than in the physical world via a kinetic attack. This makes it more difficult for a state to use the "unwilling" or "unable" criteria—with respect to the first point in the preceding paragraph—as a basis for self-defence (Blank 2013: 416).

A final related problem is that cyber-attacks are now widely being perpetrated against critical infrastructure, which is mostly privately owned. Critical infrastructure is defined as "systems and assets, whether physical or virtual, so vital to the United States that the incapacity or destruction of such systems and assets would have a debilitating impact on security, national economic security, national public health or safety, or any combination of those matters."[5] The government cannot monitor and defend all these systems on its own. This puts the civilian ownership of these networks on the front lines of any national defense effort.

13.3 Industrial Control Systems—The Holy Grail of Cyber-War

While it is still true that only a handful of powerful states possess the capacity to engage in wholesale cyber-war—namely, the US, China, Israel, Russia and India—there is evidence that some regional powers have been conducting cyber-espionage, as well as cyber-sabotage against industrial facilities and supply chains (Turns 2012: 280). This reflects the growing symmetry between the assailant and the defender with respect to the distribution of defensive capabilities and means of attack (Wittes and Blum 2015: 87). A related point is that many cyber-attacks are now directed toward critical infrastructure. These networks of industrial control systems are highly valuable because they can be used to thwart an enemy's military action, but they are also vital civilian utilities (Preciado 2012: 102).

Indeed, industrial networks are critical to the functioning of modern society. They support large portions of the national critical infrastructure, including power plants, electric grids, nuclear plants, hydro facilities, pipelines, chemical plants, manufacturing, transportation, and oil and gas facilities, as well as major business throughout the world. They also control a variety of important facilities; including power stations, water distribution, oil and gas pipelines, wastewater collection systems,

---

[5]US *Patriot Act*, Pub. L. No. 107–56, 115 Stat. 272 (2001). Note that the following sectors have been identified as critical infrastructure: agriculture, food, water, public health, emergency services, defense industrial base, government, information and telecommunications, energy, transportation, banking and finance, chemical industry and hazardous materials, and postal and shipping.

and many others. Historically, they were kept separate from the Internet. In technical terms, they were *air-gapped*, which means that they were deliberately isolated from corporate IT networks and the Internet, and by doing so, rendered them more secure.

Over the last decade though, industrial networks have been migrating from closed proprietary systems to commercial off-the-shelf technology, like Ethernet, TCP/IP, and Microsoft *Windows* (Byers n.d.: 2). This means that files must be exchanged with the outside world, as modern industry depends on a steady stream of electronic data to operate, including software updates and patches, anti-virus signatures, and so on. What this means is that these networks now contain millions of nodes, which are interconnected with other nodes, spanning corporate networks and the Internet. And, given the high stakes involved, these systems must also be kept running on a continual basis—every day and night of the year—which makes them more difficult to secure.

Keep in mind that deploying malicious code that exploits flaws in the world's software, hardware, and networking equipment, which are usually caused by coding or design errors, is the primary way that attackers gain access to networks (Schneier 2000: 205). There will always be a window of vulnerability—given the time that it takes to develop a new version of a product, or a patch—during which hackers can penetrate these holes (Hahn and Laney-Ferrer 2006: 318). When customers find out about vulnerabilities in their systems, it is up to them to apply patches or undertake other defensive measures, including the use of robust anti-virus software.

Yet, keeping the modern industrial system continuously available makes the deployment of time-honoured IT security strategies, such as patching, problematic. A company's systems administrators would need to constantly watch for and download updates, and make sure they are applied across hundreds or even thousands of computers in a single plant (Harris 2014: 99). And, corporate IT security teams may be unaware that they need to install an update or patch because the vendor may not have informed them, or they may simply have overlooked the information. Even if it were possible to isolate an ICS from the outside world, insiders still pose a threat—the human element. For example, an insider can transfer malicious files from a USB key, or an infected laptop, directly onto the plant's network. This is exactly what is reported to have happened during the *Stuxnet* attack, which was the first advanced persistent threat to focus on industry.

Stuxnet's notoriety drew the attention of the world to the vulnerability of industrial systems and devices. Before discussing this attack in more detail, several important features are worth noting: (1) it was an attack against the equipment the computers controlled, not the systems themselves; (2) it was a sophisticated nation-state attack and yet it was at least partly executed by a knowledgeable insider; and, (3) for a long while, it was not apparent to anyone that this was a cyber-attack—in fact, the virus quietly worked at sabotaging centrifuges at the uranium enrichment plant for about a year before it was discovered (Weiss 2017).

13.4 Warfare of the Future

Stuxnet was discovered in 2010 by a computer security firm in Belarus that was asked to look at why many Iranian computers were crashing and repeatedly rebooting (Zetter 2014, 2016). By that time, *Stuxnet* had been working silently away for year without drawing anyone's attention. Unlike most malware, *Stuxnet* was not trying to steal passwords, identities, or money (Zetter 2014). Instead, it looked for industrial operations using a specific piece of equipment—a Siemens programable logic controller (PLC) used to control equipment on factory floors—into which it was programmed to insert its malicious code. It is noteworthy that PLCs control many of the systems essential for modern life—assembly lines, dams, traffic lights, oil and gas pipelines, water treatment facilities, nuclear power plants, and electric companies (Whigham 2016). However, *Stuxnet* did not attack every system it infected. It was only designed to target uranium enrichment plants in Iran.

Put simply, *Stuxnet* was a sophisticated and carefully constructed cyber-weapon designed to attack Iran's top-secret uranium enrichment plant, Netanz. To get the weapon inside, the attackers infected computers at four other companies connected with the plant. It was also intended to be smuggled into the plant on an infected laptop or USB, that would in turn infect the system, disguise its presence, move through the network changing computer code, and damage the facility's centrifuges without being discovered (Zetter 2014). This is what it did. While we do not know with certainty who was behind this operation, it is widely considered to have been a join operation by the United States and Israeli governments (Kelson et al. 2012). At the same time, *Stuxnet* gave Russia, China, North Korea and others a valuable lesson in how to attack strategically important installations. Not surprisingly, since *Stuxnet* was reported, threats to industrial systems have grown steadily in both quantity and capability.

Just as espionage is an essential element of conventional warfare, spying through computers is an important precursor to taking down critical infrastructure (Harris 2014: xxii). These attacks can be just as powerful as direct attacks against critical systems by improving an attacker's ability to traverse further into an environment simply by learning about it. For example, malware campaigns *Duqu* and *Flame* were both stealthy and persistent attempts to steal valuable information from high-value targets located primarily in Europe and the Middle East (Symantec 2012). *Duqu* was labelled "the precursor to a future *Stuxnet*-like attack," not only because it had many similarities to *Stuxnet*, but because its main goal was to gather intelligence and assets, such as design documents, from industrial control systems facilities and system manufacturers to perform future attacks (Symantec 2011).

Subsequently, on December 23, 2015, a power failure hit the Ivano-Frankivisk region in western Ukraine. Over 20,000 people were plunged into darkness following a sophisticated attack that brought-down the nation's power grid (Lipovsky and

Cherepanov 2016). The attack not only disabled power in eight provinces, but also masked the activity of the attackers, and made it difficult to assess the extent of the outage. Then, in late-2016, we saw the re-emergence of *Shamoon* (W32.Disttrack), the aggressive disk-wiping malware that crippled tens of thousands of computers in the Saudi energy sector in 2012 (Symantec 2016b).

In the earlier wave of attacks, it wiped the disks of some 30,000 computers at Saudi Aramco, and replaced them with an image of a burning US flag in an effort to halt Saudi oil production (Townsend 2016). Four years later, thousands of computers in Saudi Arabia's civil aviation agency, and other Gulf State organizations, lost critical data when they were targeted by *Shamoon* (Pauli 2016). The one difference between the 2012 and 2016 versions of the malware was that the newer variant used a photograph of the body of a 3-year old Syrian refugee drowned in the Mediterranean in 2015 instead of the US flag (Pauli 2016). The consensus is that these were both Iranian state-sponsored attacks, but it is not entirely clear who was behind them.

In 2016, a hacker affiliated with the Iranian government targeted a dam in Rye Brook, New York, about thirty miles north of Manhattan (Kutner 2016). Had he been successful in causing damage to the dam, he could have caused nearby homes and businesses to flood, causing ruinous damage. The incident also shows how vulnerable the infrastructure is to these sorts of attacks, which could be launched against more significant targets pipelines, transit systems and power grids, in the future. In short, what at the end of the Twentieth Century was mostly thought to be sci-fi fantasy, now features as a genuine concern for civil society (Dinstein 2013: 281) (Fig. 13.1).

Fig. 13.1 Nations need to re-thinking traditional principles of in the cyber-sphere (Photograph by Staff Sgt. Kayla Rorick and courtesy of the U.S. Department of Defense)

13.5 Re-thinking Traditional Principles in the Era of Cyber-Warfare

To some extent, the US government is the victim of hackers who are spread around the world, continually probing its networks to insert malicious software that could cause catastrophic damage to its essential services, plunging millions of citizens and entire regions of the country into darkness, and chaos. But, how can America, or any country with an advanced economy, defend itself against so many attackers from so many locations at once? Securing widely-distributed and highly complex computer networks, which are mainly owned and operated by private entities, is an extremely difficult task for any government to do. The logical conclusion is that defending cyberspace requires the participation of the private sector, especially those in the industrial and technology industries.

The US government cannot deal with this issue without the assistance of corporate actors. Industry has long been involved in the manufacture and sale of weapons and other military technologies. Since cyber-wars require weapons, it makes sense to look to the private sector for the procurement of these devices. This is largely what has given rise to the commercial trade in zero-day vulnerabilities, which are software errors that can be exploited by an attacker yet are otherwise unknown to the wider world. They could be considered the ultimate weapon of war because they combine elements of stealth and surprise (Harris 2014: 94). More importantly, they cannot be defended against because there is no software patch, or fix for them; just as there is no protection provided by anti-virus software. *Stuxnet*, it should be noted, is reported to have exploited five zero-day attacks all at once (Wittes and Blum 2015: 86).

The US government is considered the largest purchaser of zero-day exploits, which it is reported to be stockpiling for future use. For example, it has apparently amassed thousands of zero-day exploits for potential use against China alone (Harris 2014: 96). Yet, unlike the Cold War where the world's superpowers were the sole stockpilers of nuclear weapons, there is no reason to think that the US government is amassing these weapons on its own (Harris 2014: 96). Instead, the US is competing with other nations—large and small—as well as sub-state actors, criminal groups, and privateers in a global cyber-arms race (Harris 2014: 99).

Many organizations around the world have been willing to pay substantial sums of money to acquire cyber-weapons that they can be use by themselves or used to defend against someone else's exploit (Wittes and Blum 2015: 86). The corporate vendors of these malicious applications have been eager to sell them to competing clients; pitting government agencies and military units in rival countries against each other (Harris 2014: 97). For its part, the US government could simply disclose all the zero-day vulnerabilities it finds and attempt to end the arms race altogether (Harris 2014: 98). But, it is likely to be trying to avoid the mistake made by the then-US

Secretary of State, Henry L Stimson, when he declared, "Gentlemen do not read each other's mail," then closed-down America's code breaking unit. The devastating consequence of that idealistically-driven decision became evident when the Japanese attacked Pearl Harbor. Perhaps the US sees disclosing zero-day exploits might be as ill-conceived as Stimson's logic, thereby leaving the US vulnerable to the world's cyber outlaws and adversarial states.

Despite the implications for national security, the private sector has largely been reluctant to embrace the government's determination to impose stronger cyber-security measures (Etzioni 2014: 70). Segments of the private sector consider the imposition of tougher cyber-security regulations overly-intrusive. Many consider that the private sector should be left alone to determine how much, and what sort, of cyber-security it needs (Etzioni 2014: 71). Others have suggested that if the government were to establish strict standards for cyber-security in the critical infrastructure sectors, this could impede their flexibility by forcing them to comply with costly, cumbersome, or ineffective measures. In the face of such opposition, the US government has been reluctant to impose stringent cyber-security requirements (Etzioni 2014: 73).

Nonetheless. there are scores of examples of how law enforcement agencies and military and intelligence agencies have negotiated deals with technology companies to insert *backdoors* into their products, and when it comes to the developers of encryption products, to include vulnerabilities for use in its cyber-espionage and sabotage pursuits (Harris 2014: 87). In the US laws have also been passed, such as the *Communications Assistance for Law Enforcement Act* (CALEA), and the *Foreign Intelligence Surveillance Act Amendments Act of 1978* (FAA) which require privately-owned telecommunications companies to facilitate lawful wiretaps—in the case of the former—and, to assist with the collection of data on overseas targets in the case of the latter (Wittes and Blum 2015: 74–78). This trend toward compelling private-sector entities to cooperate with cyber-security has been ongoing for some time with respect to both launching and defending against attacks.

13.6   Conclusion

Cyber-superiority is not the same as kenotic weapons superiority. States like the United States, Russia, China, the United Kingdom, Germany, France, and India cannot guarantee their national security in the cybersphere. Yet, cyberspace has made many of the traditional concepts around which our laws are based—national borders, jurisdictional barriers, sovereignty, citizenship—largely immaterial.

While the most prominent cyber-attacks of recent years appear to have been perpetrated by nation-states, now organized criminals, and just about anyone else with technical skills and a political or ideological agenda can launch attacks with the devastating force of countries with near-perfect impunity. As a result, existing domestic and international law provides little guidance about how we should characterize cyber-attacks and other military-style operations in the online environment. There is little guidance as to what sorts of offensive and defensive measures are lawful in cyberspace, whether undertaken by government or industry.

While at least one scholar has suggested the need for a cyberspace treaty, the differing agendas of the vast range of actors in this space and the disputed nature of the legal issues all render such a treaty extremely difficult, if not unlikely (Hughes 2010: 524). Still, it cannot be forgotten that international instruments like the *Geneva Convention* and the *UN Charter* were drafted in a different era with different infrastructures, utilities, and weapons. It may be time for the international community to look more closely at the issue of cyber-war and perhaps reconsider the *jus ad bellum* and *jus in bello* legal frameworks.

13.7 Principal Concepts

The principal concepts associated with this chapter are listed below. Demonstrate your understanding of each by writing a short definition or explanation in one or two sentences:

- Stuxnet;
- *Jus ad bellum*;
- Industrial control systems; and
- Zero-day exploits.

13.8 Study Questions

1. When talking about the legal authority to conduct war, the consequences of a cyber-attack can be considered against kinetic attacks in terms of producing the same or similar results. Explain whether the term *use of force* is adequate or needs to be refined to include cyber-attacks.
2. List four types of exploits against industrial control systems and explain their purpose/function for the attacker and risks to the victim(s).
3. The law of armed conflict is primarily intended to govern the conduct of war between states. The *jus ad bellum* and *jus in bello* frameworks that govern the right to wage war, and proper conduct during war, are historically tied to states. Is this framework appropriate for non-state actors who perpetrate cyber-attacks and have no interest in obeying the domestic or international law?
4. In this Chapter, we learned that one of the challenges to protecting the nation's critical infrastructure is to encourage commercial companies that run these systems to invest in cyber-security. Explain why these private entities invest more than the minimum and how might we encourage them to shore up their resources to ensure that our systems are secure?

13.9 Learning Activity

Imagine that you are the President of the United States and you want to come-up with a plan to better protect the nation against the kinds of threats discussed in this Chapter. How would you go about formulating a plan? Keep in mind that when thinking about how to protect our systems, we must first determine what is essential (i.e. to have it compromised or lost could cause catastrophic damage). Think about what information, services and other resources are vital to the functioning of society and the economy and what we could do without—either temporarily or in the long-term. Once you've determine what is critical, think about how you could build a security plan that uses the right tools and resources to safeguard it. What are we currently doing or not doing that needs to be re-thought or, perhaps, strengthened to meet this challenge?

References

Blank LR (2013) International law and cyber threats from non-state actors. Int Law Stud 89:406
Buchan R (2012) Cyber attacks: unlawful uses of force or prohibited interventions? J Confl Secur Law 17, 211
Byers E (n.d.) The industrial cybersecurity problem. International Society of Automation, https://www.isa.org/pdfs/the-industrial-cybersecurity-problem/
Carr J (2010) Cyber warfare: mapping the cyber underworld, 1st edn
Dinstein Y (2013) Cyber war and international law: concluding remarks at the 2012 Naval War College international law conference. Int Law Stud 89:276
Etzioni A (2014) The private sector – a reluctant partner in cybersecurity. Georgetown J Int Aff 15:69
Hahn RW, Laney-Ferrer A (2006) The law and economics of software security. Harv J Law Public Policy 30:282
Harris S (2014) @ War – the rise of the military internet complex. First Mariner Books, New York
Harris S (2015) @ War – the rise of the military internet complex. Houghton Mifflin Harcourt, New York
Hughes R (2010) A treaty for cyberspace. Int Aff 86:523
Ignatieff M (2000) Virtual war. Picador USA, New York
Joy B (2000) Why the future doesn't need us. Wired, April 1
Kelson R, Paganini P, Gittins B, Pace D (2012) The cyber war era began long ago," The Malta Independent Online, June 25
Kutner M (2016) Alleged dam hacking raises fears of cyber threats to infrastructure. March 30
Lee A (2011) CIA chief Leon Panetta: cyberattack could be 'Next Pearl Harbor'. Huffington Post, June 14. http://www.huffingtonpost.com.au/entry/panetta-cyberattack-next-pearl-harbor_n_875889
Lessig L (2004) Insanely destructive devices. Wired, April 1
Lipovsky R, Cherepanov A (2016) BlackEnergy Trojan strikes again: attacks Ukrainian electric power industry," *Welivesecurity*, January 4
Newman LH (2016) Trump calls for 'Crippling' cyberwar attack capabilities. Wired, October 3. https://www.wired.com/2016/10/trump-calls-crippling-cyberwar-attack-capabilities/

O'Connell ME (2012) Cyber security without cyber war. J Confl Secur Law 17(2):187

Padmanabhan VM (2013) Cyber warriors and the jus in bello. Int Law Stud 89:288

Pauli D (2016) Shamoon malware returns to again wipe Saudi-owned computers. The Register, December 2. https://www.theregister.co.uk/2016/12/02/accused_iranian_disk_wiper_returns_to_destroy_saudi_orgs_agencies/

Pool P (2013) War of the cyber world: the law of cyber warfare. Int Lawyer 47:299

Preciado M (2012) If you wish cyber peace, prepare for cyber war: the need for the federal government to protect critical infrastructure from cyber warfare. J Law Cyber Warfare 1:99

Schneier B (2000) Secrets and lies: digital security in a networked world. Wiley Computer Publishing, New York

Swoyer A (2016) Donald Trump cyber security: this is the warfare of the future. Breitbart, October 3. http://www.breitbart.com/big-government/2016/10/03/trump-touts-cyber-security-virginia-warfare-future/

Symantec (2011) W32.Duqu. November 23. http://www.symantec.com/content/en/us/enterprise/media/security_response/whitepapers/w32_duqu_the_precursor_to_the_next_Stuxnet.pdf

Symantec (2012) Flamer: highly sophisticated and discreet threat targets the Middle East," May 28. https://www.symantec.com/connect/blogs/flamer-highly-sophisticated-and-discreet-threat-targets-middle-east

Symantec (2016a) Internet security threat report. vol.21, April

Symantec (2016b) Shamoon: back from the dead and destructive as ever. November 30. https://www.symantec.com/connect/blogs/shamoon-back-dead-and-destructive-ever

Townsend K (2016) Shamoon wiper attacks return to the Gulf. SecurityWeek, December 1. http://www.securityweek.com/shamoon-wiper-attacks-return-gulf

Turns D (2012) Cyber warfare and the notion of direct participation in hostilities. J Confl Secur Law 17:279–297

Walker P (2013) Organizing for cyberspace operations: selected issues. Int Law Stud 89:341

Whigham N (2016) Alex Gibney film gives chilling insight into the world of state sponsored cyber warfare unleashed by *Stuxnet*. July 11, news.com.au

Wittes B, Blum G (2015) The future of violence. Basic Books, New York

Weiss J (2017) Industrial control systems: the holy grail of cyberwar. The Christian Science Monitor, March 24

Zetter K (2014) An unprecedented look at *Stuxnet*: the World's first digital weapon. Wired, November 3. https://www.wired.com/2014/11/countdown-to-zero-day-*Stuxnet*/

Zetter K (2016) Inside the cunning, unprecedented attack of Ukraine's power grid, Wired, March 3. https://www.wired.com/2016/03/inside-cunning-unprecedented-hack-ukraines-power-grid/

Chapter 14
Researching Cyber Weapons: An Enumerative Bibliography

Lori Fossum

14.1 Introduction

It is self-evident that fighters facing a conflict would benefit from using any means available to increase their ability to engage the enemy. Although *research* is not *conflict*, it does, to some extent, share the need to gain an advantage—after all, research is about "winning," albeit in the form of *discovery*. If a researcher is conducting a literature review, but is not able to discover material, he or she may miss vital information that might have steered their project in a different direction.

If we use the analogy of a naval captain maneuvering her Man-of-War to a destination to engage an enemy raider, the captain needs to, first, understand where her ship is in relation to the area of conflict. Then, she needs to be able plot a course to that location. But, if the captain is not able to obtain information about such things as tides, currents, reefs, storms, and other factors, her journey may not be successful.

Equally, if researchers are not aware of what has been written before, what gaps there are in the literature and what has already been studied, they are likely to embark on a journey that parallels the captain's.

In science, the arts, and in the humanities, an investigation into what has and hasn't been done in terms of research is contained in the written record of the subject literature. It contains the equivalent of the tides, currents, reefs, storms, and other factors that researchers need to be able to understand the context of their problem, and where their issue fits into the large situation.

Libraries are full of research material, but all libraries have a focus—some cater to a public community while others exist for subject specific users. For example, a law library is established and maintained primarily for legal scholars. Therefore, each collection is compiled with its mission and primary users in mind.

L. Fossum (✉)
George Washington University Law School, Washington, DC, USA
e-mail: lfossum@law.gwu.edu

© Springer International Publishing AG, part of Springer Nature 2018
H. Prunckun (ed.), *Cyber Weaponry*, Advanced Sciences and Technologies for Security Applications, https://doi.org/10.1007/978-3-319-74107-9_14

Google can bring you back a hundred thousand answers. A librarian can bring you back the right one. English author, Neil Gaiman

Literature about cyber weapons can be found in a number of sources, especially in college and university libraries. But, for the most current, reputable information, sources from conferences are particularly relevant, especially those sponsored by NATO Cooperative Cyber Defence Centre of Excellence; the International Conference on Cyber Warfare and Security; and USENIX, the Advanced Computing Systems Association conferences. Also helpful are publications from the European Intelligence and Security Informatics Conference (EISIC).

Articles published in the subject areas of computer science, engineering, export controls, law and military studies are also among the best sources of current analysis assuming they are peer-reviewed and substantiated with research sources. Books, given their longer publishing timeline, have more dated information; book-length treatment of a subject, however, is usually the most in-depth. Internet blog posts and news articles may provide timely information, but such information may be prey to mistake or lacking nuance—especially given the speed at which it is published.

14.2 Methods for Locating Information

Scholars can search for books by keywords or subject headings in publicly-accessible online catalogs, such as *WorldCat*. Searching for scholarly legal articles can also be done by subject or keywords in specialized databases as *LegalTrac*, *Legal Source*, and *Index to Legal Periodicals and Books*. There are also commercial sources such as *HeinOnline*, *Westlaw*, and *Lexis* that provide cited reference searches (*ScholarCheck*, *KeyCite*, and *Shepards*, respectively). Prior to publication, many law review articles are available on the *Social Science Research Network* or *BePress' Digital Commons* websites.

Web of Science and *Scopus* are powerful interdisciplinary citation and abstract databases that allow cited reference searching. Researchers can use these databases, as well as others, such as *ProQuest* and *EBSCO*, to identify non-legal scholarly articles, gray literature, patent applications, and government documents.

Specialized organizations provide reports, analyses, and in the case of the National Security Archive, declassified US government information. The Archive also maintains *The Cyber Vault*, a database that contains documents on cyber policy and activities, but mainly from the United States. Another important research materials resource is the NATO Cooperative Cyber Defence Centre of Excellence.

Finally, scholars should review the references cited in published books and peer-reviewed articles—such as those cited by the chapter authors of this book—and consider obtaining copies of original material if the reference appears promising.

14.3   Tides, Currents, Reefs

Returning to our earlier analogy of the Man-of-War, what is of help to most researchers in navigating to their "destination" is an enumerative bibliography. This type of bibliography is characterized by an alphabetical listing of the literature pertinent to the topic under investigation. Some bibliographies provide annotations to each citation, and are referred to as an *annotated bibliography*, while others might provide discussion about the historical context in which certain books were produced (an *analytic bibliography*). But in this chapter material was gathered using a framework of headings and subheadings that offer the researchers a logical way of viewing this material. So, this chapter offers an enumerative bibliography, albeit in a condensed form. It can be used to assist you in answering the study questions contained in the other chapters and to assist you with some of the learning activities. Any bibliographer's goal is to provide you a springboard for your own research, and in this case, an overview of the issues and implications of digital arms as seen in the current literature (Fig. 14.1).

Principal Concepts
The principal concepts associated with this chapter are listed below. Demonstrate your understanding of each by writing a definition or explanation in one or two sentences.;

Fig. 14.1 Research provides an advantage (Photograph by Airman 1st Class Ryan Lackey and courtesy of the U.S. Department of Defense)

- Analytic bibliography;
- Annotated bibliography;
- Enumerative bibliography; and
- Literature review.

Study Questions

1. The bibliography is comprised of four main genres: books, journal articles, gray literature, and government documents. Describe what other types of information are commonly cited when you research this topic. Are some genres more reliable than others? How do we determine source reliability? Discuss.
2. When researching and writing about weaponry of any kind, why is it important to consider the legal ramifications of developing and deploying such weapons? Explain which legal systems should be considered.

Learning Activity

Imagine you need to perform a literature review as you develop your research topic. As you search for and locate reputable, scholarly research material, you discover that your original thesis statement may not be supported by the published sources. Reflecting on the information you collect, find a way to develop your topic while including the information that seems to derail your thesis.

Books

Frequently Cited or Influential Books

Schmitt MN (ed) (2017) Tallinn manual 2.0 on the international law applicable to cyber operations. Cambridge University Press, Cambridge
Tallinn 2.0, "intended as an objective restatement of the *lex lata,*" (p.3) follows the influential 2013 Tallinn Manual on the International Law Applicable to Cyber Warfare. Both reflect international law experts' opinions on the current international law governing cyber operations, so neither work advances policy or the politics of any nation. *Tallinn 2.0* includes 154 "black letter" rules with commentary on each and goes beyond operations conducted as part of armed conflict to address operations more broadly
Schmitt MN (ed) (2013) Tallinn manual on the international law applicable to cyber warfare: prepared by the international group of experts at the invitation of the NATO Cooperative Cyber Defence Centre of Excellence. Cambridge University Press, Cambridge
"In 2009, the NATO Cooperative Cyber Defence Centre of Excellence (NATO CCD COE), an international military organization based in Tallinn, Estonia, and accredited in 2008 by NATO as a 'Centre of Excellence,' invited an independent 'International Group of Experts' to produce a manual on the law governing cyber warfare" (p.1). While not an official document, the *Tallinn Manual* was an attempt by a group of these experts to identify and address all the legal issues both in offensive and defensive operations

Other Influential Books

Allhoff F, Henschke A, Strawser BJ (eds) (2016) Binary bullets: the ethics of cyberwarfare. Oxford University Press, New York

Boothby WH (2014) Conflict law: the influence of new weapons technology, human rights and emerging actors. T.M.C. Asser Press, The Hague

Carayannis EG, Campbell DFJ, Efthymiopoulos MP (eds) (2014) Cyber-development, cyber-democracy and cyber-defense: challenges, opportunities and implications for theory, policy and practice. Springer, New York

Floridi L, Taddeo M (2014) The ethics of informational warfare. Springer, Cham

Green JA (ed) (2015) Cyber warfare: a multidisciplinary analysis. Routledge, New York

Heckman KE et al (2015a) Cyber denial, deception and counter deception: a framework for supporting active cyber defense. Springer, Cham

Jajodia S et al (eds) (2015) Cyber warfare: building the scientific foundation. Springer, Cham

Lemieux F (ed) (2015) Current and emerging trends in cyber operations: policy, strategy, and practice. Palgrave Macmillan, New York

Loukas G (2015) Cyber-physical attacks: a growing invisible threat. Elsevier/Butterworth-Heinemann, Waltham

Maogoto JN (2015) Technology and the law on the use of force: new security challenges in the twenty first century. Routledge, New York

Mazanec BM (2015) The evolution of cyber war: international norms for emerging-technology weapons. Potomac Books, Lincoln

Ohlin JD, Govern K, Finkelstein CO (eds) (2015) Cyberwar: law and ethics for virtual conflicts. Oxford University Press, Oxford

O'Leary M (2015) Cyber operations: building, defending, and attacking modern computer networks. Apress, Berkeley

Poindexter DF (2015) The new cyberwar: technology and the redefinition of warfare. McFarland & Company, Jefferson

Richet J-L (ed) (2015) Cybersecurity policies and strategies for cyberwarfare prevention. Information Science Reference, Hershey

Singer PW, Friedman A (2014) Cybersecurity and cyberwar: what everyone needs to know. Oxford University Press, New York

Taddeo M, Glorioso L (2017) Ethics and policies for cyber operations: a NATO Cooperative Cyber Defence Centre of Excellence initiative. Springer, Cham

Valeriano B, Maness RC (2015) Cyber war versus cyber realities: cyber conflict in the international system. Oxford University Press, New York

Zetter K (2014) Countdown to zero day: Stuxnet and the launch of the world's first digital weapon. Crown, New York

Law Review/Journal Articles

Frequently-Cited Articles

Brown GD, Metcalf AO (2014) Easier said than done: legal reviews of cyber weapons. J Natl Secur Law Policy 7(1):115–138. Written from the viewpoint of military attorneys responsible for giving concrete legal advice on cyber war to commanders, the authors claim that "treating all cyber techniques as weapons is impractical" (p.116). Instead, the article proposes the assessment of cyber events in context since most do not rise to the level of an armed attack

Blake D, Imburgia JS (2010) "Bloodless weapons"? The need to conduct legal reviews of certain capabilities and the implications of defining them as "weapons.". Air Force Law Rev 66(1):157–204. Provides a relatively early, comprehensive overview of cyber weapon development's legal considerations, pre-*Tallinn Manual*. Gives an overview of which legal regimes control in one's analysis

Other Relevant Articles

Allan C (2015) Targeting cyber arms dealers who directly participate in hostilities. Southwest J Int Law 21(2):341–374

Anderson K (2016) Why the hurry to regulate autonomous weapon systems–but not cyber-weapons? Temple Int Comp Law J 30(1):17–42

Bradbury S (2011) The developing legal framework for defense and offensive cyber operations. Harv Natl Secur J 2(2):629–651

Brecher AP (2012) Note. Cyberattacks and the covert action statute: toward a domestic legal framework for offensive cyberoperations. Mich Law Rev 111(3):423–452

Cayón Peña J, Armando Garcia L (2014) The critical role of education in every cyber defense strategy. Northern Kentucky Law Rev 41(3):459–469

Chayes A (2015) Rethinking warfare: the ambiguity of cyber attacks. Harv Natl Secur J 6 (2):474–519

Davis PK (2015) Deterrence, influence, cyber attack, and cyberwar. New York Univ J Int Law Polit 47(2):327–356

Gross ML (2015) Nonlethal weapons, noncombatant immunity, and the principle of participatory liability. Case Western Reserve J Int Law 47(1):201–216

Hakim M (2015) Defensive force against non-state actors: the state of play. Int Law Stud Ser US Naval War Coll 91:1–31

Harrington SL (2014) Cyber security active defense: playing with fire or sound risk management? Richmond J Law Technol 20(4):1–41

Harrison Dinniss HA (2015) The nature of objects: targeting networks and the challenge of defining cyber military objectives. Israel Law Rev 481(1):39–54

Henriksen A (2015) Lawful state responses to low-level cyber-attacks. Nordic J Int Law 84 (2):323–352

Herr T, Rosenzweig P (2016) Cyber weapons and export control: incorporating dual use with the PrEP model. J Natl Secur Law Policy 8(2):301–320

Hiller J (2014) Civil cyberconflict: microsoft, cybercrime, and botnets. Santa Clara High Technol Law J 31(2):163–216

Hodgson G (2016) Cyber attack treaty verification. I/S: J Law Policy Infor Soc 12(2):231–260

Keen JF (2015) Conventional military force as a response to cyber capabilities: on sending packets and receiving missiles. Air Force Law Rev 73:111–150

Koh HH, Buchwald TF (2015) The crime of aggression: the United States perspective. Am J Int Law 109(2):257–295

Kovach CM (2014) Beyond Skynet: reconciling increased autonomy in computer-based weapons systems with the laws of war. Air Force Law Rev 71:231–278

Lilienthal G, Ahmad N (2015) Cyber-attack as inevitable kinetic war. Comput Law Secur Rev 31 (3):390–400

Lin H (2010) Offensive cyber operations and the use of force. J Natl Secur Law Policy 4(1):63–86

Lowe TK (2015) Mapping the matrix: defining the balance between executive action and legislative regulation in the new battlefield of cyberspace. Scholar: St Mary's Law Rev Race Soc Justice 17 (1):63–94

McFarland T, McCormack T (2014) Mind the gap: can developers of autonomous weapons systems be liable for war crimes? Int Law Stud 90(1):361–385

McGhee J (2014) Hack, attack or whack; the politics of imprecision in cyber law. J Law Cyber Warf 4(1):13–41

McGee S, Sabett RV, Shah A (2013) Adequate attribution: a framework for developing a national policy for private sector use of active defense. J Bus Technol Law 8(1):1–48

Mele S (2014) Legal considerations on cyber-weapons and their definition. J Law Cyber Warf 3 (1):52–69

Moore A (2015) Stuxnet and article 2(4)'s prohibition against the use of force: customary law and potential models. Naval Law Rev 64:1–26

O'Connell ME (2015) 21st century arms control challenges: drones, cyber weapons, killer robots, and WMDs. Glob Stud Law Rev 13(3):515–534

Richardson JC (2011) Stuxnet as cyberwarfare: applying the law of war to the virtual battlefield. John Marshall J Comput Infor Law 29(1):1–28

Richmond J (2011) Evolving battlefields: does Stuxnet demonstrate a need for modifications to the law of armed conflict? Fordham Int Law J 35(3):842–894

Schmitt MN (2015a) The law of cyber targeting. Naval War Coll Rev 68(2):11–29

Schmitt MN (2015b) The notion of 'objects' during cyber operations: a riposte in defence of interpretive and applicative precision. Israel Law Rev 48(1):81–109

Singer PW (2015) Stuxnet and its hidden lessons on the ethics of cyberweapons. Case Western Reserve J Int Law 47(1):79–86

Sullivan C (2016) The 2014 Sony hack and the role of international law. J Natl Secur Law Policy 8 (3):437–468

Trautman L (2016) Congressional cybersecurity oversight: who's who and how it works. J Law Cyber Warf 5(1):147–306

Walker P (2013) Organizing for cyberspace operations: selected issues. Int Law Stud 89:341–361

Waxman MC (2013) Self-defensive force against cyber attacks: legal, strategic and political dimensions. Int Law Stud 89:109–122

Non-law Articles and Book Chapters

Frequently-Cited Article

Lin H (2009) Lifting the veil on cyber offense. IEEE Secur Priv 7(4):15–21. Based on a 2009 National Research Council report, "Technology, Policy, Law, and Ethics Regarding US Acquisition and Use of Cyberattack Capabilities," this article highlights the lack of information about US offensive capabilities and the uncertainty surrounding offensive cyberattacks as instruments of US policy

Other Relevant Articles and Chapters

Almeshekah MH, Spafford EH (2014) Using deceptive information in computer security defenses. Int J Cyber Warf Terrorism 4(3):63–80

Bartos CA (2016) Cyber weapons are not created equal. U.S Naval Inst Proc 142(6):30–33

Barzashka I (2013) Are cyber-weapons effective? Assessing Stuxnet's impact on the Iranian enrichment programme. RUSI J: R United Serv Inst Defence Stud 158(2):48–56

Bencsáth B et al (2012) The cousins of Stuxnet: Duqu, flame, and gauss. Futur Internet 4(4):971–1003

Bergin DL (2015) Cyber-attack and defense simulation framework. J Defense Model Simul: Appl Methodol Technol 12(4):383–392

Boothby B (2016) Cyber weapons: oxymoron or a real world phenomenon to be regulated? In: Friis K, Ringmose J (eds) Conflict in cyber space: theoretical, strategic and legal perspectives. Routledge, New York, pp 165–174

Butrimas V (2014) National security and international policy challenges in a post Stuxnet world. Lithuanian Annu Strateg Rev 12(1):11–31

Czosseck C, Podins K (2012) A vulnerability-based model of cyber weapons and its implications for cyber conflict. Int J Cyber Warf Terrorism 2(1):14–26

Denning DE (2012) Stuxnet: what has changed? Futur Internet 4(3):672–687

Droege C (2013) Get off my cloud: cyber warfare, international humanitarian law, and the protection of civilians. Int Rev Red Cross 94(886):533–578

Farwell JP, Rohozinski R (2011) Stuxnet and the future of cyber war. Survival: Glob Politics Strategy 53(1):23–40

Flowers A, Zeadally S (2014) US policy on active cyber defense. J Homeland Secur Emerg Manag 11(2):289–308

Gartzke E, Lindsay JR (2015) Weaving tangled webs: offense, defense, and deception in cyber-space. Secur Stud 24(2):316–348

Geers K (2010a) The challenge of cyber attack deterrence. Comput Law Secur Rev 26(3):298–303

Geers K (2010b) Cyber weapons convention. Comput Law Secur Rev 26(5):547–551

Gjelten T (2013) First strike: US cyber warriors seize the offensive. World Aff 175(5):33–43

Grant TJ (2013) Tools and technologies for professional offensive cyber operations. Int J Cyber Warf Terrorism 3(3):49–71

Heckman KE, Stech FJ, Schmoker BS, Thomas RK (2015b) Denial and deception in cyber defense. Computer 48(4):36–44

Iasiello E (2014) Hacking back: not the right solution. Parameters 44(3):105–113

Jang-Jaccard J, Nepal S (2014) A survey of emerging threats in cybersecurity. J Comput Syst Sci 80 (5):973–993

Jenkins R (2013) Is Stuxnet physical? Does it matter? J Mil Ethics 12(1):68–79

Kello L (2013) The meaning of the cyber revolution perils to theory and statecraft. Int Secur 38 (2):7–40

Kelly D et al (2012) Exploring extant and emerging issues in anonymous networks: a taxonomy and survey of protocols and metrics. IEEE Commun Surv Tutorials 14(2):579–606

Kenney M (2015) Cyber-terrorism in a post-Stuxnet world. Orbis 59(1):111–128

Lachow I (2011) The Stuxnet enigma: implications for the future of cybersecurity. Georgetown J Int Aff 12:118–126

Lewis JA (2012) In defense of Stuxnet. Mil Strateg Aff 4(3):65–76

Lindsay JR (2013) Stuxnet and the limits of cyber warfare. Secur Stud 22(3):365–404

Lucas GR Jr (2014) Ethics and cyber conflict: a response to JME 12:1 2013. J Mil Ethics 13(1):20–31

Lupovici A (2016) The "attribution problem" and the social construction of "violence": taking cyber deterrence literature a step forward. Int Stud Perspect 17(3):322–342

Maitra AK (2015) Offensive cyber-weapons: technical, legal, and strategic aspects. Environ Syst Decis 35(1):169–182

Peterson D (2013) Offensive cyber weapons: construction, development, and employment. J Strateg Stud 36(1):120–124

Rid T, McBurney P (2012) Cyber-weapons. RUSI J 157(1):6–13

Rowland J, Rice M, Shenoi S (2014) The anatomy of a cyber power. Int J Crit Infrastruct Prot 7 (1):3–11

Rustici RM (2011) Cyberweapons: leveling the international playing field. Parameters 41(3):32–42

Stevens T (2016) Cyberweapons: an emerging global governance architecture. Palgrave Commun 2:160102. https://doi.org/10.1057/palcomms.2016.102.
Tripathi S et al (2013) Hadoop based defense solution to handle distributed denial of service DDoS attacks. J Inf Secur 4(3):150–164

Gray Literature

Frequently-Cited Report

Mandiant (Firm) (2013) APT1: exposing one of China's cyber espionage units. Mandiant, Alexandria. Security firm Mandiant, now a Fireeye company, issued this report after extensive research, concluding APT1 is likely sponsored by China and has been implicated in wide-ranging cyber espionage operations since 2006

Other Relevant Reports

Bilge L, Dumitras T (2012) Before we knew it: an empirical study of zero-day attacks in the real world. In: Proceedings of the 2012 ACM conference on computer and communications security. pp 833–844
Black K, David M (2016) War in 1s and 0s: framing the lexicon for the digital age. Proceedings of the 11th international conference on cyber warfare and security. pp 31–36
Caballero J, Grier C, Kreibich C, Paxson V (2011) Measuring pay-per-install: the commoditization of malware distribution. USENIX security symposium. pp 1–15
Center for Cyber and Homeland Security (2016) Into the gray zone: the private sector and active defense against cyber threats. George Washington University, Washington, DC
Chen J, Duvall G (2016) On dynamic cyber defense and its improvement. In: Proceedings of the 11th international conference on cyber warfare and security. pp 74–80
Colbaugh R, Glass K (2012) Proactive defense for evolving cyber threats. Sandia National Laboratories, Albuquerque/Livermore
Conklin C, Bahney BW (2012) More than meets the eye: clandestine funding, cutting-edge technology and China's cyber research & development program. Lawrence Livermore National Laboratory
De Falco M (2012) Stuxnet facts report. A technical and strategic analysis. NATO CCD COE Publications, Tallinn
Giles K, Hartmann K (2015) Cyber defense: an international view. Strategic Studies Institute and US Army War College Press, Carlisle
Herr T (2014) PrEP: a framework for malware and cyber weapons. Proceedings of the 9th International Conference on Cyber Warfare and Security ICCWS-2014. pp 84–91
Hershey PC, Dehnert RE Jr, Williams JJ, Raytheon (2017) Digital weapons factory and digital operations center for producing, deploying, assessing, and managing digital defects. Patent no. 9,544,326, USA
Huntley WL (2016, January) Strategic implications of offense and defense in cyberwar. 2016 49th Hawaii International Conference on System Sciences HICSS. pp 5588–5595
Kaspersky Lab, Global Research & Analysis Team (2017) Lazarus under the hood. 59 pp

Leed M, Lewis JA, McCreary JD (2013) Offensive cyber capabilities at the operational level: the way ahead. Center for Strategic and International Studies, Washington, DC

Li JJ, Daugherty L, National Defense Research Institute US (2015) Training cyber warriors: what can be learned from defense language training? RAND, Santa Monica

Libicki MC, Ablon L, Webb T (2015) Defender's dilemma. RAND, Santa Monica

National Research Council (2010) Proceedings of a workshop on deterring cyberattacks: informing strategies and developing options for US policy. National Academies Press, Washington, DC

Rattray G, Healey J (2010) Categorizing and understanding offensive capabilities and their use. In: Proceedings of a workshop on deterring cyberattacks: informing strategies and developing options for US policy. pp 77–97

Shakarian P (2017) The enemy has a voice: understanding threats to inform smart investment in cyber defense. New America Foundation, Washington, DC

Tyugu E (2012) Command and control of cyber weapons. 2012 4th International Conference on Cyber Conflict, CYCON 2012 – Proceedings

Wassenaar Arrangement on Export Controls for Conventional Arms and Dual–Use Goods and Technologies (2017) Public documents volume II: list of dual-use goods and technologies and munitions list. pp 1–234

Zhioua, S. 2013. The Middle East under malware attack dissecting cyber weapons. Proceedings – International conference on distributed computing systems pp. 11–16.

Government Documents

Frequently-Cited Government Documents

United States (2015a) Chapter XVI cyber operations. In: Department of defense law of war manual. General Counsel of the Department of Defense, Washington, DC. The *Manual* represents the position of the Department of Defense, not necessarily the US government as a whole. Chapter XVI, "Cyber Operations," comprises only 15 pages of the 1,220–page-long Manual but provides more transparency about the Department of Defense's cyber operations generally. Some of the *Manual*'s positions on international law differ from those seen in the *Tallinn Manual*

United States Air Force (2011) Air Force Instruction 51-402, Legal Reviews of Weapons and Cyber Capabilities. The instruction was issued to reflect "a change in the Air Force definition of 'weapon' and requires a legal review of cyber capabilities intended for use in cyberspace operations" (p.1)

Other Relevant Government Documents

Canada (2010) Canada's cyber security strategy

Government Accountability Office, Washington DC, Belkin P (2014) NATO's Wales summit: expected outcomes and key challenges

Los Alamos National Laboratory & United States (2015) What is the current state of the science of cyber defense? United States. Dept. of Energy, Washington, DC

Ministry of Defence (2016) The cyber primer, 2nd edn. Ministry of Defence, London

Russian Federation (2011) Conceptual views regarding the activities of the armed forces of the Russian Federation in information space

Sandia National Laboratories & United States (2015) Evaluating moving target defense with PLADD. United States. Dept. of Defense, Washington, DC

United Kingdom (2010) A strong Britain in an age of uncertainty: the national security strategy

United Kingdom (2011) The UK cyber security strategy: protecting and promoting the UK in a digitized world

United States (2011) Strategy for operating in cyberspace. Department of Defense, Washington, DC

United States (2010) The White House. National security strategy

United States (2013) Joint publication 3–12 on cyberspace operations. Department of Defense, Washington, DC

United States (2014) Army techniques publication 3–36 (FM3–36). Electronic warfare techniques.

United States (2015b) Defense cybersecurity: opportunities exist for DOD to share cybersecurity resources with small businesses. United States Government Accountability Office, Washington, DC

United States (2015c) Defense infrastructure: Improvements in DOD reporting and cybersecurity implementation needed to enhance utility resilience planning. United States Government Accountability Office, Washington, DC

United States (2015d) The department of defense cyber strategy. Department of Defense, Washington, DC

United States (2017) Army field manual 3–12, Cyberspace and electronic warfare operations

US Strategic Command (2009) The cyber warfare lexicon: a language to support the development, testing, planning and employment of cyber weapons and other modern warfare capabilities. Version 1.7.6

Index

© Springer International Publishing AG, part of Springer Nature 2018
H. Prunckun (ed.), *Cyber Weaponry*, Advanced Sciences and Technologies for
Security Applications, https://doi.org/10.1007/978-3-319-74107-9

Printed by Printforce, the Netherlands